Dark Victorians

Dark Victorians

VANESSA D. DICKERSON

University of Illinois Press
URBANA AND CHICAGO

♾ This book is printed on acid-free paper.

Library of Congress Cataloging-in-Publication Data
Dickerson, Vanessa D.
Dark Victorians / Vanessa D. Dickerson.
p. cm.
Includes bibliographical references and index.
ISBN-13 978-0-252-03256-1 (cloth : alk. paper)
ISBN-10 0-252-03256-X (cloth : alk. paper)
1. African Americans—Relations with British—History.
2. African Americans—Great Britain—History—19th century.
3. African Americans—Intellectual life—19th century.
4. African Americans—Attitudes—History—19th century.
5. British—Attitudes—History—History—19th century.
6. Great Britain—Intellectual life—19th century.
7. Transnationalism.
8. Du Bois, W. E. B. (William Edward Burghardt), 1868–1963—Political and social views.
9. Carlyle, Thomas, 1795–1881—Political and social views.
I. Title.
E185.61.D53 2008
305.800941—dc22 2007030319

Contents

Acknowledgments

I wish here to acknowledge the investment others have made in this work and in me. This book would not have been possible without the instruction of U. C. Knoepflmacher who trained me as a Victorianist. The book was arguably under way as soon as I stepped into his classroom at Princeton. I would also like to recognize historian Ken Goings who, early on, saw the value of my work on black Victorians and encouraged me to persist in the exploration of my ideas. I owe thanks to the many librarians who assisted me along the way. These include the librarians at Rhodes College, the University of Memphis, DePauw University, the New York Public Library, the Schomburg, Howard University, the Library of Congress, and the British Library. I also wish to thank Irene Ferguson, assistant archivist at the University of Edinburgh. A grant by the Faculty Development Committee at DePauw University and the generosity of Neal Abraham, the vice president of Academic Affairs at DePauw, enabled me to complete this work. I am grateful, too, for the professionalism and assistance of acquisition editor Joan Catapano and her editorial staff. Finally, I wish to extend a special thanks to Yanna and, now here at the end of this process, to Darrel, for loving me and keeping me sane.

Dark Victorians

Introduction

Crossing the Big Water between White Victorians and Black Americans

In *The Wind Done Gone* (2001), Alice Randall's parody of Margaret Mitchell's 1936 plantation novel *Gone With the Wind,* the female protagonist Cynara sums up the black experience in an assertion as historical as it is poetic in its impetus. "We are a sailed people," Cynara explains in the diary in which she proposes "to write down everything. Something like Mr. Frederick Douglass." By identifying blacks as sailed or sold people, Randall's character not only evokes the horrors of the middle passage ("We sailed to America. We taste the path of our abduction in our tears," Cynara continues), but she also anticipates her own personal reversal of that passage as she plans to marry her white lover then cross the Atlantic to live with him in London ("We are sailing to London. I am and he is, the sail and the wind, and the old city"). Whereas in America, Cynara can never be more than her lover's black concubine; in London, Cynara can cross the color line, pass as a white woman, and live as a married lady (7, 156, 157, 158). London, England, holds the prospect of a fuller, richer life informed by respectability. Little wonder that Cynara hungers for the city that has haunted her readings.

As it turns out, the fictional Cynara never crosses the Atlantic with her lover, opting instead to remain a black woman in the city on the Potomac instead of a white lady in "the city on the Thames" (157). She may only continue to visit the old city in the pages of the novels she reads; Randall's bondswoman can in some sense still travel to England. Such was not the case for many of the enslaved, dehumanized, and illiterate nineteenth-century blacks in America for whom books about England, let alone travel to England, were nigh inaccessible and inconceivable. For those African Americans who were fortunate enough to entertain the prospect of making it abroad, the

England that serves in Randall's novel as merely an enticing option for the character Cynara proved in reality, if not a lifeline, then a much more serious proposition in the nineteenth and early twentieth centuries. Thus, Frederick Douglass, and some others like him, "went as a fugitive across the waves" (Douglass Papers. Reel 13. Travels. Folder 29). Having escaped to England, Douglass declared in an 1847 speech in London, "I have reason to love England." His powerful and heartfelt sentiment about this nation was to become a declaration that resounds literarily and discursively in the lives of blacks in America.

Indeed, England has played a special if not always obvious role in the lives of African Americans since the founding of the United States. Thus one of the earliest African American writers, a seafaring black named Briton Hammon, after finding himself a captive first of the Native Americans then the Spanish, reveals himself to be one of the first African American anglophiles when the English come to his aid. In his captivity narrative, Hammon identifies the captain who rescues him as "a true *Englishman,*" who, when confronted by the Spanish, declined to return Hammon and the others who made it to his ship, averring that he could not in good conscience "deliver up any *Englishmen* under *English* Colours" (423). The use of italics here is indicative not only of the uncommon store Hammon and his white editor and readers set by England and the English but also—to the extent that Hammon himself shaped the content of his of his narrative—to Hammon's great and earnest pleasure in being himself styled an Englishman.[1] Be that as it may, Hammon had further reasons to appreciate the English, for, until he finally rejoined his master, he would work and sail on English ships on more than one occasion and the English would do, Hammon noted, the "honorabl[e]" thing and pay him "wages due to me" (424).

Whereas for Briton Hammon, the English fortuitously served as protectors and employers, for black slave prodigy and revolutionary poet Phillis Wheatley, the English were intellectual models and mentors. That is, the English and Englishness were arguably a significant part of who Wheatley was intellectually and artistically. Writing poems influenced—as scholars Vernon Loggins, John C. Shields, and others have pointed out—by seventeenth- and eighteenth-century English poets such as John Milton, Alexander Pope, and Thomas Gray, Phillis Wheatley litters her poetry with references to English luminaries such as evangelist George Whitefield, King George III, English commander Samuel Hood, and the Right Honorable William, Earl of Dartmouth. Among her papers are letters to such British personages as Lord Dartmouth, the Right Honorable Selina Hastings, Countess of Huntingdon, as well as to London merchant John Thornton.

The English, then, have a marked presence in the writings of Wheatley whose poetic efforts to "paint the *British* shore, / And vast *Atlantic*" no doubt owe much to her Eurocentric training (Wheatley 91). However, the trip Wheatley took to England in 1773 to restore her health also accounts for the notable presence England and the English have in her literary life. After all, it was in London that she not only began to regain physical health but also to secure her reputation as a published writer. A volume of her poems would first be published in London, England in 1773 when Wheatley was approximately nineteen years old. The city and some of its more prominent citizens were, for Phillis Wheatley, the gateway to Europe and an Europeanness that provided her with a means of "assimilat[ing] into the dominant culture" (Kendrick 71). This means, the city of Boston, and the Wheatleys, for all their fondness for their talented slave, could neither match nor gainsay. "The toast of London," as Henry Louis Gates styles the young black poet in *The Trials of Phillis Wheatley*, could never be the toast of prerevolutionary or, for that matter, of revolutionary Boston, United States of America (33). However, once Wheatley had received the adulation of the English, the Americans were bound to take greater and more serious notice, if not confer more respect. Certainly, having found a publisher in England, Wheatley, thanks no doubt to the efforts of her owners, was able to call upon several eminent Bostonians to further validate her authorial powers and help her market her book. Shields identifies some of the "prominent Bostonians of the day" who vouched for Wheatley as "Thomas Hutchinson (then Governor), James Bowdoin (a founder of Maine's Bowdoin College), John Hancock (signer of the Declaration of Independence), Charles Chauncy, Samuel Mather, and, not the least, Mather Byles," nephew of Cotton Mather (387). This garnering of signatures may be said to have placed Wheatley at the center of a veritable maelstrom of white authoritative males who, as critic M. A. Richmond so aptly describes them, were "men of substance all, conscious of it, affixing their valuable signatures to the ponderously drawn affidavit designed to impress even the most skeptical with its judicious restraint" (34). In any event, this gathering of signatures constitutes the first time so many prestigious white American fathers came to the aid of a black female, if not to defend her honor, then to verify the truth of her mental endowments.[2] One trip to England had, in large measure, made this extraordinary turn of events possible.

The early experiences of such blacks as Briton Hammon and Phillis Wheatley constitute embryonic engagements with the British that culminate in Frederick Douglass's articulation of his love for England. What makes Douglass's declaration that he had "reason to love England" so compelling is that it is voiced during a century that saw that nation colonize other, often darker-skinned people and that also saw Britain contribute its share of so-called empirical evidence to the European underwriting of biological determinism and scientific racism.[3] The Britain of philanthropy and reform was also the Britain of empire, an empire that extended British rule over nearly a quarter of the earth's population. If the movement of Britain into imperialism during the nineteenth century only seemed to put African Americans and white Britons at odds and to bring these two people to the brink of a great divide, then the physical barrier of the Atlantic Ocean would seem only to underscore that gaping divide. Yet African Americans did cross the big water, whether they did so literally as the Briton Hammons, Phillis Wheatleys, and Frederick Douglasses did or whether they crossed figuratively as Alice Randall's character Cynara does in readings that leave her longing for the Thames, Hampton Court, and the Tower of London, "all the things I read about in those Walter Scott novels and those slow Jane Austen pages" (157).

This book attempts to effect a crossing of the Victorian Atlantic by recognizing, among other things, black America's romance with Victorian Britain. The fact that African Americans from the nineteenth to the early twentieth century, roughly from 1830 to 1914, had, as Douglass puts it, reason to love England has been broached in cursory and indirect fashion by various scholars such as Cornel West, David Levering Lewis, Paul Gilroy, and Eric Sundquist in works that range from studies of British and American abolitionists, European and American travel, and individual African American and British writers. There has been, however, no study that assembles the pieces and fragments to present a sustained study of the relations between African Americans and Victorian Britons and of how African Americans and British Victorians approached, engaged, and thought about one another.

Instead, more recently, scholars such as Michelle M. Wright and Brent Hayes Edwards have been considering the crossings or intersections of blackness and of black folk in key European centers such as Germany and France. In *The Practice of Diaspora* (2003), Edwards traces what he calls the "rise of black internationalism" identifying interwar France as a nodal point for black connectivity. He describes Paris, France, as a city that "resonates in the cultures of black internationalism because it came to *represent* certain kinds of crossings, certain extensions of the horizon, even for populations that did not travel" (4). In the essay "Others-From-Within From Without: Afro-German Subject Formation and the Challenge of a Counter-Discourse" (2003), Wright approaches black transnationalism via the idea of black diaspora identity formation, focusing on how blacks are "Othered" in Western discourse (296). Both Edwards and Wright treat diasporic identity and linkages involving black populations in Europe and America. These studies of how postcolonial and interwar blacks made connections and had transatlantic encounters with each other are one thing; the study of intercultural relations between whites and blacks, more specifically between black Americans and British Victorians, is another.

Much of the groundwork for these studies of diasporic transnationalism and black internationalism as well as the study undertaken here of mainly interracial and intercultural connectivity has been laid by such intellectuals as cultural scholar Paul Gilroy and postcolonial scholars Edward Said, Homi Bhabha, and Benita Parry, for example, who have consistently concerned themselves with the way the Europeans or Westerners have crossed and recrossed these oceans. The operative word here is "cross" in all its variations as journey (to go across), as encounter (to come across), as change (to crossover), as violence and extermination (to cross out), even as writing, which, in the words of one French poet and essayist, requires an exquisite journey of pencil and hand across the page: "C'ést que le fait d'écrire, intrinséquement parlant, est lui aussi voyage. On part, avec en main, la plume qui trace sur le papier, on s'arrête pour respirer et réfléchir, on repart à nouveau, on s'arrête une fois de plus, toujours plume en main, comme s'accomplissent les diverse étapes d'une péregrination qui . . . comme l'écriture . . . se détache de A pour aller vers Z, en traversant les diverses lettres d'un alphabet réel et imaginaire à la fois, en zigzaguant à travers lui, en faisant de larges detours, ou en empruntant des raccourcis. . . . (Stétié 8).[4] The European act of crossing the oceans, recording the "discovery" of the lands of indigenous peoples, then double-crossing the natives and writing them out of existence often in the name of king and cross (religion) is a crucial factor in the phenomena of colonization, nationalism, and imperialism, which inform such works as Said's *Orientalism* (1978) and *Culture and Imperialism* (1993), Bhabha's *Nation and Narration* (1990) and *The Location of Culture* (1994), Chinua Achebe's "Colonialist Criticism" (1975), Eric Cheyfitz's *The Poetics of Imperialism* (1991), and black British cultural scholar's Paul Gilroy's *The Black Atlantic* (1993). As Said asserts in *Culture and Imperialism*, "All the energies poured into critical theory, into novel and demystifying theoretical praxes like the new historicism and deconstruction and Marxism have avoided the major . . . determining, political horizon of modern Western culture, namely imperialism," which constitutes the real and insidious crossing of borders to control, amass, and redefine the people and resources of an othered nation (60). Postcolonial studies, fed by cultural studies of transatlantic crossings and by travel writing "read as glimpses into colonized societies . . . colonial viewpoints and racist assumptions" (Paravisni-Gerbert and Romero-Cesareo

2), do not participate in the "massive avoidance [which] has sustained a canonical inclusion and exclusion," but rather are about the business of exposing the "protracted, complex, and striated work of empire" (Said 60). Since its emergence as a distinct critical discourse in the late 1980s through the 1990s, one of the aims of postcolonial studies has been to debunk the myth of Eurocentric universality that constitutes no more and no less than the chauvinistic marginalization of non-Western cultures to underpin what Achebe calls the "narrow, self-serving parochialism of Europe" ("Colonialist Criticism" 76).

A study of the relations between nineteenth-century African Americans and Victorian Britain would seem to be at odds with critical and theoretical approaches that eschew Eurocentrality. This is to say that at this point in time a study of nineteenth-century blacks and the British Victorians may lie uncomfortably near those writings of the "latter-day colonialist critic," who, according to Achebe, being "equally given to big-brother arrogance, sees the African [African American or other non-European] writer as a somewhat unfinished European" (69). However, such a study engages itself at the point where these other discourses such as cultural and postcolonial studies explore linkage and disruption, continuities and discontinuities, and where these studies describe, as Gilroy puts it, "the processes of cultural mutation and restless (dis)continuity" (2). As Daniel Howe even more clearly explains, "A culture can reach out beyond the social group with which it originates and become a vital element in the consciousness of others." What is more, those adopting the other culture can "sometimes . . . retain [. . .] the ability to appreciate and perpetuate their original cultural heritage as well as their new one" (10, 11). African American culture is not, to borrow Edward Said's expression, "antiseptically quarantined from . . . worldly affiliations" (xiv). Surely black Americans are as much a crossed as a sailed people. To understand the situation of African Americans in the nineteenth and early twentieth centuries one must do so with an awareness not only of the roles America and Africa but also with a sharper awareness of the role Europe, especially Britain, played. To appreciate nineteenth-century blacks' experience both as a colonized people living within what had been a white colony and as hyperhybridized people or at least as the cultural wards and orphans, not only of Africa and America, but also of Britain, it is necessary to read and think, as Edward Said insists, "contrapuntally," in a way that "convey[s] a more urgent sense of the interdependence between things" because the historical experience of empire has made "all cultures . . . involved in one another; none is single and pure, all are hybrid, heterogeneous, extraordinarily differentiated, and unmonolithic" (18, 61, xxv).

A contrapuntal reading of Victorian blacks might do well to begin with the British engagement with Africans, a reading that Patrick Brantlinger so deftly begins to undertake in his essay on the genealogy of Africa as a dark continent, "Victorians and Africans." Here Brantlinger demonstrates how a country that made substantial contributions to the grand narratives of emancipation and enlightenment created a damning narrative about a barbaric, savage, and ignorant Africa in need of the civilizing guidance of the imperial metropolis. In describing the Victorian scripting of Africa as a dark continent, Brantlinger brings to the fore one of the problematic factors of a study that purports, as this one does, to limn a special connection between British Victorians and African Americans. For if, as Brantlinger avers, England experienced a transvaluation of values marked in its shift from the abolitionism of the 1830s to imperialism, which gets underway in 1884 with the Berlin Conference which officially launches the "scramble for Africa," and if, as Brantlinger further and convincingly argues, "abolitionism contained the seeds of empire," then what are the ramifications for nineteenth- and early twentieth-century black Americans who embraced England and its Victorianism (185, 186)? Critic Paul Gilroy starts down this road of African American connections to the British when he points to a need "to reconsider Frederick Douglass's relationship to English and Scottish radicalisms and to meditate on the significance of William Wells Brown's five years in Europe as a fugitive slave, on Alexander Crummell's living and studying in Cambridge, and upon Martin Delany's experiences at the London congress of the International Statistical Congress in 1860." Finally, we need to understand, Gilroy continues, "such difficult and complex questions as W. E. B. Du Bois's childhood interest in Bismarck, his investment in modelling his dress and moustache on that of Kaiser Wilhelm II, his likely thoughts while sitting in Heinrich Von Treitschke's seminars, and the use his tragic heroes make of European culture" (17). Some of the questions that best formulate the gist of this call for a reconsideration, if not a reconciliation, of strange bedfellows are as follows: How did Britain and its Victorian ideas help or hinder black negotiation of prejudice and racism in America? How did the presence and agitations of blacks in the United States affect the British Victorians? How did England square its support of African Americans with its imperialism? In what sense are blacks belated Victorians? Such inquiries and interrogations shape and inform the substance of this study of two groups of people seemingly worlds apart.

Indeed, it is not so much a postcolonial awareness of how political discontinuities might seem to outweigh any real, significant, or notable connections between blacks in American and the Victorians in England as it is the sheer differences in status and social condition of the two groups that interfere with the perception of African American and Victorian British continuities. Thus, in England in 1837, this, the year of Queen Victoria's ascension, would officially mark the beginning of a transition that would eventually see the British nation riding the crest of a rationalism and an empiricism that took its impetus from and found its most immediate source in the eighteenth-century enlightenment and the onset of industrialization. In the nineteenth century, the Victorians were confident and triumphant. The English people (I am speaking especially of white Britons) in greater numbers than ever before enjoyed increased leisure and wealth. Indeed, the material progress of the nation was something of a marvel, a matter of pride if not complacency. As critic Richard L. Rapson has noted, "Many an Englishman felt compelled to proclaim with . . . rhapsodic exaggeration his satisfaction with his world, his country, and his future" (18). By 1882, Englishman Frederic Harrison writing for the *Fortnightly Review* would reflect with such rhapsody upon the "magnificent epoch" in which he was privileged to have been born:

> Surely no century in all human history was ever so much praised to its face for its wonderful achievements, its wealth and its power, its unparalleled ingenuity and its miraculous capacity for making itself comfortable and generally enjoying life. British Associations, and all sorts of associations, economic, scientific, and mechanical, are perpetually executing cantatas in honour of the age of progress, cantatas which (alas!) last much longer than three hours. (412).

Victoria's "subjects" looked remarkable in other ways too. They tended to be optimistic, dogmatic, earnest, and enthusiastic. Bowling forth in the physical universe with all the force that steam engines, railroads, and electric telegraphs could lend them, the Victorians also passed democratic reforms that signaled a concomitant social and political progression, every bit as exciting as the industrial, technological, and scientific one. I do not mean to suggest that the Victorians had found utopia. They paid a price for their prosperity; they knew anxiety, and they felt tensions that have been documented and chronicled in their literature and by twentieth-century critics such as Walter Houghton. Even though it may indeed be true that the best of times can also be the worst of times, the point is that, on the whole, the white nineteenth-century Victorian was part of a nation, an empire, and a group that felt itself to be approaching a pinnacle, an intellectual and cultural apotheosis.

On the other side of the Atlantic Ocean in the United States of America in 1837, no story could have been more different from that of the white Britons than that of African Americans. Whereas the white Britons were subjects of the queen, black Americans were the objects of the masters. Here was a people still not free (ironically not free in the midst of a democracy), and even later on in the nineteenth century when black Americans were emancipated, that emancipation would only mean the exchange of physical chains for just as substantial if "invisible" fetters. Though they made increased leisure and wealth possible for white Americans, though their bodies insured material and even intellectual progress for others, they could not and did not reap the benefits of their own labor. Progress, wealth, power, and comfort were not for them. For the most part, illiterate and propertyless (being property themselves), black Americans could only say that it was the worst of times and had been since their arrival in America. If the white British were a nation of people with dominion, then what made black Americans, in the words of Robert Stepto, "national" was the fact that they were a people "without dominion" (77). Indeed, during the nineteenth century, no beings ever looked so opposite, so removed from each other by ocean and experience as the white Briton and the African American. These two were truly, to borrow Ronald Takaki's words "from different shores."

Yet, this division is arguably not so stark as it appears. In *Black Atlantic,* Paul Gilroy has made great strides to overcome the division, exclusivity, and "ethnic absolutism" among the diasporic blacks, particularly among blacks separated by the Atlantic Ocean (2). What remains is an interrogation of the division between and exclusivity of white Britain and black America. This is to say that just beyond Gilroy's concept of a geocritical space called the Black Atlantic, there lies a Victorian Black Atlantic that signifies how profoundly, if at times subtly and imperceptibly, Victorian ideas shaped and were shaped by those diasporic blacks who lived across the Atlantic in the United States of America.

For Victorian Britain is deeply and complexly implicated in the lives of nineteenth- and twentieth-century black Americans. British influence on abolitionist societies in America has been well-documented. Like the northern states of the United States and neighboring Canada, Britain was, especially in the minds of nineteenth-century blacks in the South, a geopolitical mecca. Yet, unlike these other liberatory spaces, England stood apart as a land simultaneously too far and too near. This is to say that the British Isles were not only physically less accessible to American blacks by some 3,000 miles of ocean but that Britain itself was also historically contiguous to white Americans as the motherland of the American colonies. Forever aligned, if not allied with America, Britain was an important force in the cultural identity of a white America that by the nineteenth century was firmly steeped in the slavery from which the British had just managed to pull away. What remains to be done is what this book sets out to do—to study the relations of the African

American to Victorian Britain. For Britain served not only as what Paul Gilroy calls the "parental culture" for white America, but also a parental culture for black Americans, as important cultural connections between the Briton and the African American grew despite Victorians' (whether British or American) efforts, in the words of Stanley Coben, "to exclude certain other ethnic groups perceived as alien from full membership in either the established culture or the nation" (Gilroy 2; Coben 4). Long before interwar France, "allowed," as Brent Hayes Edwards argues, "boundary crossing, conversations, and collaborations that were available nowhere else to the same degree," Victorian Britain itself served as a vortex for such crossings, conversations, and collaborations between African Americans and British Victorians (4). The Victorians and Victorianism would become so insinuated in the life of African Americans that by the beginning of the twentieth century, W. E. B. Du Bois in his biography of the race, *The Souls of Black Folk,* prefaced the chapters of this work by pairing bars of black sorrow songs with snippets of poetry or prose by Victorian writers. As late as 1969, Maya Angelou in the best-read book of her multivolumed autobiography, *I Know Why the Caged Bird Sings,* describes black girls in the small southern towns of the 1930s caught in a time warp of Victorian values: "While white girls learned to waltz and sit gracefully with a tea cup balanced on their knees, we were lagging behind, learning the mid-Victorian values with very little money to indulge them" (87). Blacks also embraced Victorianism. It remains for scholars to understand how and why. Driven by such questions, *Dark Victorians* studies discursive and cultural cadences, kinships, and correspondences. It describes a romance between African Americans and Britain by examining the works of such distinguished sociocultural brokers as Harriet Martineau, Thomas Carlyle, Charles Dickens, Elizabeth Barrett Browning, Frederick Douglass, Ida B. Wells, and W. E. B Du Bois to learn about the conditions, circumstances, and events that yield the phenomenon of a Black Victorianism. A phenomenon that comes about in part because, as Victorian Thomas Carlyle admitted, "I now perceive more clearly than ever, that any man's opinions depend not on himself so much as on the age he lives in, or even the persons with whom he associates"—associates, I should add, not only by means of personal contact but also, especially and subtly, by means of literature and discourse, which Michel Foucault describes as power (30).

The purpose of this study, then, is not to revisit the history of abolitionism, though *Dark Victorians* does, to some extent, just that. Rather, the aim of this study is to take stock of the response of British visitors to slavery in America and, even more important, to note how major African American thinkers and doers from Frederick Douglass, William Wells Brown, Harriet Jacobs, Martin Delany, Alexander Crummel, and others right down to

Ida B. Wells and W. E. B. Du Bois reacted to their travels to and sojourns in Britain. In gauging these responses and reactions, the study seeks to limn a filiation or to describe a mutuality of influence between black Americans and white Britons. The subject is complex, treating over nearly a century and a half of transatlantic connections, multiple writers, two races, and two nations. However, in taking up some of the threads of a complex transatlantic tapestry, the book always remains invested in the effort to locate linkages, to find, as William S. McFeely would put it, "both critical and common ground" in the relations of African Americans and British Victorians (22). To this end, the first chapter provides a context for British and African American interactions by reviewing the history of England's relations with the United States and American and England's history of encounters with blacks. More specifically, the first chapter examines how British writers, both those who came and those who did not come to America, engaged through their writings the institution that defined life for black Americans in the nineteenth-century—slavery. The second chapter reverses traffic across the Victorian Atlantic. Whereas chapter 1 sees the British traveling to or looking across the Atlantic at blacks in the United States, chapter 2 considers black Americans who cross over to the British Isles. In exploring the travels of prominent black individuals to Britain, the chapter spells out some of the sociohistorical imperatives for African American travel during the Victorian age. The next two chapters treat the relations between African Americans and Victorians by looking at two prominent figures—one white and British, the other black and American—who may both be described as Victorian and who furthermore may be literally or figuratively, culturally or physically described as dark Victorians. The critical and common ground between the African American and the British Victorian is more specifically represented in these final two chapters on Thomas Carlyle and W. E. B. Du Bois, respectively. Arguably among the most influential, colorful, and celebrated men of their time, race, and country, these two cultural prophets appear as oppositional as black and white can make them, given the fact that one was convinced of the inferiority of blacks, the other committed to black uplift. The goal of chapter 3 and chapter 4 is to underscore the study's major premise—that the transatlantic travel, if not drift of bodies and discourse, ensured that the disparate worlds of the African American and the British Victorian did not, after all, lie so terribly far apart. Queen Victoria's kingdom, in its formulations of nationalistic England and imperialistic Britain, would help unlock more social, cultural, and political doors for African Americans than the newly founded democracy in the United States, and African Americans, in turn, would factor into Victorian philanthropy and contribute to the shaping of Victorian discourse on reform and race.

1. On Coming to America

The British Subject and the African American Slave

The primary objective of most early nineteenth-century British travelers to the United States was not to take tea with the country's slaves. However, upon their arrival, these visitors inevitably came face to face with the institution of slavery and the blacks subjected to that institution. These British encounters were ultimately colored by Britain's own peculiar history with blacks and slavery as well as by the ties the British had to America. It is helpful to read British writings about nineteenth-century African America in the context of at least a basic understanding of this history and these ties. To do so is to realize that, in their commentary about black Americans, the British subjects who literally or figuratively crossed the Atlantic did not write out of a strict solidarity with white Americans but rather out of a unity or fraternity qualified by the history of what had happened to Africans on English soil and finally in British colonies. On coming to America, British men and women found one of the main attractions to be the African Americans, who lived under a system if not completely alien to, then certainly outlawed on English soil by 1772 and rendered commercially obsolete in the British West Indies by the 1830s. America, which had won its independence from monarchal England in 1776 and which in its democratic governance and society appeared so new, so daringly experimental, was lagging behind on the issue of human bondage.

Still, if, strictly speaking, America did not completely bedazzle, it certainly held great magnetic appeal for nineteenth-century middle- and upper-class Britons. After all, between America and Britain there was literally and figuratively blood, both good and bad. British novelist Anthony Trollope described these ties of history, money, and blood in 1861 at a time when the threat of war loomed between England and a U.S. government already embroiled in a war of secession: "Family connections between the States and the British Isles are almost as close as between one of those islands and another. The commercial intercourse between the two countries has given bread to millions of Englishmen. . . . These people speak our language, use our prayers, read our books, are ruled by our laws, dress themselves in our image, are warm with our blood. They have all our virtues; and their vices are our own too, loudly as we call out against them. They are our sons and our daughters, the source of our greatest pride, and as we grow old they should be the staff of our age" (290). These commonalities of shared family, language, history, and economy did not preclude, as Trollope understood, national differences. Thus, even at the beginning of the nineteenth century, "the contrast [of the New World] with the Old World was," as William J. Baker declares, "dramatic." Government, physical space, and class-structure differed: "In Europe hereditary monarchs still reigned, supported by an aristocratic tradition and state religions which controlled education. No physical, unclaimed frontiers existed. Society was highly class-structured, and few Europeans thought seriously in terms of social equality. Families were paternalistic. . . . At every point this prior cultural conditioning . . . ran headlong against American ideas and institutions" (11). By the opening decades of the nineteenth century, slavery would prove one of the most important American institutions against which British law and some influential members of British society would run headlong.

When the American colonies broke away from British rule in the 1780s, the British fascination with America began. "It was a trauma the British could never forget," declares Ronald Hyam in his study of the British Empire and its expansion, *Britain's Imperial Century, 1815–1914* (1976). "The Great Experiment challenged, fascinated, dogged them." Some Englishmen no doubt thought the American experiment "constitutionally enriching in the realm of political thought," an "embod[iment of] the cause of freedom, equality and anti aristocracy"; however, "to some Tory English aristocrats the success of American democracy was seen as a threat" (52, 53, 54). So in the nineteenth century, one of the reasons Britons crossed the Atlantic was to check on the young country, which "was the seat of democracy, a new, bold experiment in the affairs of modern civilization" (Baker 11). However, British men and women also sailed to America for reasons as multifarious as monitoring investments, fleeing or easing financial distress, ameliorating connubial relations, sightseeing, collecting information for travel books, asserting independence, and experiencing the culture.[1] Some antebellum travelers, such as Charles Dickens and William Makepeace Thackeray, went back for second visits, no small undertaking considering the expense and inconvenience, if not peril, involved in a transatlantic crossing during this period, especially "before 1850 [when] a voyage from Liverpool to New York was a hazardous and wearying experience. Only those with high motivation, unusual courage, ample time, substantial income, or a specific mission dared risk the [watery] passage" (Rapson 25), which perhaps more than any other form of travel "was physically disturbing to the stomach, bowels and skin" (Morgan 12). As Mary Suzanne Schriber observes in her study of middle- and upper-middle-class white female travelers, "travel required sacrifice and penance. All travelers tolerated inconveniences and many of them withstood considerable discomfort for travel's promised privileges. Whether crossing the Atlantic or the Pacific . . . travelers not only suffered from dreaded and often excruciating sea-sickness, but from the worries occasioned by the fatal accidents to which ships were subject, such as fires, icebergs, and collisions with other ships" (18). Though the first transatlantic crossings by steamship were made in the 1830s, it would be a century later, during the years between the two World Wars with the advent of the transatlantic steamer as an established mode of travel by sea, that "travel . . . by ocean liner" would become, according to Paul Fussell, "one of the cheapest ways of living, certainly for a freelance writer who carried his office with him and could work in his cabin or in a saloon" (71). From 1839 until the turn of the century, however, the Cunard Line—successfully launched when Samuel Cunard of Halifax, Novia Scotia, landed a contract to transport mail along with passengers between Great Britain and North America—proved the best buy for the money and for safety. Still, as one history of the Cunard liners reports, although the Cunard venture was subsidized by the British government, the "penalty for missing a sailing was £15,000, and a delay of more than twelve hours could cost £500. The initial fares were quoted as 34 guineas to Halifax, 38 guineas to Boston. However, costs were far higher than at first anticipated" (Rentell 3). Early Victorian visitors to the United States and black abolitionists traveling to Great Britain would sail in one of a succession of Cunard liners, including the *Britannia, Arcadia, Caledonia, Columbia, Cambria, Hibernia, America, Niagara, Europa,* and *Canada.* The conservative company would work hard and successfully to establish a record of safety.[2]

No matter what the reason for the journeys or the logistics of the voyage, on coming to America, the British found one compelling feature of the United States to be its red and black men and women. Accordingly, in the travelogues, essays, and books on America from the 1830s and 1840s, these visitors upon their return home tended to comment upon the status of these two groups.[3] Though British writers were anything but oblivious to the position of Native Americans, they were especially attuned to the blacks in America who underwrote the Southern economy and notions of Southern gentility. As late as 1853, Thackeray still experienced black Americans as one of the signal defining features of the country. In a letter written to his mother during the first of his two trips to the United States, he confessed that "I feel as if my travels had only just begun—There was scarce any sensation of novelty until now when the slaves come on to the scene; and straightaway the country assumes an aspect of the queerest interest" (*Letters and Private Papers* 3: 198–99). During the first half of the nineteenth century, the mention of or reference to the subjugation of blacks in the travel literature of English visitors to the United States was practically obligatory.

British writers often remarked upon and singled out African Americans in the travel works for several reasons. One of these was that the customary trip of the British traveler to the South, especially before the Civil War, not only meant a confrontation with the presence of blacks (there were blacks to be met with in the Northern cities), but also a more direct if not intense encounter with the formidable institution of slavery. Like the black spokespersons who visited England as part of the abolitionist societies that emerged in the United States in the 1830s, the British traveler to America who came into contact with blacks could in their writings make those blacks "convenient vehicles for British scorn of American life and values" (Pease 49). British writers tended to register the black presence in the United States because "the color line" (so named by W. E. B. Du Bois) was so sharply and rigidly drawn in the United States. In addition, American society was so preoccupied with its blacks that, as writers such as Dickens and Martineau would argue, the position of blacks was almost steadily kept before the traveler: in conversations warning British travelers to the South to steer clear of the subject of slavery and abolition and in public notices and newspapers advertising the sale of slaves or calling for the apprehension of runaways. The English actress Fanny Kemble wrote, "The Southern newspapers, with their advertisements of negro sales and personal descriptions of fugitive slaves, supply details of misery that it would be difficult for imagination to exceed" (10). Englishman George Combe, who made a "phrenological visit" to the States from 1838 to 1840, exclaimed that "nothing in the United States has surprised me so much as the general tone of the public mind and the press on the subject of slavery" (1: 158). In *American Notes* (1842), novelist Charles Dickens, who, according to Peter Ackroyd, would "implicitly . . . support the South in the Civil War" (Ackroyd 971), underscored the ugliness of slavery by quoting among other things "a few specimens of the advertisements in the public papers" for runaways such as "the negro Manuel . . . Much marked with irons"; "the negro Jim Blake" who "has a piece cut out of each ear, and the middle finger of the left hand cut off to the second joint"; "my man Isaac" with "a scar on his forehead, caused by a blow; one on his back, made by a shot from a pistol"; the two children and a black woman identifiable because "A few days before she went off, I burnt her with a hot iron, on the left side of her face. I tried to make the letter M"; "the Mulatto wench Mary. Has a cut on the left arm, a scar on the left shoulder, and two upper teeth missing" (Dickens 273–274, 275). Exposed to similar media fare, Harriet Martineau remarked how "the traveller in America hear[ing] on every hand of the fondness of slaves for slavery," nevertheless read numerous advertisements for runaways: "If he [the traveller in America] points to the little picture of a runaway prefixed to advertisements of fugitives, and repeated down whole columns of the first newspaper that comes to hand, he is met with anecdotes of slaves who have been offered their freedom, and prefer remaining in bondage" (1: 242). Supporters of slavery told one story, and newspaper advertisements told another.

In addition to long columns of advertisements for runaways and a goodly share of anecdotes about happy slaves, Martineau found "there was no end to the kind cautions given me against travelling through the Southern States" not only "because of the badness of the roads and the poverty of the wayside accommodations" but also because of her "opinions on slavery." Though Martineau confesses in *Retrospect of Western Travel* (1838) that she had "observed somewhat of the degradation of the blacks," she recalls that her "mind had not yet been really troubled about the enmity of the races." Her "awakening," as she calls it, "began just before I left Philadelphia" en route to the Southern states. In a conversation with a lady about interracial marriage, Martineau found herself decried as an "amalgamationist." The "denunciations," reports Martineau, "spread rapidly from her." So that the day before her departure from Philadelphia, Martineau's "old shipmate, the Prussian physician . . . lost no time in calling to tell me, with much agitation, that I must not go a step farther south; that he had heard on all hands, within two hours of his arrival, that I was an amalgamationist, and that my having published a story against slavery would be fatal to me in the slave states." These and similar circumstances only prove, as Harriet Martineau so succinctly put it, "how irritable the minds of the people are upon this topic" of slavery and how this irritability resonated so equivocally in the minds of English travelers (1: 139, 140, 225, see also 208–9). As Una Pope-Hennessy in *Three English Women in America* (1929) has remarked about British who traveled to the United States in the opening decade of the nineteenth century, "The slave States . . . presented an irresistible lure for Europeans. With feelings compounded of curiosity, repugnance, and sentimentality they plunged into Virginia, easing themselves into a kind of acquiescence in conditions which theoretically they abhorred, when they saw the beaming negro in aristocratic houses and stables" (14).

Naturally, English men and women finding the American people so agitated by the subject of black Americans and slavery felt compelled to write about the matter, even if that writing about slavery proved, according to historian Thomas D. Clark, uneven, brief, and "hit-and-miss" (737). Although a British subject such as Fanny Kemble, who married a Southern slave owner and lived with him on his plantation, may be counted among those all too few "patient, methodical, and persistent" observers, it is true that even those British travelers who "rarely did . . . actually observe slavery through day-to-day or season-to-season operation," and those Europeans travelers who "were satisfied to record conclusions" about slavery "drawn from casual street, roadside, and tavern-room and drawing-room conversations, cursory visits to farms and plantations, and wayside talks with planters"—the Europeans who at least traveled to American and read its print media on the subject of African Americans—were still better informed than if they had remained back in England (Clark 737). Finally, however, the British who traveled to America, then sailed back to England where they published an account of their experiences in the New World tended to treat the African American as an obligatory if not integral part of their narratives because ultimately blacks were yet another link between the British and the Americans. This is to say, the British had their own history of relations with blacks that duly influenced their perceptions and reactions to the black presence in the United States.

Despite Britain's relatively late arrival on the scene of the transatlantic slave trade, it became not only the main supplier of slaves to the colonies but also a great beneficiary of the trade. With the Asiento of 1713, an agreement between Spain and England that gave the slave trading monopoly that was formerly Spain's to the English, "England became the leading slave mistress, slave trader, and slave carrier of the world" (Shyllon 8). As such, they were instrumental in establishing slavery in the New World and in paving the way to their own imperial expansion. More recently, British historian James Walvin has written in *Making the Black Atlantic* about the "crucial" role of the British "in the shaping of the enslaved Atlantic," reminding readers of just how entrenched and reprehensible the British were: "British ships carried millions of Africans into slavery across the Atlantic; British colonies and settlements were made viable by absorbing larger numbers of African slaves; British material well-being was greatly enhanced by the sweat of those same slaves." Continuing to strike this chord, Walvin reiterates his claim that "at the height of the Atlantic slave system, the British shipped more Africans than any other nation; their slave colonies disgorged produce (and its associated prosperity) on an unparalleled scale, and Britain itself benefited from slavery to a degree which largely goes unrecognized" (x). Yet the English would abolish the slave trade by 1807 and end slavery itself in the British realm in 1838, nearly three decades before the United States. Historian Michael Craton accounts for this sociopolitical precocity mainly by pointing out that the British behaved like humanitarians because slavery was no longer economically profitable or feasible. As he puts it, "Commercial success . . . was its own morality" (*Sinews of Empire* xix). In *England, Slaves, and Freedom, 1776–1838* (1986), James Walvin does an excellent job of tracing the web of economics, religion, and politics that prompted England to dispense with first the slave trade then slavery itself. Another interesting point, Walvin makes elsewhere is that because the British experienced slavery in their own peculiar way—at a distance in their colonies, as "an institution which thrived 5,000 miles away" (*Black Ivory* 304–5)—they became neither hardened, inured to this outrageous savagery of the peculiar institution, nor did they become dependent on slave labor in the same way as did whites especially in the southern states of America. This is not to say that there were no slaves in England itself. As Folarin Shyllon reminds us, "blacks . . . brought into Britain in their [*sic*] thousands [during the seventeenth century, in fact] were . . . the merest of chattels, obliged to wear collars like dogs, freely and shamelessly bought and sold, and freely and callously bequeathed to relatives" (11). Indeed, as late as the first quarter of the nineteenth century, in a land of absentee plantation owners, slaves were too often at the mercy of whites, whom Michael Craton has described in *Testing the Chains* as "a case-hardened crew of salaried managers and bookkeepers" (269–70). However, by the end of the eighteenth century, slavery was taking a turn toward dissolution. Though there were free and enslaved Africans in Britain, "until 1772," Shyllon reports, "the great majority were slaves. From then onwards, the number of free blacks increased until 1834 when black slaves in both Britain and the colonies were emancipated" (75). British slaves lived in "plantation households"—those of West Indian planters or officials who "had brought back to England some of their household body-servants," or the slaves lived in "non-plantation households"—those "of Englishmen who had never been to the West Indies, but had acquired blacks as an 'index of rank'" (78). The slavery of American colonialists was ultimately not the slavery of old world imperialists. As Robin Blackburn instructs in *The Overthrow of Colonial Slavery*, "The species of slavery that prevailed in the Americas in the eighteenth century should not be seen as a relic of the Ancient or medieval world." Blackburn goes on to explain: "The colonial systems were of very recent construction and were highly commercial in character . . . The slaves were drawn exclusively from Africa and the great majority of them were subjected to harsh labour regimes. By contrast previous forms of slavery had been less far-flung, less commercial and more heterogeneous. The slaves of the New world were economic property and the main motive for slaveholding was economic exploitation; to this end at least nine tenths of American slaves were put to commodity production" (7). Although England was complicit in the slavery of New World planters, its feudal history and its "*extensive* system of imperial exploitation contrasted with the *intensive* regime of micro-exploitation on the slave plantations elsewhere in the Americas" (Blackburn 9–10). The crucial point is that in England there were no plantations—the main establishments that lent relations between blacks and whites in the United States their peculiarly intense and pernicious quality.

Instead, in England, which had had an earlier and longer contact with Africans, the British would be exposed to Africans and Anglo-Africans on a variety of terms that demonstrated, among other things, black intellectuality. The blacks that had been in England before 1772 were not only there as slaves, but as thinkers, visitors, and scholars. As Shyllon makes clear in one of the chapters of his study of blacks in Britain between 1555 and 1833, African kings sent their sons to England to be educated as did West Indian planters who had fathered children by black women. Furthermore, the British were no strangers to the reality of black scholars and poets such as the black Arabic scholar Suleiman Diallo or, as he is best known, Job Ben Solomon; polymath and polyglot George de St. Georges; or the black Latin poet who studied at Cambridge University, Francis Williams. England would also have its Olaudah Equiano before America had its Frederick Douglass and so experience much earlier than the United States, where black literacy was illegal, the tradition of the homegrown slave's narrative written by him or herself, the slave narration being, as Charles T. Davis and Henry Louis Gates, Jr. assert, "the millennial instrument of transformation through which the African would become the European, the slave become the ex-slave, the brute animal become the human being" (xxvii). By the last quarter of the eighteenth century, the autobiographies and writings of such prominent black figures as Ukawsaw Gronniosaw, Ottobah Cugoano, Ignatius Sancho, and Olaudah Equiano affected British perceptions of blacks in ways that pointed to, if it did not ensure, the brotherhood of blacks and whites. Finally, the number of blacks in Britain ought also to be factored into the account of British relations with blacks. Demographically, because there were so few blacks in England, especially in the eighteenth and early nineteenth centuries, the British felt neither particularly served nor threatened by the black presence in the homeland. In light of the particular way British relations to Africans unfolded economically, geographically, literarily, and demographically, it was easier for Britain to emancipate its blacks.

Those British men and women traveling to the United States earlier in the nineteenth century had their own national orientation toward blackness and, what is more significant, were sensitized to the plight of darker peoples because between 1807 and 1838 England was grappling itself with its relations to its own black populations. According to scholar Mary Louise Pratt, by the late eighteenth century "Euroimperialism faced a legitimation crisis" as "the histories of broken treaties, genocides, mass displacements and enslavements became less and less acceptable as rationalist and humanitarian ideologies took hold." In Europe, "particularly after the French Revolution, contradictions between egalitarian, democratic ideologies at home and ruthless structures of domination and extermination abroad became more acute." The winds of change were stirring; however, as Pratt so cleverly adds, "the demands of capital remained" (74). Nevertheless, by the early nineteenth century, slavery was one of the institutions to which increasingly industrialized, reform-minded, and democratic Englishmen "were giving a great deal of thought" (Rapson 18, note). The British abolitionist movement, which would influence similar movements across the sea in America, was ultimately a part of the great wave of belief in "social amelioration," in the ability of men to "correct social abuses and to refurbish outmoded institutions" (Brantlinger, *Spirit of Reform* 1). As James Walvin has surmised in *Black Ivory*, "To end slavery would be to strike a blow for reform; it would be a step towards a more just society. It would assuage the Christian conscience, would exonerate the sense of national virtue, please the supporters of new economic theories and confirm the justice of popular demand. An end to slavery would unite more Britons than any other issue. It was a victory for morality, for religion and good economic sense" (306). By 1838, the dilemma of the monarchal democracy—to emancipate or not to emancipate—had been resolved so that, Britain could now sit back and observe the vicissitudes of social progress in the States.

This is exactly what that great writer of books and sea tales such as *Frank Mildmay* (1829), *Peter Simple* (1834), and *Mr. Midshipman Easy* (1836), Captain Frederick Marryat, who traveled to America in 1837, so clearly does when he concedes that "slavery did commence when the colonies were subject to the mother country" but nevertheless thinks it "singular that the Americans at the time of their Declaration of Independence, took no measures for the gradual, if not immediate, extinction of slavery." Marryat, who upon visiting the United States, found free black Philadelphians "superior . . . in intelligence and education to what, from my knowledge of them in our West India islands, I had ever imagined them capable of" did not believe that blacks would "ever attain to the same powers of intellect as the white man, for I really believe that the race are not formed for it by the Almighty" (275, 149). His fictions such as *Midshipman Easy* and *Peter Simple* in which foolish characters find it difficult to defend the rights of men, his disdain for black intelligence, and his belief in white superiority did not prevent him from pointing out the legal, political, and moral contradictions in and culpability of slaveholding democracy. Marryat contended that it was "useless" for Americans "to exclaim . . . that it was England" who had bequeathed them slavery. It was useless to "reproach" the British for "having originally introduced the system among them" because "there was nothing to prevent immediate manumission at the time of the acknowledgement of their independence by Great Britain." Marryat concluded strongly and defensively that "the Americans have no right to revile us on being the cause of slavery in America. They had the means, and were bound, as honourable men, to act up to their declaration; but they entered into the question . . . and decided that they would retain their ill-acquired property at the expense of their principles" (275, 278). As far as Marryat was concerned, if America was going to set itself apart in its declarations of independence, democracy, and freedom, then it was obligated to act on those declarations.

Not all British comers to antebellum America saw the American decision not to manumit its slaves as a singular failure or an ungentlemanly lapse of principles. The spirit of reform was indeed abroad, but the fact remained that early visitors to America were coming from what had traditionally been a highly class-structured society in which few Europeans thought seriously about social equality among the members of their own race. Given that the British were still very much the product of a hierarchical sociopolitical system and given the additional fact of what Christine Bolt identifies in *Victorian Attitudes to Race* as a "belief in Anglo-Saxon solidarity and supremacy" (39) that was supported by Victorians sciences such as anthropology, the mixed response of some British travelers to slavery in the United States may do more finally to suggest the nature of one of the tensions between England and America than to demonstrate a British concern with the plight of blacks in America.

One British visitor to America who may be said to have quarreled bitterly with the young nation was Frances Trollope, mother of civil servant and novelist Anthony Trollope who himself made four or five trips to America, publishing in 1862 after his first real sojourn in North America a book by that name that constitutes a work sensitive to and corrective of his mother's rendering of America. Interestingly enough, though Frances Trollope was practically reviled after the publication of her travel account, *Domestic Manners of the Americans* (1832), she, "who so enraged American vanity" with criticism of "cockroaches, spitting, poor table manners, and execrable taste," she, too, who offended Americans with her criticism of that which she herself termed "the jarring tumult and universal degradation which invariably follow the wild scheme of placing all the power of the state in the hands of the populace," did little to vex Americans on the question of slavery (Mooney xi, xiv; Trollope xix).

One of the inducements for Frances Trollope's three-year sojourn in America was financial (as it had been for Dickens who hoped to reap the whirlwind of his popularity and increase his monetary store). Trollope hoped to recover the bankrupt fortunes of her family by opening an "emporium for [the sale of] fancy goods in the West." After the resounding failure of the bazaar she had finally opened in Cincinnati, Trollope, upon her return to London, would publish *Domestic Manners* in what James Mooney calls "the face of a squalor and deprivation that she was never again to know" (xii, xiii). Although money was one of the enticements for Trollope and her children's three-and-a-half-year residence in the United States, another had been a striking young idealist and friend, Scotswoman Fanny Wright, who not only encouraged Trollope's visit to a country she praised mightily, but who also accompanied Trollope and her children across the waters. Wright shared with Frances Trollope her plans to set up an alternative plantation in Tennessee where she, Fanny, would educate blacks and whites together and thereby disprove black mental inferiority. Trollope herself confesses that though she left England with certain ideas about slavery, "with feelings so strongly opposed to slavery, that it was not without pain I witnessed its effects around me," once she learned more about the "real situation" of the American slaves, she "often smiled at recalling" how she initially "at the sight of every Negro man, woman, and child that passed . . . wove some little romance of misery, as belonging to each of them" (8–9). It would seem, that unlike Fanny Kemble, who was mistress of a Southern plantation, or Fanny Wright, who finally freed and sent to Haiti the slaves she had meant to educate on an estate in Tennessee, Frances Trollope's exposure to the institution was not as abhorrent or objectionable as it had been for her two fellow countrywomen. She did not feel passionately about Fanny Wright's "suffering Africans" (12). Thus, when considering the prospect of a visit to Fanny Wright's experimental establishment, Nashoba, Trollope did not anticipate an opportunity to participate in Wright's effort to correct a wrong but rather she "expected for my children and myself both pleasure and information . . . watching the success of her [Wright's] experiment" (12).

Frances Trollope perceived the contradiction inherent in the slavery at the heart of the American experiment, commenting that "the effect produced upon English people by the sight of slavery in every direction is very new, and not very agreeable, and it is not the less painfully felt from hearing upon every breeze the mocking words, 'All men are born free and equal.'" However, Trollope, who recognized distinctions between slaves living in the North and those in the South, concluded, "the condition of domestic slaves . . . does not generally appear to be bad." Though sadly, "they *may* be sent to the *south* and sold" into harsher conditions, though domestic slaves regrettably "have no power to change" their condition, and may become disaffected if not "kept in that state of profound ignorance which precludes reflection," these slaves "are, generally speaking, tolerably well fed, and decently clothed . . . rarely exposed to the lash," and "carefully nursed in sickness" as "valuable piece[s] of property" (190, 191, 192). Eschewing too close a look at the subject of slaves in the cotton, rice, or sugarcane fields or slaves sold south, Trollope, focusing instead on domestic slaves, was convinced that being a slave in the home of a gentleman was better than being hired help, especially if one was born into slavery. "All free servants in America," she concluded tended to be given to "pining discontent," but those born into servitude were more accepting of their lot (192).

Americans, especially slaveholding Americans, who read *Domestic Manners,* needed not resent Trollope for her abolitionist views. She conceded that slavery had "injurious" aspects for both master and slave; nevertheless, emancipation was unthinkable. "To emancipate them entirely throughout the Union cannot, I conceive, be thought of, consistently with the safety of the country," she declared. What was needed was a kinder, gentler mode of treating blacks who were "very sensible to kindness, and might . . . be rendered more profitably obedient by the practice" of ameliorative treatment based in "wisdom, justice, and mercy" (193, 195).

Phrenologist George Combe was one Briton who did not find emancipation unthinkable. Like Marryat, granting the "historical fact" that slavery in America "originated with England," Combe still argued that American persistence in the pernicious practice of slavery was morally and humanely indefensible. Though "every candid mind must acknowledge that there are great and formidable difficulties in the way of their abolishing it," America's "attempt to defend wrong and call it right" was "only postponing the time when the evil must be dealt with in a different spirit" (1: 160, 161). Slavery was not only a "canker in the moral constitution of the country, that must produce evil continually until it is removed," but it was also a canker on the legal constitution of the country, specifically, as Combe saw it, on the Declaration of Independence, which states that the "just power of government" comes from "the consent of the governed." It followed, Combe reasoned, that "*Slavery is a form of government.* The slaves have never consented to it: It is therefore unjust, and ought to be abolished" (1: 158, 2: 96). America persisted in doing wrong. He concluded that England, however, had righted herself as "on 1st August 1834 . . . she at length did tardy justice to the negro race by declaring them free in all her colonial territories." It was the Americans who were truly remiss. Combe believed, "The true friend of the United States, therefore, while he regards them as having inherited from the British government the great evil of slavery, must acknowledge it to be a calamity, and desire its termination" (1: 161).

Though Combe definitely saw himself as a "true friend of the United States," it is not clear that his friendship extended to the black American. As a practitioner of phrenology, a pseudoscience that purported to read moral and intellectual character through the size and shape of the head, the contour and heft of the brain, George Combe would go beyond the exterior body to take the measure of the crania and living heads of black Americans with results just as racialized not only as some of Dickens's, Kemble's, Thackeray's, or Trollope's descriptions, but also as many of his brethren in the legitimate sciences. Phrenologically speaking, the blacks, as Combe saw it, had been enslaved because they were more tractable than Native Americans: "The Negro is . . . naturally more submissive, docile, intelligent, patient, trustworthy, and susceptible of kindly emotions, and less cruel, cunning, and vindictive than the other race [Native Americans]." Consequently, "the white men can oppress him far beyond the limits of Indian endurance, and still trust their lives and property within this reach; while he is so intelligent that his labor is worth acquiring." Combe goes on to state what the descriptions of Dickens and even Kemble have merely implied—white superiority: "In both [the African American and the Native American], the brain is inferior in size, particularly in the moral and intellectual regions, to that of the Anglo-Saxon race, and hence the foundation of the natural superiority of the latter over both." Though Combe expected and called for abolition of slavery, a "subject . . . deeply distressing" to him, he did so out of a noble conviction that slavery in the States was morally, religiously, philosophically, and legally wrong, but he also supported the idea of black emancipation out of a practical conviction that the African American would pose no real threat to whites. It was Combe's "conviction . . . that the very qualities which render the Negro in slavery a safe companion to the White, will make him harmless when free" (1: 260, 265).

Some British travelers to America during the early decades of Victoria's reign found the treatment of black people in the new nation unequivocally deplorable if not diabolical. Political activist and writer Harriet Martineau, for instance, who sailed to America in 1834 just three years before Victoria ascended the throne, was appalled by the exploitation of black bodies and the ruin of their moral and intellectual being. As a member of a "Unitarian minority . . . that, despite their [*sic*] often substantial economic and professional success and frequently high educational attainments," as British historian David Turley puts it, "nurtured [such] a consciousness of having suffered discrimination for their beliefs" that they referred to themselves as "theological Negroes," Harriet Martineau was especially attuned to the plight of the African American (57). A Unitarian intellectual and an avid abolitionist, Martineau, who had written moral histories to promote black emancipation as well as a hero-worshipping historical novel about Toussaint L'Ouverture, *The Hour and the Man* (1841), was not only morally but intellectually put off by slavery and its hypocrisies and contradictions. Having witnessed the "hatred of the whites to the blacks in America," she marveled at white "contempt for" black bodies that were "taken for dissection" because the exploitation of black bodies in this way (bodies, I should add, already exploited in barns, fields, kitchens, bedrooms, and closets) was tantamount to an admission of black humanity. After all, "with the exception of the colouring of the skin," the "bodily structure" of blacks "can be . . . thus assumed to be the pattern of that of the whites." Martineau could not understand how "the exquisite nervous system, the instrument of moral as well as physical pleasures and pains" though assumed "analogous with that of the whites" did not afford whites any clue to their shared sensibilities with blacks who were after all their "brethren" (1: 140–41). She was sorely disheartened when she stopped at a boarding house where a slave, a little Negro-child, a "brighteyed, merry-hearted child; confiding, like other children, and dreading no evil, but doomed, hopelessly doomed, to ignorance, privation, and moral degradation" played about her feet. "A horror" came over Martineau that "sickened my very soul" as she "thought of the fearful disobedience to the first of moral laws, the cowardly treachery, the cruel abuse of power involved in thus dooming to blight a being so helpless, so confiding, and so full of promise" (1: 142). Though Martineau, while traveling in America, heard "on every hand of the fondness of slaves for slavery," she undoubtedly questioned the validity of this assertion especially after a visit she paid to the slave market, "a place which the traveller ought not to avoid to spare his feelings" (1: 242, 235). Having gone straight from the auction block into the "fine houses" of white Americans, Martineau came away with an understanding of how at any given moment there were "ministers of the Gospel . . . agreeing to deprive persons of colour of all religious education," or some "distant Lynch mob . . . outraging the person of a free and innocent citizen" (1: 236–37). She was an English traveler who found that "To see slaves is not to be reconciled to slavery" (1: 142).

British actor, Frances Anne Kemble, or Fanny Kemble as she was called, not only saw slaves, but also lived among them as the mistress of a plantation after marrying a slaveholding American, one Pierce Butler of Philadelphia. Before her residence on her husband's cotton and rice plantation in Georgia, Fanny Kemble admitted that though "Assuredly I *am* going prejudiced against slavery, for I am an Englishwoman, in whom the absence of such a prejudice would be disgraceful," she went to the plantation "nevertheless . . . prepared to find many mitigations in the practice to the general injustice and cruelty of the system" (15). When Kemble took up residence on her husband's property on the coast of Georgia in 1838, the same year Martineau published her book on her travels to America, she found anything but a mitigated system. Although "the negroes on . . . [the] estate [were] generally considered well off," she found them living in the darkness of degradation, suffering, sickness, ignorance, and filth (65). She witnessed, as she reports in the journal she kept for her friend Elizabeth Dwight Sedgwick, a "contempt and neglect" so marked that "these poor [black] people are used to make the commonest expression of human sympathy appear a boon and gracious condescension" (41). Indeed, slavery was for both slave and master an "accursed system" that bred misery "even under the best and most humane administration of its laws and usages" (97). As Una Pope-Hennessy declares, "The whole system of 'managing' slaves was abhorrent to Fanny, and the more she knew the worse it seemed. A maximum amount of work had somehow to be dragged out of lazy, shiftless, indifferent human beings" who had little incentive to work: "What incentive could there be to work hard if the work had no end and benefited neither them nor their children, even though they had toiled for thirty or forty years.'" The whip became the motivator, because food, property, or the very lives of the slaves could not be used to compel slave labor. Slaves had little to lose; however, "they did fear suffering, and suffering was hanging like a sword of Damocles always above their heads" (Pope-Hennessy 196–97). Fanny Kemble had great compassion and pity for those beings whose lives so powerfully determined the quality of her own: "with shame and grief of heart I say it, by their unpaid labour I live—their nakedness clothes me, and their heavy toil maintains me in luxurious idleness" (Kemble 73). To this Englishwoman, the blacks on her husband's plantation were her "most injured benefactors." She felt that "the least I can do is to hear [them] . . . indeed, so intense in me is the sense of injury they receive from me and mine, that I should scarce dare refuse them the very clothes from my back, or food from my plate, if they asked me for it" (Kemble 73–74).

Ultimately, the year Fanny Kemble spent on the plantation contributed to the dissolution of her marriage.

Interestingly enough, even Fanny Kemble's moving journalistic testimonial to the meanness of slavery does not preclude a racist assessment of the black body. Before observing that, "the black babies of a year or two old are very pretty . . . hav[ing], for the most part, beautiful eyes and eyelashes, the pearly perfect teeth, which they retain after their other juvenile graces have left them," Kemble comments that "grown negroes" are not very "admirable for their personal beauty (in my opinion, at least)." She did think "their skins are all (I mean of blacks generally) infinitely finer and softer than the skins of white people," and this "characteristic . . . might be accepted as some compensation for the coarse woolly hair." She also found that "the nose and mouth, which are so peculiarly displeasing in their conformation in the face of a negro man or woman, being the features least developed in a baby's countenance, do not at first present the ugliness which they assume as they become more marked." Finally, "another peculiarity" Kemble "remarked among the [black] women" with which she came in contact was the "very considerable beauty in the make of the hands." She noted, too, the handsome figures of some of the women and "their carriage . . . erect and good," though "their feet are very generally ill made, which must be a natural, and not an acquired defect, as they seldom injure their feet by wearing shoes." Granting blacks some redeeming physical features, Kemble was yet struck by displeasing conformations and defects that were the staple of a detrimental stereotyping. Despite her "sympathy for . . . [blacks'] misfortunes, love for their virtues, and respect for their common nature," Fanny Kemble could not completely transcend the racialized body (32, 40, 41, 42).

Charles Dickens's encounter with American slavery in 1842 would not prove personally as remarkable or devastating as Kemble's was, but its potential to transform public opinion about the institution was exponentially higher. By the time Charles Dickens arrived in slavery-ridden America, he was, as John O. Jordan has argued in "Dickens and Diaspora," if not of imperial stature, then a vessel of British character and suasion, "a form of cultural capital exported from Britain to the world" and a figure who by the "post-1945 era of British imperial decline . . . emerged [indeed I would contend reemerged] as an important vehicle for consolidating and reasserting English national identity both at home and abroad" (240). However, during Dickens's 1842 visit, it was what Sidney P. Moss styles Dickens's "quarrel with America" over copyright laws that seemed to preoccupy the lionized British writer during his trip to America. As a matter of fact, while he was in America, Dickens had, in keeping with other English tourists, decided to say nothing about slavery "except in private and when provoked." The result was that "while Dickens was in America, he was outspoken enough on the subject of copyright, but about slavery he had nothing to say." Still, upon returning to the safety of England, Dickens felt, as the editors of the Penguin edition of Dickens's *American Notes* point out, "obliged to include a full chapter on slavery in *American Notes*" (13), a chapter to which Frederick Douglass would later refer his British audience: "Starvation, the bloody whip, the chain, the gag, the thumb-screw, cat-hauling, the cat-o'-nine-tails, the dungeon, the blood-hound, are all in requisition to keep the slave in his condition as a slave in the United States. If any one has a doubt upon this point, I would ask him to read the chapter on slavery in Dickens's *Notes on America*" (*My Bondage and My Freedom* 253). In the chapter on slavery to which Douglass alludes, Dickens contends what Fanny Kemble must have determined about her slave-owning husband that slavery blights and brutalizes. The masters over "the biped beasts of burden," he argued, exercise an "unnatural power" and "a reckless license" that results in "the worst deformity and ugliness" and renders these "men who rule the slaves" what Dickens called "freeborn outlaws." Dickens goes on to inform his readers of "The man . . . born and bred among its [slavery's] wrongs," the man who has seen, as Dickens informed his readers, "husbands obliged at the word of command to flog their wives; women, indecently compelled to hold up their own garments that men might lay the heavier stripes upon their legs," women "becoming mothers on the field of toil, under the very lash itself," the man who "has read in youth, and seen his virgin sisters read, descriptions of runaway men and women, and their disfigured persons. " That man, declared Dickens, "is a coward in his domestic life, stalking among his shrinking men and women slaves armed with his heavy whip," that man can be, "will be a brutal savage" when provoked (180, 270, 283).

However, the slave owner was not alone in his crime. The chapter in which Dickens, according to Sidney P. Moss, "expressed himself explosively on the subject" would also take to task public opinion, which Dickens determined through references to advertisement and newspapers, was deeply implicated in the horror of slavery. Moss has shrewdly argued that Dickens's treatment of slavery in America is vehicular, his true purpose having been "not so much to expose the evil of slavery as the evil of public opinion in America; the same public opinion that had denied him copyright" (178–79). The point is, whatever Dickens's reasons for the chapter on slavery (whether he was adhering to the tradition of the English traveler who went to America and made obligatory reference to slavery, whether he was most anxious to reveal slavery in its nefariousness and reprehensibility, or whether he merely availed himself of another opportunity to criticize indirectly the absence of copyright laws), the fact that he emphatically positions this chapter near the end of the book leaves the reader with an impression not only of the "darker side to Anglo-American relations," but also of a moral "duplicity and chicanery," a terrible "decay and dissolution" that Dickens found bodied forth in the institution of slavery (Whitley and Goldman 13, 28, 33). Ultimately, slavery played no small part in Dickens's quarrel with America.

Still much like Kemble, some of the attitudes Dickens holds about the black body in general, about the physical person of African Americans in particular were unsympathetic and unflattering, if not insulting. Thus Dickens, who having looked upon slavery and "went upon [his] way with a grateful heart that [he] was not doomed to live where slavery was, and had never had [his] senses blunted to its wrongs and horrors in a slave-rocked cradle," could not resist making the American black the butt of a humor that features a black driver "with his eyes starting out of his head," "black drivers . . . chattering . . . like so many monkeys" (though admittedly, the description is offset by white drivers "whooping like so many drovers"), another black driver "twirling his head round and round like a harlequin, rolling his eyes, shrugging his shoulders, and grinning from ear to ear." In *American Notes,* Dickens also refers to a black steward he happens upon when he "take[s] another step forward, and slip[s] upon the shining face of the black" who "jumps up" from the floor where he had been sleeping, and "grins, half in pain and half in hospitality." The Dickensian humor also includes the description of a "fat negress, particularly favoured by nature in respect of bustle" (175, 176, 177, 179, 183–84). Dickens's talent for exaggerating phiz, in these instances, gives stronger currency to negative stereotypes about the very people with whom he would commiserate.

Dickens's propensity to mock in *American Notes* the victims of the system he would denounce foreshadows the shift in his attitude toward blacks that would occur over the next twenty or so years. As Michael Goldberg has observed, "Whereas in 1842 Dickens felt an unequivocal horror for the 'accursed and detested system' of slavery and was glad to turn his back on the states where it was practised, by 1865 he was confessing himself a 'Southern sympathizer to this extent—that I no more believe in the Northern love of the black man, or in the Northern horror of slavery having anything to do' with the beginnings of the Civil War" (149). Although Dickens's biographers, Edgar Johnson and Fred Kaplan, can rightly argue that Dickens sided with neither North nor South during the Civil War, one may also justifiably contend that Dickens, who supported Governor Eyre's bloody suppression of the blacks during the Jamaican rebellion, lost no love on the black race. If we grant what

Peter Ackroyd submits, "There are times when he is more reactionary than any of his contemporaries (with the possible exception of Carlyle), but there are also occasions when he condemns the evils of the nineteenth century in tones that recall the most liberal reformers of the time," then surely by 1865, we may concede that Dickens's regard for blacks had taken on what critic Arthur Adrian in the title to his essay on Dickens and slavery terms a "Carlylean slant" (Ackroyd 378). Ackroyd notes that "he was violently opposed to what he now called 'that platform-sympathy with the black—or the Native, or the Devil . . .' and believed that it was wrong to deal with '. . . Hottentots, as if they were identical with men in clean shirts at Camberwell . . .'" (971). What Goldberg recognizes as his "progressive" attitude and feeling for the slaves has, after emancipation, dwindled into something less generous. So that Goldberg himself is compelled to remark how "Arthur Adrian is stating the case mildly when he says that Dickens' 'earlier commiseration for the oppressed Negro . . . showed strange signs, after the Civil Wars, of having lost its erstwhile fervor'" (149). The fact is, as Bolt puts it, "Abhorrence of slavery did not always imply sympathy for the Negro, in either American or Englishman" (29).

The second half of the nineteenth century saw first-time visits to the United States by such celebrated literary figures as William Makepeace Thackeray, Anthony Trollope, and much later, near the turn of the century, Rudyard Kipling. In keeping with the changing tide of race relations that characterized British thinking during the nineteenth century, each of these celebrities proves increasingly strident and racist in their respective views on blacks.[4] As scholars have noted, there was a decidedly unfavorable shift in the general thinking about race during the last half of the nineteenth century, which went from "statements about responsibility to those about superiority" (Palmegiano 1). According to British historian Peter Fryer, "Ideas of Teutonic destiny developed by philologists and German nationalists mingled with ideas of inherent white superiority developed by phrenologists and anthropologists to swamp common sense in a flood of racial arrogance." Indeed, Fryer insists, "Hardly any British writers came out openly against racism in the last quarter of the nineteenth century . . . Few bothered to give the subject extensive consideration" (181, 187).

William Makepeace Thackeray did not by any means go untouched by the brush of racism. As John Peck points out, the last chapter of Thackeray's last completed novel, *Phillip*, is "extraordinarily distasteful" in its racist treatment of the wealthy, propertied mulatto character, Woolcomb. Peck, who admits that "*Phillip* is not the only Thackeray novel marked by racism," finds, however, that "the hatred [in *Phillip*] is so extreme as to unbalance the work." Still he observes that "for the most part," the racism Thackeray expressed in his fiction was "incidental" (127). Nevertheless, Thackeray's racism was not that of the Briton who had neither contact with nor interest in black Americans. In the wake of Charles Dickens's *American Notes* (1842) and *Martin Chuzzlewit* (1843), the author of *Vanity Fair* (1848) took, before the internecine war fought over slavery, two tours of the United States from 1852 to 1853 and from 1855 to 1856, during which times he was anything but oblivious to the black American slave. Deborah A. Thomas argues in her study, *Thackeray and Slavery* (1993), "The subject of slavery is especially pertinent to Thackeray, who seems to have been fascinated with it" because in the 1830s, "the subject of slavery was in the air," because Thackeray had an "Anglo-Indian upbringing," and because his mother subscribed to evangelicalism, a religious movement that proved oppositional to slavery, all these influenced the writer (xv, 7, 13). Interestingly enough, Thomas, who does an impressively thorough job of tracing Thackeray's literal and figurative representations of slavery in the novels, contends that the idea of slavery that informed Thackeray's creative work became a less compelling force in Thackeray's fiction after he came into "contact with bondage in real life in the American South" (xvi). In 1859, Thackeray would publish the only one of his novels, *The Virginians,* that could be truly said to directly touch upon America and slavery. Set partly in America and partly in England, the novel, which follows the fortunes of two Virginian cousins who end up fighting on different sides during the American War for Independence, never centers on the question of slavery but manages in its references to that institution to create some stereotypical images of blacks.

Although it is important and interesting to analyze the creative uses to which Thackeray put slavery in his fiction, it requires an examination of Thackeray's letters to determine more clearly how he reacted to the nineteenth-century African American, especially because he "refrained from public comments on the slavery issue both in the United States and [back home in England] after his visits" (Thomas 121). On his first lecture tour to the United States, Thackeray recognized how black slaves were indigenous to the distinctive shape of the American social landscape as they, to his mind, made America take on "an aspect of the queerest interest" (*Letters and Private Papers* 3: 198–99). By the time Thackeray begins trading letters with the Baxters, an American family he had met in 1852, it is clear that though he never, as Thomas avers, morally approved of slavery (15), he betrays a racist-mindset increasingly prevalent in the later part of the Victorian age as he believed blacks were an inferior but amusing race with great appeal to his whimsical side. Thus, he sketches an "Ebony femme de chambre" he came across in a Baltimore hotel room, exaggerating her Negroid features even as he draws attention to the pipe, which Thackeray recognizes as her signature possession. "She makes the beds with that pipe in her mouf and leaves it about in the rooms" (*Thackeray's Letters to an American Family* 34). The blacks added spice to his American travels and were a special source of amusement that he recorded as such not only in drawings like that of the black femme de chambre but also in his letters. To Mrs. Baxter, Thackeray wrote upon his arrival in Richmond, Virginia, in a letter dated March 3, 1853, that he was "delighted with the comfortable friendly cheery little town—the picturesquest he has seen in America—that the negroes instead of horrifying me I am sorry to say amuse me with their never ending grotesqueness and please me with their air of happiness." One week later in a letter from Charleston, South Carolina, to Mrs. Baxter's daughter, Lucy, Thackeray reports that he has just sent a letter to his daughter Minny in England in which he writes among other things about Negroes. He confesses that though he should not dwell on the subject, it is one he is hard pressed to relinquish because the black Americans "interest me very much especially the little pickaninnies with their queer faces and ways which are just exactly half way between the absurd and the pretty, and so create in my mind a strange feeling between pleasure & pity." He goes on to describe his encounter with the black slave children, "Yesterday where I dined I felt my elbow pinched by a very little hand, and looking down saw such a little elfin bit of a brat with such a queer smile and grimace holding me up a silver basket with bread—And the day before at dinner there was one little negro-boy with a great peacock's feather fan whisking the flies away, whilst another niggerkin yet smaller was deputed to do nothing but watch the process of the dinner, which he did standing back against the sideboard and making endless faces at the child with the fan." On this occasion, Thackeray found in the delightfully entertaining antics of the "pickaninnies" and "niggerkin" evidence that conditions were not as bleak for the enslaved black as some represented them to be. "The goodness of the masters to these children is very pleasant to witness. I wish some of our countrymen could see it. I wish we knew many things about America at home; where there will be one person before very long please God who will be able to say that people here are not all cruel . . ." (*Thackeray's Letters to an American Family* 47, 51–52).

Thackeray, for whom the American black was such an object of interest that he would "sit up in my room, and draw pictures of niggers & saunter about & get through the day as we can," wrote in a manner that seems all the more contradictory given the letters that betray the pleasure he takes in the oddity of the blacks he encounters in America. Just three months after the letter posted from South Carolina, having just met the author of *Uncle Tom's Cabin* but not having yet made the effort to "buckle to Uncle Tom and really try to read it," Thackery writes, "I told Lord Shaftesbury though (who seems to worship Mrs. Stowe) that there were other people besides blacks in America & that there were 23 millions of whites who interested me still more than the niggers" (*Thackeray's Letters to an American Family* 53, 72). In fact, the black Americans Thackeray observed proved a source of conflict in the writer. He cannot, for instance, tell what to make of their condition and his reaction to their physical being. "I don't know whether it is terror, pity or laughter that is predominant" he muses in a letter to his mother. The blacks he met were not necessarily as long-suffering and unhappy as Harriet Beecher Stowe had made them out to be but rather were "grinning & joking in the sun; roaring with laughter as they stand about the streets in squads." Having verified for himself the figure of the "happy darky," Thackeray also notes the appeal of black Americans who are "very civil, kind & gentle, even winning in their manner when you accost them at gentlemen's houses, where they do all the service." Yet Thackeray simply cannot identify physically, mentally, or socially with the African American. "They are not my men & brethren, these strange people with retreating foreheads, with great obtruding lips & jaws: with capacities for thought, pleasure, endurance quite different to mine." In the same letter, he again insists on the gulf he simply cannot negotiate: "But they don't seem to me to be the same as white men, any more than asses are the same animals as horses; I don't mean this disrespectfully, but simply that there is such a difference of colour, habits, conformation of brains, that we must acknowledge it, & can't by any rhetorical phrase get it over." His feelings of total estrangement, if not repulsion, war with his moral sense as he struggles to explain: "Sambo is not my man & my brother; the very aspect of his face is grotesque & inferior. I can't help seeing & owning this; at the same time of course denying any white man's right to hold this fellow-creature in bondage & make goods & chattels of him & his issue" (*Letters and Private Papers* 3: 199). In describing this "fellow-creature," that is, no fellow or brother that he can own, Thackeray rather lamely concludes that at least enslaved blacks in America have not been treated as badly as they were in Africa. He ultimately found the slaves of his American hosts to be merry and well fed. Although he fundamentally disapproved of slavery, he saw no need for immediate emancipation, as he believed that the economic wrongness would bring about the natural collapse of the institution.[5]

A century later, the whimsical and conflicted racism of Thackeray did not prevent Trinidadian writer C. L. R. James from crediting the Victorian novelist with educating him in the ways of Englishness. In *Beyond a Boundary,*

James recalls, "I laughed without satiety at Thackeray's constant jokes and sneers and gibes at the aristocracy and at people in high places. Thackeray, not Marx, bears the heaviest responsibility for me." James further remarks that he took imperceptibly and for granted from Thackeray's *Vanity Fair*, things that were "enduring: the British reticence, the British self-discipline, the stiff lips, upper and lower" (39).[6] Thackeray, who did not hesitate to take to task "the aristocracy and . . . people in high places," was not, when he traveled to America, above casting the barbs of his sneers and jokes upon the lowly, enslaved, and bedeviled African Americans; his "stiff lips, upper and lower," trembled all too often with mirth in racialized descriptions ultimately as damaging as any Carlylean invective.

Anthony Trollope, son of the author of *Domestic Manners*, Frances Trollope, came to America, visiting the country several times between 1858 and 1876. It was after his first substantial sojourn in the United States at the opening of the Civil War in 1861 that Trollope penned the travel work, *North America*, in which he was compelled by dint of the historical moment of slavery and of the Civil War to consider the role and condition of blacks in America. With greater conviction than Thackeray, Trollope believed the black race inferior. The West Indian blacks, for example, were, Trollope surmised, a race so predisposed to "decline" work as to require that they be forced to labor. As Victoria Glendinning put it in her biography of Trollope, "Anthony was amazed by their lack of financial greed" (250). As for the black American cursed by the system of slavery, Trollope declared that he "does not comprehend the object and purport of continued industry" and "is a child in all things" (*North America* 359). Whereas Thackeray was more or less amused by African Americans, Trollope was confounded by their coloring, the various shades of which made it difficult for him to categorize them as full-blooded (i.e., intellectually irredeemable, lesser) or half-blooded—colored or mulatto (i.e., not quite as diminished as his thoroughly Negroid counterpart). He remarks, "In the West Indies . . . I always believed myself able to tell a negro from a coloured man. Indeed the classes are to a great degree distinct there, the greater portion of the retail trade of the country being in the hands of the coloured people. But in the States I have been able to make no such distinction. One sees generally neither the rich yellow of the West Indian mulatto, nor the deep oily black of the West Indian negro. The prevailing hue is a dry, dingy brown,—almost dusty in its dryness" (362). Problematic and diminished as blacks were, Trollope swore that "The name of slave is odious to me. If I know myself I would not own a negro though he could sweat gold on my behoof. I glory in that bold leap in the dark which England took with regard to her own West Indian slaves." For all that, Trollope felt he could not condemn the South for its unfortunate choice to cling to slavery: "I will not call them wicked, impious, and abominable, because they now hold by slavery, as other nations have held by it at some period of their career. It is their misfortune that they must do so now,—now, when so large a portion of the world has thrown off the system, spurning as base and profitless all labour that is not free" (355). The point to be made is that even though Trollope felt the full-blooded Negro to be "the white man's inferior through laws of nature," he just as strongly believed that such men needed neither social nor political equality but rather "social tolerance and social sympathy" (361). Glendinning's assessment of Trollope's view on blacks, with whom "he had never been in contact" until his 1859 visit to the West Indies, is concise, gracious, if not generous to a fault: "He was always against slavery, but he thought it would take a very long time before black people would be the equal of whites" (249, 250).

Perhaps one of the most unsympathetic and offensive assessments of the African American comes much later in the century from the British writer, Rudyard Kipling who published his own *American Notes* in 1891. Here, in what one reader of the *Notes* calls the "seem[ingly] supersarcastic" tone that characterizes the work, Kipling "draw[s] breath" at one point to "curse the negro waiter, and through him the negro in service generally." In fact, Kipling launches into a racial diatribe about "this woolly one, whose race has been the butt of every comedy on the native stage since the beginning." Kipling who found that his black waiter was "as complete a heavy-footed, uncomprehending, bungle-fisted fool as any *mem sahib* in the East ever took into her establishment," saw that this one waiter, "did his thinking in English, but he was a Yoruba negro, and the race type had remained the same throughout his generations." Having identified the waiter as one of "the race type" from the wrong side of Africa, Kipling, observing that "there are six million negroes . . . in the States, and they are increasing," comments that "the American, once having made them citizens, cannot unmake them." Suggesting that blacks are hereditary Neanderthals, the British writer announces that despite American attempts to "elevate [. . .] by education" the Yoruba man, "it is likely to be a long job, because black blood is much more adhesive than white, and throws back with annoying persistence" (8, 46, 47–48).

Betraying in himself an annoying inclination to participate in what he identifies as the tradition of denigrating the black race and making it "the butt of every comedy on the native stage since the beginning," Kipling then looks briefly at the Negro who, when he "gets religion . . . returns directly as a hiving bee to the first instincts of his people." Segregated in their churches in this country, the black congregation prays, "moved by the spirits to groans and tears," and a dance "up the aisle to the mourners' bench," a dance that reminds Kipling of "a Zanzibar stick dance." As he watched, Kipling declares, "the links that bound them to the white man snapped one by one, and I saw before me the hubshi (woolly hair) praying to a God he did not understand": he saw what were, in his opinion, "savages, neither more nor less" (49). Kipling does not stop here with the savagery of the so-called black citizen he ultimately defines in opposition to Americans, but rather he wonders, "what . . . the American [will] do with the negro" who "will not disappear." Kipling predicts, "He will continue as a problem." Then he concludes sarcastically, "It is not good to be a negro in the land of the free and the home of the brave" (50).

On coming to antebellum America, the British visitors considered here encountered an institution that was neither wholly alien nor necessarily uncongenial to them. Some, even those most critical of slavery, still betrayed the very attitudes about race that underpinned black subjugation. The immediate impact of British visitors on nineteenth-century African American slaves varied as British contact ranged from brief and superficial to sustained and more intimate. Ultimately, for African Americans, the most significant outcome of British crossings was the body of writings—the essays, journals, travelogues, and books these subjects of Queen Victoria published upon their return home. These literary productions afforded America an outside perspective on its homegrown institution and probably provided the young nation one of its earliest experiences with international accountability (the self-styled democracy was not treating some of its people democratically). These literary productions also provided insight for British Victorians, who, Douglas A. Lorimer contends, being "remote from the inter-racial contacts of the Empire, and rarely meeting blacks in Britain . . . perceived the physical characteristics of the Negro largely through the verbal descriptions of lecturers and writers" (*Colour, Class and the Victorians* 17). The condition of black Americans was not just the topic with which members of that special group, the abolitionists, concerned themselves, but rather it was a subject that the British visitor to America often found compelling because it helped him or her to define points of contact between the United States and Britain and shed further light on Britain's own "uniquely British experiences with Africanist people" (Gerzina 6). In the opening decades of the nineteenth century, the travel writings of writers such as Dickens, Marryat, Martineau, Trollope, or the phrenologist Combe—writers without an emancipatory mission, but writers with public appeal—these personages did much to raise the African American in British consciousness, even if they did not uplift the race. Though they did not popularize, the writings of these British citizens helped give black Americans a presence in Britain.

A number of nineteenth-century British writers who did not make transatlantic voyages still managed an imaginative crossing of sorts by creatively broaching the subject of race and slavery. Just as Charles Dickens's *Martin Chuzzlewit* or William Thackeray's *The Virginians* raises, though cursorily, the topic of slavery, such works as Mary Shelley's *Frankenstein,* George Eliot's *Daniel Deronda,* Charlotte Brontë's *Jane Eyre,* Emily Brontë's *Wuthering Heights,* Elizabeth Gaskell's "An Accursed Race," and Robert Browning's "Caliban Upon Setbos," to name a few, have all been identified as works invested to various degrees in issues of race and slavery. Scholars and critics have explored these and similar creative works about race in such critical texts as Christine Bolt's *Victorian Attitudes to Race* (1971); Douglas A. Lorimer's *Colour, Class and the Victorians* (1978); Patrick Brantlinger's *Rule of Darkness: British Literature and Imperialism, 1830–1914* (1988); Anita Levy's *Other Women: The Writing of Class, Race, and Gender, 1832–1898* (1991); Deborah A. Thomas's *Thackeray and Slavery* (1993); H. L. Malchow's *Gothic Images of Race in Nineteenth-Century Britain* (1996); and Shearer West's edition of *The Victorians and Race* (1996). Although these critical but more especially these literary texts reveal the degree to which race mattered in Victorian England, one work by poet Elizabeth Barrett Browning proves of special interest as it can be studied as evidence of that British author's particular engagement with the plight of the African American slave. That is to say that unlike Mary Shelley's depiction of the monster as a new and rejected race of being, Thackeray's representation of blacks in *The Virginians* as minor if not superfluous characters, the Brontës's representation of the genteel slavery of their white female protagonists, or George Eliot's complex treatment of the Jew in *Daniel Deronda,* Elizabeth Barrett Browning's "The Runaway Slave at Pilgrim's Point" (1848) encompasses more poignantly and specifically the position of the nineteenth-century African American. The idea here is not to credit Barrett Browning with an abolitionist fervor that surpasses that of other white Victorian writers and artists who opposed slavery, but rather to pay attention to a work by a writer who, without setting foot upon American soil, found her ancestry, marriage, and family wealth inflected by black blood. This is to say that Elizabeth Barrett Browning's treatment of the subject is of particular interest because, unlike the other Victorians discussed in this chapter, her gender, her genealogy, even her marriage and economic history link her in some interesting ways to blacks.

The daughter of Edward Moulton Barrett whose wealth, like that of his grandfather Charles, was drawn from a Jamaican plantation, the poet Elizabeth Barrett Browning not only, in the contemporary coinage of Edward Ball, had "slaves in the family" but also, by eloping with and marrying the poet Robert Browning, joined her life to a man who also probably had some black ancestry.[7] So that the antislavery poem that Barrett Browning wrote during her honeymoon resonates in some telling, complex, and, to borrow a word from one of Barrett Browning's biographers, Julia Markus, some "peculiar" ways (92). To review the peculiarities that Markus herself notes in the biography on the Brownings's marriage, the poem Elizabeth Barrett Browning wrote at the request of American abolitionists could not have been written at an odder time or by a more singular personage. Barrett Browning was a famous yet, until her elopement with Browning, a sickly and reclusive woman so uncannily situated that she herself proved not only a runaway daughter but also a white female whose family's money and prominence rested squarely on the backs of slaves. She was, moreover, a white female Briton through whose blood, it seems, there coursed at least one damning black drop. So that in writing this poem for the abolitionist cause, Elizabeth Barrett Browning was likely also writing out of her own experience of genteel slavery. This is to say she was likely writing out of her own experience of being contained and immobilized, if not enslaved, hurt, if not denied by a paterfamilias who may well have feared that his daughter's marriage and children born of that marriage might expose the sable strains of ancestry. In any event, the concepts of "running" and "emancipation" were not without personal relevance to her.

In "The Runaway Slave," Barrett Browning imaginatively enters the world of the black American slave. Although, as Markus has astutely argued, Elizabeth Barrett Browning's representation of the locale evokes Jamaica as much as it does America (93), in writing the poem, she clearly meant to speak about slaves in the United States "at Pilgrim's Point" not Montego or Morant Bay, as she places the black female speaker of the poem at a historically recognizable location instead of some obscure spot in the States. "I stand on the mark beside the shore / Of the first white pilgrim's bended knee" (ll. 1–2), declares the poem's speaker in the opening lines of the poem. The next lines are replete with irony and contradiction if not plain paradox, for the liberty for which the exiled pilgrims pray on bended knees is the very freedom the speaker also seeks but is denied by the descendents of the pilgrims. The speaker, in effect, identifies with the pilgrims whose children and heirs are her enslavers when she reenacts the movements of pilgrims newly landed on America's shores: "I bend my knee down on this mark" which the first pilgrims made (l. 6). By her acts, the speaker acknowledges that these white pilgrims are not only fellow runaways but also and ultimately her ancestors just as surely as one of the heirs of the pilgrims will become her child's father. Kneeling as they have knelt before her, the black runaway feels the souls of the pilgrims surround her whose supplications, however, are not a blessing but a curse: "And thus I thought that I would come / And kneel here where ye knelt before, / And feel your souls around me hum / In undertone to the ocean's roar; / And lift my black face, my black hand, / Here, in your names, to curse this land / Ye blessed in freedom's, evermore" (ll. 15–21). In these lines, the speaker is clearly set apart from the white pilgrims by her black face and black hands, but she draws near them by lifting these black features to call upon them as the ancestors they are, to "in your names . . . curse this land / Ye blessed in freedom's" name. The tensions that will not permit complete identification persist. Though the runaway is also a pilgrim for freedom, her pilgrimage can never completely resemble that of the Europeans. Where they have blessed, she needs must curse. The soul movements of the pilgrims are "proud and slow" to survive, but hers must be furtive and fast: "I have gasped and run / All night long from the whips of one / Who in your names works sin and woe! (ll. 12–14). The souls of black folk are shut out from life, comfort, and—as the speaker finds to her devastation, that most transformative and redeeming human gift—love. The runaway woman cries, "Our blackness shuts like prison-bars: / The poor souls crouch so far behind / That never a comfort can they find / By reaching through the prison-bars" (ll. 39–42). Reach, the speaker does, nevertheless, as she "once . . . laughed in girlish glee" at the prospect of "one of my colour" who dares to love her (ll. 58, 59). However, the nature of slavery is such that, as Barrett Browning apparently understood, control over one's body and therefore intimacy is not allowed:

> We were black, we were black,
> We had no claim to love and bliss,
> What marvel if each went to wrack?
> They wrung my cold hands out of his
> They dragged him—where? I crawled to touch
> His blood's mark in the dust . . . (92–98)

As the speaker declares, "Wrong . . . [is] followed by a deeper wrong" as her oppressors not only lynch her black lover but dispose of the speaker herself by raping her and burdening her with the shame of bearing a white child she ultimately experiences as an erstwhile albatross around her neck: "I wore a child upon my breast, / An amulet that hung too slack" (ll. 99, 107–8). Instead of her black lover, she is left with a little white body that she "carried . . . to and fro, / And it lay on my heart like stone, as chill" (ll. 165–66). The slave woman kills "the babe who lay on my bosom . . . far too white, too white for me" (ll. 115–16) because it reminds her of the master and because she wants to spare it the whips and curses of the master. She lashes and asphyxiates the master's offspring, her very own baby, with a shawl and a kerchief that symbol of a slave woman's positioning in the field and the kitchen instead of the dining room and parlor, that symbol of a life of servitude not of ladyhood. Ironically, as she smothers and sends into darkness the white face of a child, which lifts its face to her as she has lifted her face to the pilgrims, the speaker has another chilling moment of identification. The "white child wanted his liberty" just as the pilgrims and the speaker herself had wanted theirs: "Ha, ha! he wanted the master-right" (ll. 125, 126). Her laughter may suggest dementia, but the speaker assures us that she is "not mad . . . [but] black," that her response to her lack of liberty looks extreme and excessive only to those who prize liberty without ever knowing what it is to be deprived of it politically, social, economically, physically, and spiritually not only for the duration of one's life but also for the lifetime of one's progeny (l. 218).

As with the white pilgrims, the white angels of Christianity, who also landed at Pilgrim's Point with those pilgrims, prove just as problematic where the notion of freedom is concerned. Those so-called angelic hosts, who are, according the white man's religion, supposedly closer to God than any beings—especially a black woman "lifting a leaf of the mango fruit"—are neither saviors nor true liberators but rather tricksters or indeed vampires plucking and sucking the life of the speaker and her child as surely as slavery underwritten by white Christianity fed upon the bodies and souls of black people. "Your fine white angels (who have seen / Nearest the secret of God's power) / And plucked my fruit to make them wine, / And sucked the soul of that child of mine / . . . Ha, ha the trick of the angels white! / They freed the white child's spirit so" (ll. 154, 157–60, 162–63). In a hellish transubstantiation, the white master in the name of Christianity has used not only the body but also the issue or fruit of the speaker's dark body to commandeer and ensure his own freedom, his own leisure, his own prosperity, his own wine, as it were. Any freedom the speaker and her mulatto child can achieve is somehow fraudulent, a ruse, a pyrrhic emancipation, as it were, because it cannot really be had at Pilgrim's Point but rather can be gained only in death.

Yet Pilgrim's Point is, as it were, the sticking point. As the symbolic gateway to unprecedented democracy and freedom heralded to the world by the United States not Jamaica or England, it is the only thing to which the runaway slave has to return, the only hope that remains while there is life left in her body. Herein lies the great paradox: that in the land of the free there are men and women who are not free, that one mark left by a bended knee beside the shore at Pilgrim Point stands for freedom, but a similar mark left on the same shore by the bended knee of the black speaker stands for subservience and servitude. The marks similar as they are have different meanings for the dark race and the "Washington-race":

> I am not mad: I am black.
> I see you staring in my face—
> I know you staring, shrinking back,
> Ye are born of the Washington-race,
> And this land is the free America,
> And this mark on my wrist—(I prove what I say)
> Ropes tied me up here to the flogging-place. (ll. 218–24)

The speaker's position is such that her bid for freedom looks to the "shrinking . . . Washington-race" like madness. The speaker, however, insists that she is not mad and the proof of her assertion is in the markings on her wrist, which constitute the inscription of slavery upon her black body, marks scored into her flesh by "ropes [that] tied me up here to the flogging-place." She is not insane. She is a black person who ironically is, like the white Christ, crucified and that daily. She also experiences a true transubstantiation as her body is broken, and her blood is shed frequently for the white oppressors. However, unlike Christ, as the runaway slave hangs figuratively and literally upon her cross, she does not bless her persecutors ("Lord forgive them, they know not what they do," pleaded Christ) she curses them, for, after all, "Whips, curses; these must answer those" (l. 232):

> You think I shrieked then? Not a sound!
> I hung, as a gourd hangs in the sun;
> I only cursed them all around
> As softly as I might have done
> My very own child . . . (ll. 225–29)

To curse one's own child is to experience the strong but conflicting emotions of love and anger, to pass inexplicably from parent to would-be executioner much as water amazingly turns to wine and as, in the poem, "exile turned into ancestor" (l. 3). In another transformative moment in this poem replete with irony, ironic identifications, and odd sympathies, the speaker, up until now so poignantly solitary and personal in her wounds and suffering, turns outward from her cross, Joan-of-Arc-like, to rally the troops, if not to incite rebellion: "from these sands / Up to the mountains, lift your hands, / O slaves, and end what I begun! (ll. 229–31). However, as soon as the speaker calls for an uprising another shift takes place, as, facing her pursuers, she dissociates herself from white crucifixion. That is, she will not allow white men to crucify and sacrifice her in the name of their religion.

Our wounds are different. Your white men
Are, after all, not gods indeed,
Nor able to make Christs again
Do good with bleeding. *We* who bleed
(Stand off!) we help not in our loss!
We are too heavy for our cross,
And fall and crush you and your seed. (ll. 239–45)

Freed of a cross that cannot account for or accommodate the weight of her horrendous experience, the speaker still considers the course of retribution inherent in the fact that the enslavement of blacks gravely injures whites and their posterity: "*We* . . . Fall and crush your and your seed." Finally, motherhood not Christianity prevails and marks the way to the runaway's redemption—such as it is—in the heart of the runaway slave. Falling and swooning, "as if I should die / Of liberty's exquisite pain," the speaker "in the name of the white child waiting for me," lifts, though with a heart broken with disdain, her curse on the Washington-race, granting an emancipation of sorts which her oppressors have yet to extend to her: "White men, I leave you all curse-free" (ll. 248–50, 252).

Although some British writers such as Elizabeth Barrett Browning did not actually sail to America where they could see for themselves the damage done to blacks and to American democracy, they could in their imaginative crossings of the Atlantic take part in the neutralization of the young nation's curse. For a writer such as Browning, to make such a crossing was also to conduct a more personal literary pilgrimage into the ancestral British heart of darkness. The experiment in the New World was tainted by an old evil from which Browning, the great-great granddaughter of a West Indian slaveholder, chose ultimately to distance herself by identifying with the slave instead of the enslaver. The point is that whether or not Victorian writers were sympathetic to the predicament of blacks in the New World, each book, article, essay, or poem the Victorians wrote about the black American helped agitate the race-infested waters of the Atlantic. The real and imagined journeys of Victorian British writers to the United States of America and thereby often into the lives of African Americans were ultimately injections, if I may play upon the title of a book by Mia Bay, of the black image into the white mind.[8] Indeed, Victorian writers such as Browning may be said to have discursively transported African Americans to British shores at a time when African Americans themselves could hardly make it beyond the Pilgrim's Points of the New World, let alone travel beyond the Atlantic.

2. Hail Britannia
African Americans Abroad in Victorian England

For nineteenth-century British travelers, the United States of America was a brave new world, and for African Americans, England was the land situated somewhere near the second star to the right. This perception of England and of Europe as a kind of Neverland, a cherished place to which travel was an extraordinary venture, is evident as late as 1899 when educator, race leader, and accommodationist Booker T. Washington questioned about whether he had ever considered a trip to Europe, exclaimed that "it was something entirely beyond me." In his autobiography, *Up From Slavery,* Washington goes on to express his feeling that travel to Europe was a white entitlement; such travel was one of the "luxuries [that] had always seemed to me to be something meant for white people, not for my race" (271, 272–73). Washington confesses to having "always regarded Europe, and London, and Paris, much as I regard heaven" (*Up from Slavery* 273). By the time Washington made his second trip to Europe in 1910 to study the condition of the poor and working Europeans who were emigrating in increasing numbers to America and competing as it were with blacks, he would not be as in awe of London and Paris as he had been ten years earlier when he believed European cities such as London to be transcendental spaces.[1]

This glorification of London and Europe must have proved even more of a tendency among African Americans during the first part of the century when most blacks in the United States, enslaved and illiterate, could not and did not travel abroad. Thus while Queen Victoria's subjects journeyed in appreciable numbers to America, very few African Americans were in a position to travel to Britain. Still, some blacks managed the trek across the Atlantic, though they traveled on terms very different from that of the British. On the one hand, the crossing of white Britons to American no matter how physically perilous and financially taxing was made in the assurance of both a welcome predicated upon shared whiteness and Europeanness and a return to a homeland where he or she was free. On the other hand, the earlier crossings of black Americans was an affair informed not only by the physical and economic difficulties of sea transit but also by all the anxieties attendant upon being racial pariahs often in flight from the homeland. Getting to the British Isles would generally prove a formidable task for African Americans and being there a taste of paradise.

Getting There: The Sociohistorical Politics of Black Travel to Europe

During the first half of the nineteenth century, most of the African Americans who crossed the Atlantic to Great Britain did so under very different circumstances from British travelers and with different sociocultural imperatives. Antebellum blacks, whether slave, fugitive, or free, often traveled overseas as freedom fighters or seekers. Whether officially abolitionists or not, African Americans traveling abroad were leaving behind a country that enslaved blacks and discriminated against them for a country where they could find respite and reprieve. This is to say that, unlike the British or the white Americans who crossed the ocean in the nineteenth and early twentieth centuries, black Americans found their passage troubled in more ways than one. Thus, those nineteenth-century blacks whose celebrity status approximated that of British visitors to the United States, such as the Marryats and Martineaus, tended not be travelers with "ample time" and "substantial income" (Rapson 25). Forced to "seek a refuge from republican slavery in monarchical England," Frederick Douglass, for example, depended on the financial backing of his antislavery activist friends during his "twenty-one Months in Great Britain" (*My Bondage and My Freedom* 223). Ultimately enabled to go "roaming in freedom over . . . the most interesting spots on the earth's surface," Douglass declared, "I shall never be done [thanking] the abolitionists for their agency" (Douglass Papers). Later in the century, Ida B. Wells, who traveled twice to England, would visit Great Britain: first, at the behest of Scottish patron Isabelle Fyvie Mayo (a.k.a. author Edward Garrett) and, later, at the invitation of the Society for the Furtherance of the Brotherhood of Men, which had been formed during the occasion of Well's first two-month visit to Great Britain. Both the patron and the society extended invitations to Wells assuring her of their willingness to, in Isabelle Mayo's words, "find the money for [Well's] expenses and provide opportunity for airing this intolerable condition" of lynching in the United States (Wells 85). "The invitation which was the cause of my going to England," wrote Ida B. Wells, "said that the committee would guarantee all my expenses but could pay me nothing for my services. They loyally kept faith with me, since every item of expense had been met by them" (109–10). Despite the financial assistance of the society, Ida Wells must have breathed a little easier when the editor of the Chicago *Inter-Ocean* gave her the opportunity to write for the paper while she was overseas, making her "the first, and so far as I know, the only one of my group who was a regular paid correspondent of a daily paper in the United States" (125). Blacks, who often needed help getting overseas, had to piece together the terms of their travel abroad, often parlaying patrons, donations, subscriptions, invitations, and, in Ida B. Wells's case, a writing assignment just to get there.

Even if blacks secured passage across the sea, there remained the issue of sustaining one's self and, in some instances, one's family while abroad. A contemporary of Frederick Douglass, William Wells Brown, who traveled to France, England, and Ireland, was one of the few, if not the only, fugitive slaves to boast the distinction of achieving some financial autonomy while abroad. "Most of the fugitive slaves, and, in fact, nearly all of the colored men who have visited Great Britain from the United States," the author's memoirs reports, "have come upon begging missions, either for some society or for themselves. Mr. Brown has been almost the only exception. With that independence of feeling which those who are acquainted with him know to be one of his chief characteristics, he determined to maintain himself and family by his own exertions—by his literary labors, and the honorable profession of a public lecturer" (W. Brown 90). However, it should be noted that in 1849, abolitionists sent Brown abroad to an International Peace Congress in Paris as an official delegate of the American Peace Society, and along the way Brown was not adverse to graciously accepting "a subscription . . . hastily set on foot on his behalf" (W. Brown 91).

On the issue of sponsorship, British scholar Fiona Spiers concedes that some black abolitionists became "independent through royalties, lecture fees, or some other form of industry," despite initial reliance on the "philanthropy or hospitality from such benefactors as the Estlins in Bristol" or the ministrations of "men like [abolitionists] Joseph Sturge and Louis Chamerovzow, or professionals like George Thomson." Spiers concludes, however, that many blacks who could have supported themselves chose not to do so "preferr[ing] . . . instead to remain on the lecture circuit, living off philanthropy, donations and collections" because the lecture tours, "arduous" as they may have been, "generated an excitement which the speakers seem to have found addictive." Spiers adds that, by remaining so situated, these black abolitionists were "brought . . . into contact with a variety of eminent and famous people whom they could never otherwise have met" (84, 85). Even if, to put it more generously as Audrey Fisch does, some "African-Americans found that abolitionism formed a wide arena in which one could both get a living and satisfy one's political goals," the fact remains that for a number of fugitive slaves, uneducated but skilled in the growing of tobacco and cotton or sometimes in such trades as carpentry and building, it was difficult to find work in England (5). Those fugitive slaves conscripted to speak on the lecture circuit found even this venture at best an unreliable means of securing a living as the lecture season was brief, lasting a few months from November to May, and the returns were neither consistent nor guaranteed. Thus Josephine Brown recalls that her father Williams Wells Brown, like most African Americans abroad for any extended lecture tours, found lecturing so "precarious," that "he must adopt some other mode of providing support for himself and his daughters" (82). Therefore, Brown began writing for the English press.

Another fugitive from America, John Brown—whose experience of slavery was such that his master at one point had conducted experiments upon him to discover how deep his blackness went—arrived in England eager to make his own way. Eschewing the idea of receiving what he called "charity help," he understood the difficulty he faced finding employment in the great metropolis. "I have no education, and until I can settle down I am not likely to pick up much." Although he identifies himself as a "handy fellow" willing to do carpentry and to grow cotton to get a living, John Brown, much like Williams Wells Brown, is compelled to write and "to realize sufficient for this by the sale of my Narrative" (John Brown 207, 208), which contributed to the swell of "tales of slavery [which became] . . . indeed a 'staple' in the Victorian literary marketplace: at least twenty American slave narratives appeared in English editions by mid-century" (Fisch 52). The commodification of the slave's story is not only testimony to British interest in the fate of black Americans but is also indicative of black efforts for fiscal survival abroad.

The fact is that African Americans, such as John Brown and William Wells Brown who journeyed overseas, did not tend to travel in luxury or comfort. Even with the financial backing of societies, committees, and patrons, travel abroad was typically a financial strain. William Wells Brown found this strain very much in evidence after he shared his half-shilling with another African American fugitive who could not find employment in England. "The last sixpence," he wrote, "had been spent for postage-stamps, in order to send off some letters to other places, and I could not even stamp a letter in answer to the one last from Worcester. The only vestige of money about me was a smooth farthing that a little girl had given to me at the meeting at Croyden, saying, 'This is for the slaves.' I was three thousand miles from home, with but a single farthing in my pocket! Where on earth is a man without money more destitute? The cold hills of the Arctic regions have not a more inhospitable appearance than London to the stranger with an empty pocket. But whilst I felt depressed at being in such a sad condition, I was conscious that I had done right in remitting the last ten pounds to America. It was for the support of those whom God had committed to my care, and whom I love as I can no others" (135). A taste of freedom served up without requisite funds could be trying.

Identity could prove as problematic as money as some black Americans sought to come to terms with the meaning of home. As scholar Mary Louise Pratt and others have determined, Anglo-American travelers went abroad with a strong sense of belonging, of identification with home. Nineteenth-century British travelers, in particular, part of a vast empire of whose greatness they partook and felt proud of, tended to be cultural chauvinists who wanted to remake other countries in their image or, at least, to quickly take the measure of the foreign country with that imperialistic "cultural yardstick [which] has always been the most important piece of equipment in travel writers' suitcases or rucksacks" (Gruesser 735). With her focus on American women travelers, Mary Suzanne Schriber, also remarks how even American women traveled and wrote about that travel in psychological cocoons of superiority: "Once having traveled, women wrote for the same reason as many American men; that is, they wrote to promote the superiority and the manifest destiny of American political and spiritual values, for which the travel book was a fit form. Paul R. Baker explains that American travelers of either gender judged American life superior to any other, whether in religion or in morality, particularly as they expressed themselves on the topics of the American family; the treatment of women; the work ethic; the system of commerce; and, above all, the American system of government" (*Telling Travels* xxii). Blacks who went abroad challenged this claim to moral and spiritual superiority as they represented the failure of America to live up to its touted high standards, at least where black people were concerned. For in the United States, the black family was neither fostered nor valued; black women were neither protected nor cherished. Forced slave labor had undergirded the work ethic and the system of commerce, especially in the South, and the government that sought to secure freedom and justice for all proved, to put it mildly, undemocratic in its practices toward its black population. Nineteenth-century black transatlantic travelers were all too often taking temporary leave from a homeland that abused, disowned, and disinherited them, a country that had, for the most part, foreclosed on black humanity. If any traveler had the need to confirm that "there are far distant, deeper, and provocative shapes to our lives," it was surely the African American traveler of the nineteenth and early twentieth centuries (Caesar 18). When Douglass, Brown, and Wells went abroad, they tended literally to go without the sanction of the powers that be and often despite strong domestic disapproval. Unsurprisingly, when nineteenth-century African Americans who had embarked for foreign shores with a mission to reveal the ugly truth about American treatment of blacks encountered white American travelers along the way, they were not always above threat and menace. White Americans from New Orleans and Georgia, sailing on the same ship as fugitive slave and antislavery speaker, Douglass, "went so far as to threaten to throw me overboard." When the captain put an end to what Douglass himself styled a "*melee*" with "its tragic and comic peculiarities," the white gentlemen having landed in Liverpool immediately went to the British press to "denounce me as a worthless and insolent negro" (*My Bondage and My Freedom* 224). William Wells Brown found his passage overseas similarly affected by white Americans "much annoyed at the fact that I was a passenger, and enjoying the company of white persons." These individuals "not only insulted" Brown but also made offensive comments such as the following, which bluntly suggested that Brown ought to stay in the place to which his white countrymen had consigned him: "'That nigger had better be on his master's farm,' and 'What could American Peace Society be thinking about, to send a black man as a delegate to Paris?'" (110).

Although journalist and antilynching activist Ida B. Wells, who had received her invitation to go abroad when she was a guest at the home of Frederick Douglass, reported no insults during the first of her two Atlantic crossings, she would find that she, too, "had many a set-to with the ubiquitous Americans traveling or living abroad" (190). She also discovered that "many cultured English persons who had visited our shores and had been splendidly entertained by our best people" sided with these hostile Americans so that "hardly a day passed without letters in the daily papers attacking and discrediting my assertions" (190). Some of the most powerful oppositions and objections to Well's presence and activities overseas were mounted by the American press, which sought to cast her to both the American and the British public as a "Negro Adventuress," a disreputable source, "a Negro sycophant" (*Crusade for Justice* 168, 181, 182). The *Memphis Daily Commercial* was particularly strident in its "obscene" and libelous repudiation of Wells, so much so that the London post described the *Commercial*'s references to Wells as "very coarse in tone," containing such "language . . . as could not possibly be reproduced in an English journal" (*Crusade for Justice* 186, 183). Both at home and abroad, African Americans understood white American color prejudice to be particularly virulent and distinct. "The truth is," Frederick Douglass commented during his European sojourn, "'the people here know nothing of the republican negro hate prevalent in our glorious land . . . Whatever may be said of the aristocracies here, there is none based on the color of a man's skin. This species of aristocracy belongs preeminently to 'the land of the free, and the home of the brave.' I have never found it abroad, in any but Americans. It sticks to them wherever they go. They find it almost as hard to get rid of, as to get rid of their skins'" (*My Bondage and My Freedom* 227). White American contempt for black skin was so doggedly strong that it may be said to have hounded blacks such as Frederick Douglass and Ida B. Wells from the American ports to the British docks and back again.

Little wonder that from the time some blacks set foot aboard ship to sail for England until the time they reboarded to sail back to America, they were compelled to reflect upon where they belonged. Many African Americans began firmly with the notion that the United States was for them a point of origin. Thus, men such as Martin R. Delany and Alexander Crummell, who both became emigrationists, asserted, in opposition to colonizationists, that African Americans had, by virtue of birth and memory, an automatic stake in the United States. Delany, for instance, averred the United States to be "our common country": "Here were we born, here raised and educated; here are the scenes of childhood; the pleasant associations of our school going days; the loved enjoyments of our domestic and fireside relations, and the sacred graves of our departed fathers and mothers. . . ." He insisted, "We are Americans, having a birthright citizenship—natural claims upon the country—claims common to all others of our fellow citizens—natural rights, which may . . . be obstructed, but never can be annulled" (*The Condition, Elevations, Emigration* 48–49). Crummell, who eventually went to live in Liberia, also declared at one point, "We are American citizens. We have no other country; it is evidently one of the certainties of both our own and of [our] children's lives that we shall go on . . . bound up with all the interests of this country. As a people we are here to stay; and the possibility of our removal from this land is just about as great as the uprooting of the giant forests of California . . ." (*Destiny and Race* 241). Although it is true that disillusionment with American life took its impetus from domestic treatment, it is also true that disillusionment with American citizenship could just as likely originate or at least intensify with travel abroad. This is to say the routes taken abroad problemized the black American's sense of rootedness in the United States.[2] Douglass's European voyage, for example, gave him occasion to examine his allegiance to America. In doing so, he found that he could see another land without bias as he was "influenced by no prejudices in favor of

America." He continued in his letter to abolitionist William Lloyd Garrison, "I think my circumstances all forbid that. I have no end to serve, no creed to uphold, no government to defend; and as to nation, I belong to none. I have no protection at home, or resting-place abroad." Identifying himself as "outcast from the society of my childhood" and as "outlaw in the land of my birth," Douglass felt that although love of home or patriotism was "perfectly natural," he had been unnaturally disabused of such an inclination: "If ever I had any patriotism, or any capacity for the feeling, it was whipped out of me long since, by the lash of the American soul-drivers." Whenever he feels the tug of love for America's "bright blue sky, her grand old woods, her fertile fields, her beautiful rivers, her mighty lakes, and star-crowned mountains," he is pulled back into "unutterable loathing" by the memory of the outrages inflicted upon his people in "such a land" (*My Bondage and My Freedom* 225). Douglass and other travelers like him could never be accused of being cultural chauvinists as they were too conflicted by the love they felt for their homeland and the hatred they felt for the abuses they had suffered there.

William Wells Brown best articulates the ambivalence Douglass seeks to express. Standing upon the deck of the Cunard steamship *Canada*, which sailed for Liverpool on July 18, 1849, Brown admits, "I had supposed that I would leave the country [the United States] without any regret; but in this I was mistaken, for when I saw the last thread of communication cut off between me and the land . . . I almost regretted that I was not on shore." Brown lays claim to the home that is no home, explaining, "Whatever may be the fault of the government under which we live, and no matter how oppressive her laws may appear, yet we leave our native land (if such it be) with feelings akin to sorrow" (95, 96). Fugitives such as Douglass and Brown as well as a crusader such as Ida B. Wells must have felt emotions akin to those exiles experience. Certainly, their equivocal response to departure can be attributed in part to the fact that, as Edward Said reminds us, "exile is predicated on the existence of, love for, and a real bond with one's native place; the universal truth of exile is not that one has lost that love or home, but that inherent in each is an unexpected, unwelcome loss" (*Culture and Imperialism* 336). What is even more to the point is that, as Alasdair Pettinger puts it in the introduction to his collection of Black Atlantic travel writing, "for many [black] authors [of travel writing] . . . it is not always clear where 'home' is. And for that reason it is the subject of a much wider range of emotions—nostalgia, indifference, exasperation, perplexity, embarrassment" (xvii). Black nineteenth-century travelers sailed with their double-consciousness intact.

At the root of the ambivalence some black travelers experienced was the historical retardation of travel for African Americans. During the eighteenth and for much of the nineteenth century, African Americans, as a subjugated people, had very limited mobility. Given the fact of the Middle Passage, during which millions of Africans were forced under horrendous conditions to sail across the Atlantic into slavery, and given the force of African American desire for freedom, it may well be that "travel has always played a strategic thematic and metaphorical role in [such] African American literature" as slave narratives, black autobiographies, and fictions of migration (Gruesser 735).[3] However, it is also true that the geography of slavery was such that travel, if not an alien concept, was a term to which few nineteenth-century Americans of African descent could attach any real or personal meaning or derive any sense of empowerment. As John Torpey has remarked in his study of the passport, "Slavery, even when it did not involve actual shackles, entailed that slaveholders held the power to grant their slaves the right to move" (8). Like the act of reading, the local, let alone the foreign, peregrinations of blacks were severely restricted, even outlawed, because such activity could invite the questions, comparisons, knowledge, discontent, and agency—the mental and physical mapping—that might very well result in escape or revolt. Thus, orator, editor, and former slave Frederick Douglass in the appendix to his second autobiography, *My Bondage and My Freedom* (1855), lists some of the laws meant to contain slaves and to deter their movements: "for visiting a plantation without a written pass, ten lashes; for letting loose a boat from where it is made fast, thirty-nine lashes for the first offense; and for the second, shall have cut off from his head one ear . . . for traveling in any other than the most usual and accustomed road, when going alone to any place, forty lashes; for traveling in the night without a pass, forty lashes" (257). An Alabama slave, Jenny Proctor, also sheds light on the circumscribed movements of African Americans when she comments that her fellow bondspeople and she "didn't know nothing 'bout going to town" and that "the only way any slaves on our farm ever goes anywhere was when the boss sends him to carry some news to another plantation or when we slips off way in the night" (Boyd 62, 63). Certainly before the Civil War, the experience of traveling, let alone traveling abroad, was so unlikely that going to the big house, one of the most important geographical points of reference for the plantation slave, meant traversing a great distance, probably the only remarkable distance many slaves would undertake short of being sold farther down South. As Frederick Douglass recalled in his first and best-known autobiography, *Narrative of the Life of Frederick Douglass: An American Slave, Written by Himself* (1845), "The slaves selected to go to the Great House Farm, for the monthly allowance for themselves and their fellow-slaves, were peculiarly enthusiastic" (46). These privileged slaves celebrated their election by "mak[ing] the dense old woods, for miles around, reverberate with their wild songs, revealing at once the highest joy and the deepest sadness" (46). A mere jaunt even if only 100 yards from the slave quarters to the plantation's domestic seat of power—a place that conjured up fear and awe in the mind of the slaves—was a journey in and of itself, a "going away": "I am going away to the Great House Farm! / O, yea! O, yea! O!" (46, 47). Understandably, travel abroad proved a dubious, if not alien concept for the slave who from childhood felt, like Douglass, "doomed to drag out a miserable existence as a slave, chained to one hated spot on the earth" (Douglass Papers). The bondsman or woman in the United States was not just bound; he or she was practically riveted in place.

For a people forced at one time to cross the Atlantic Ocean into bondage, a trip back across those waters was rare, as were indeed narratives of such voyages, especially book-length accounts of such voyages. So even though the numbers of Americans making international excursions increased during the nineteenth century, the percentage of blacks who undertook such trips remained relatively, strikingly, but understandably low. Mary Suzanne Schriber reports, "A total of some 1,765 books of travel were published in the United States between 1830 and 1900, 325 of them before and 1,440 of them after the Civil War." Of middle- to upper-class white women, Schriber writes that "thousands . . . left the home shores for foreign parts." The same cannot be said of black folk, let alone black women who did not easily come "into possession of the raw material for travel writings: travel itself" (*Writing Home* 4, 12–13; *Telling Travels* xxii). Although R. J. M. Blackett claims, "Black Americans visited Britain in significant numbers in the thirty years before the Civil War," it is doubtful that their numbers can be typified as being in the thousands (*Building* 4). Indeed Blackett, who in the writing of his book *Building an Antislavery Wall* identified by name some one hundred black visitors to Britain, only gives a partial list of twenty-two in the appendix to that work. Historian Benjamin Quarles, who remarks a "sharp increase" in the number of black reformers traveling to the British Isle after 1830, also indicates that these numbers are, relative to the number of whites making similar crossings before the Civil War, still not in the thousands: "Certainly the mission-bent blacks who crisscrossed the British Isles were most cordially received. Small in number and transients for the most part, they posed," Quarles observes, "no threat to the laboring man or to the purity of the national blood stream. Hence they received that heartiest of welcomes that comes from a love of virtue combined with an absence of apprehension" (136). Little wonder that blacks published only a handful of these travel texts and much of what scholars can learn about the earlier travels of African Americans is not in texts readily identifiable as travel literature (i.e., travel journals, travelogues) but instead must be gleaned from slave narratives, autobiographies, and such. So unlikely was the prospect of travel for the antebellum black that in an introduction to the uncommon travel narrative of David Dorr—a quadroon slave who wrote about his trip around the world as if he was a gentleman abroad in the company of a master before whom he felt himself every bit an equal— Malini Johar Schueller in a provocative but legitimate moment of consternation wonders, "Can a slave write a travel narrative?" Schueller answers his own rhetorical question, just barely, conceding the wondrously slight possibility of such a phenomenon as a traveling, writing black slave. At the height of slavery, many of those black Americans who went abroad accompanied the white masters, mistresses, and families who owned them; it is doubtful that many of these slaves had the wherewithal to record the events of their travel in servitude. As part of what Schueller identifies as an "entourage," slaves, having "unequal rights of access" to those "sights and cultural spaces that . . . get reported in travel narratives," did not travel abroad as visitors, voyeurs, agents, but rather were carried along as property, servants, or conveniences. "Slaves, like the servants of Victorian bourgeois travelers," Schueller asserts, "scarcely ever achieved the status of 'travelers'" because, to put it simply, they were not white: "Being a traveler meant assuming mobility, and the complex network of race, class, and gender privileges accruing a genteel (Anglo) identity," and writing a travel narrative meant having "the power to comment and interpret," which was "largely an 'Anglo' privilege" (ix). Still there were some blacks who made it abroad without being part of the entourages of white travelers, and some of these African Americans achieved a degree of repute. Thus, students and scholars of American and African American studies will recognize in the following list some of those blacks who traveled to Britain: Paul Cuffe, the businessman who went to England in 1811 to further plans for colonization in Africa; New Englander Prince Saunders who visited England in 1814 and went on to spend time in Haiti; Minister Nathaniel Paul who sailed for Britain in 1832 to raise money for the Wilberforce settlement; and abolitionist speakers Robert Purvis and Charles Lenox Remond who visited England in 1834 and 1840, respectively. There were also slaves, former slaves, and reformers such as the Reverend James W. C. Pennington who made three trips to England in 1843, 1849–1852, and 1861; Moses Roper who spent roughly eight years in England from 1835 to 1844 lecturing against slavery; the radical Henry Highland Garnet who arrived in England in 1850 to advance the cause of the Free Produce Association and later to argue for African emigration; Garnet's second cousin, Samuel Ringgold Ward who went to Britain in June 1853 to raise money for antislavery efforts in Canada; James Watkins, a fugitive from Maryland who was in Great Britain during the 1840s and 1850s; Josiah Henson who traveled to Britain in the 1850s to raise money for the Dawn community; Henry "Box" Brown who made it to England in 1850 after being smuggled out of slavery in a box; William Wells Brown who spent five years in Britain from 1849 to 1854; William and Ellen Craft, the fugitive couple that settled in England in 1851; Harriet Jacobs who would travel to England three times in 1845, 1858, and 1868; and David Dorr whose 1850 account of his tour of the world's major cities begins in England. Additionally, there were free and postbellum blacks such as Zilpha Elaw who went to preach in Britain in 1840 and ended up spending five years there; J. McCune Smith who, during the five years he spent in Great Britain, studied at the University of Glasgow and became a founding member of the Glasgow Emancipation Society; Robert Douglass, Jr. who having come to England with a letter of introduction from the portrait painter Thomas Sully attended classes at the Royal Academy of Arts in the early 1840s; professor William G. Allen who went to England in 1853 and became active in the antislavery movement in England where he and his white wife, a quondam student of his, settled; William H. Day who spent five years in England from 1859 to 1863; Sarah P. Remond who was the sister of abolitionist Charles Lenox Remond; emigrationist, novelist, coeditor of Douglass's *North Star*, and touted father of black nationalism Martin R. Delany whose academic pursuits led to a seven-month stay in Europe where he attended in 1860 the International Statistical Conference at London, the Congress of the National Association for the Promotion of Social Science in Glasgow, and the Royal Geographic Society; and finally Episcopalian priest Alexander Crummell who went in 1848 to England where he set about raising money for his New York church and earning his baccalaureate degree from Queens College, Cambridge in 1853.[4] Black pre–Civil War travelers such as Frederick Douglass and William Wells Brown, for example, went overseas to escape slavery or to wage an oral and literary war on it there by advancing the abolitionist cause. Similarly, later in the century, Ida B. Wells went abroad to campaign against lynching. Though by no means exhaustive, this list does garner the names of a number of individuals who have become recognizable in the annals of black history to suggest a correlation between black emancipatory activities and European travel. Likewise, the list suggests that many of the nineteenth-century African American men and women who achieved some measure of prominence traveled to Britain at some point in time, whether as abolitionists, students, educators, or business people.

The point is that blacks made it abroad, and, like their white countrymen and -women, they did so with an awareness that, of all the European countries that lay across the big water, Britain was the place to go, because it was a social and cultural mecca. For one thing, "much of what happened in Great Britain was almost as important in the lives of North Americans as what happened at home" (Brebner 109). Anglo-American relations were such that for white Americans, Great Britain was a touchstone. Thus, "Practically every major American literary figure in the first half of the nineteenth century had to make the inevitable pilgrimage to Great Britain. While the American visitor to England often went not to judge (as did the Englishman in America) but to find himself" (Rapson 5). This is not to say that Americans were completely and indiscriminately enthralled by England and the English. As David Dorr—the only slave known to have toured the world with his master and represented himself as being as genteel and leisured as the master he accompanied and ultimately escaped—recalls, while in Liverpool, "I had been taught at Orleans that the 'English could whip all the world, and we could whip the English,' and that England was always in great danger of being starved by us, and all her manufactories stopped in double quick time by Southern cotton-planters. But, the greatest absurdity of all was, that England was very much afraid we would declare war against her, and thereby ruin what little independence she still retains" (14). Couched in this unpopular view of England is criticism qualified by admiration for England's power and its past. According to Una Pope-Hennessy, the "traditions of the War of Independence and the vivid stories of the war . . . gave most American men and women a subsoil of antipathy in the make-up of their minds" (17). Still, as Ann Douglas contends, "nineteenth-century America was, in certain senses also usually considered pejorative, more Victorian than other countries to whom the term is applied" (3). England was the country by which nineteenth-century Americans took their measure; they looked at this country, identified as the mightiest in the world, and proudly recalled that revolutionary moment in 1776 when monarchal England became the springboard to their own empowerment and democratic freedom. As one critic has so aptly remarked, "Although Americans did not have Victoria as their queen, they were Victorian in their economy, industry, and culture" (Palmer 169). American affiliation with the British was such that, for Americans, "Europe often reduces to England" (Weisbuch xvii). Identifying himself as a "rude, uncultivated fugitive slave . . . driven, by stern necessity" to England, Frederick Douglass understood what England meant to white American males, in particular. It was "that country to which young American gentlemen go to increase their stock of knowledge, to seek pleasure, to have their rough, democratic manners softened by contact with English aristocratic refinement" (*My Bondage and My Freedom* 223). Frederick Douglass, who would himself come away from Great Britain even more "the quintessential high Victorian gentleman, always impeccably dressed and elegantly behaved" (McFeely 17), was one of a number of blacks who went abroad to England with an understanding of the role Europe played in the cultural identity of America. This understanding was no less salient in the twentieth century when historian Nathan Huggins, cleverly writes, "The simple matter is that Americans have been a provincial people, forever self-conscious of themselves and their society in the making, and pulled by the powerful gravity of the European civilization to which they are heir and, despite claims to independence, which they emulate. Negroes, no less than other Americans, have suffered this same condition. Even more so, in fact, for Afro-Americans have inhabited a special ethnic province within provincial America. They have been perplexed by the desire to emulate the European-entranced white American and by the equally appealing dream of self-definition through the claiming of their inheritance of African culture" (8). Because white American Anglophilia was so pronounced, black Americans logically saw Britain as important if not central to any strategies for overcoming and circumventing impediments to black freedom and self-realization in the United States. White American Anglophilia could be put to the service of deconstructing Negrophobia or at least to securing black emancipation in the United States. Black Americans who traveled to the British Isles before the Civil War could locate a chink in the wall of Western solidarity that had held blacks as natural slaves. In the first half of the nineteenth century, blacks and abolitionists in the United States found England to be the place where "meaningful difference must arise out of a primary unity," a place where America and its most heartily acknowledged source of "cultural continuity"—England—did not always see eye to eye (Weisbuch xviii, xiii). Blacks found that to have the English eye upon members of the race who made it abroad was to gain visibility back home in white America. Thus, historian David Howard-Pitney writes that at the end of the nineteenth century, Ida B. Wells "was initially more successful in attracting notice among Afro-Americans than among whites. It was only when she traveled to the British Isles to criticize and embarrass America abroad for its 'national crime' that she began to gain wide national and international attention" (74).

No wonder that, by far, most of the African Americans who went abroad during the nineteenth and early twentieth centuries traveled to England, which, despite its imperialist and slaveholding past, was perceived as a haven for those who would be free. Thus as early as 1829, the revolutionary and nationalist author of *Appeal in Four Articles*, David Walker, exhorted African Americans who were thinking of emigration not to return to Africa but to "go to those who have been for many years, and are now our greatest earthly friends and benefactors—the English" (qtd. in Moses 16). England was ultimately much more than a sanctuary. It was the land of appeals or better yet the amplifier of publicity; years later W. E. B. Du Bois would proclaim in a speech about the South that publicity was one of the most formidable instruments of reform. In Britain, African Americans could generate, to borrow Du Bois's terms, "blatant publicity," a "publicity to force the truth into their ears," a truth that would "make it impossible for any human being . . . not to realize the barbarities that prevail here" ("Behold the Land" 364). Frederick Douglass formulated this point earlier and more succinctly, recognizing that through the agency of England, fugitives such as himself returning to America could hope to "shame them [Americans] into a sense of decency upon this subject" of slavery (Papers, London Tavern, March 30, 1847). He anticipated questions about his focus on Britain. "I may be asked, why I am so anxious to bring this subject before the British public—why I do not confine my efforts to the United States?" In response to this question, he listed several reasons, among them the fact that slavery is "so hardening," "so corrupting," "so deleterious," and "so overwhelming in its power, that no one nation is equal to its removal." He felt that Britain had the wherewithal to help extirpate the "sapping" and "gigantic evil" of slavery. "I am here," he explained, "because you have an influence on American that no other nation can have." Douglass believed that "the denunciations against slavery, uttered in London this week, may be heard in a fortnight in the streets of Boston," and that "there is nothing said here against slavery that will not be recorded in the United States." Douglass also understood the special way in which Britain empowered him. He explained that he was in Britain "because the slaveholders do not want me to be here." Having learned "never to occupy ground which the enemy would like me to occupy," Douglass, by being in Britain, acquired leverage with which to "summon the people of Britain," to "make known to them the conduct of the slaveholders," and thereby "cut [. . .] them to the quick . . . produc[ing] a sensation such as would be produced by nothing else." As he so deftly put it, "The power I exert now is something like the power that is exerted by the man at the end of the lever; my influence now is just in proportion to the distance that I am from the United States. My exposure of slavery abroad will tell more upon the hearts and consciences of slaveholders, than if I was attacking them in America" (*My Bondage and My Freedom* 259–60). However, as Blackett has argued, Douglass wanted to do more than expose slavery: He wanted to build an antislavery wall, to discipline, if I may borrow philosopher Michel Foucault's terms, rather than punish the United States. Thus antebellum blacks who went to Britain, Blackett points out, "were interested not in raising arms and men to combat oppression, but in erecting a moral cordon around America that would isolate her from the international community" (6).

After the Civil War, there may no longer have been a need to erect an antislavery wall, but there undoubtedly remained a need to maintain a moral cordon around America. From 1865 to 1900, the sociopolitical climate changed significantly in both the United States and in Britain. Thus, the slave narratives that had served to arouse British sympathy for beleaguered blacks practically went off the radar of the larger public for nearly sixty years as scholars Charles Davis and Henry Louis Gates, Jr., point out in their introduction to *The Slave's Narrative.* The American Antislavery Society would effectively shut down by 1870, leaving some blacks such as Sarah Remond to shift the antislavery focus of her work in England to calls for aid for the freedmen.[5] The failure of Reconstruction in the United States would give way to Jim Crow laws and lynchings that would reach unparalleled heights in the 1890s. Some blacks would seek to escape the postwar, post-Reconstruction South by becoming part in the 1870s and 1880s of the Exoduster movement of blacks to the West. Meanwhile Britain, contending with its own racial upheaval in the form of the Jamaican rebellion and the ensuing 1865 Governor Eyre controversy, would also in the 1870s and 1880s start to become deeply agitated over the issue of Irish Home Rule, which would allow the Irish their own parliament and give them seats in the English parliament. Both the United States' and Great Britain's fascination with spiritualism, mesmerism, and psychic research would be part and parcel of a pseudoscience that would underpin racism, and the movements to gain suffrage for working class men and finally women would take place during the decades of the 1880s and 1890s. Given these developments, it is fair to say that the relations between the British and the African Americans were affected. Certainly no list of antilynching campaigners can be produced that is comparable to the list of African American abolitionists who went abroad to stoke the fires of reform that burned brightest for African Americans in Victorian Britain. Granted the success of Ida B. Wells in raising British consciousness about lynching in the States, there were no doubt times in the 1880s and the 1890s when the British looked to be more interested in scrambling for the dark continent of Africa than in mitigating the plight of recently emancipated blacks. However, as David Brion Davis has argued in *Slavery and Human Progress,* Britain's scramble for Africa had become deeply intertwined with its international antislavery mission during the last decade of the nineteenth century, a period that saw "the waning commitment to the idea of progress itself, a disenchantment encouraged by the excesses of industrialism, imperialism, and nationalistic rivalry" (305, 307). This is not to say that blacks stopped traveling to Britain or that the British with their new international focus on antislavery and empire became oblivious to the existence of black Americans. Rather, this is to say that in the midst of the social, political, and spiritual foment that took place during the last half of the nineteenth century, blacks would remain behind the veil though not entirely invisible as groups such as the Fisk's Jubilee Singers and, more germane to this study, prominent individuals such as Booker T. Washington, Ida B. Wells, and, by the turn of the century, black scholar W. E. B. Du Bois went abroad to Britain and Europe during the last quarter of the century.

Being There: What Being on British Soil Meant to African Americans

For many blacks who traveled overseas during the nineteenth century, first contact with the people of the British Isles proved talismanic, especially for those who were and felt themselves to be fugitives from slavery and injustice. Having escaped slavery and the sexual advances of her master, Harriet Ann Jacobs, who, in 1845, sailed for twelve days aboard the *Britannic* to England where she would care for her benefactor's young daughter, describes her arrival as a heady, liberatory experience: "My situation was indescribably more pleasant. For the first time in my life I was in a place where I was treated according to my deportment, without reference to my complexion." Feeling as if a "millstone had been lifted from my breast," Jacobs recalled how she "laid [her] head on [her] pillow, for the first time, with the delightful consciousness of pure, unadulterated freedom" (183). England afforded her a sweet oblivion from which she was jarred only when she looked to America's shore: "Indeed, I entirely forgot it [color prejudice], till the time came for us to return to America" (185). Turning from the liberating wonder of Britain to the harsh reality of America, Jacobs could only comment, "It is a sad feeling to be afraid of one's native country" (186). Frederick Douglass also bespoke the magic of the British Isles, marveling at the transformation contact with the isles effected; he "look[ed] with wonder and amazement on the transition," exclaiming, "but now behold the change! Eleven days and a half gone, and I have crossed three thousand miles of the perilous deeps." He had found the opposite of the United States, a transformative and Edenic land: "Instead of a democratic government, I am under a monarchical government. Instead of the bright, blue sky of America, I am covered with the soft, grey fog of the Emerald Isle. I breathe, and lo! The chattel becomes a man." As far as Douglass could tell, gone were the questions about his humanity, gone were the insults, the disrespect, the reminders of his complexion, and the ubiquitous reminders that "*We don't allow niggers in here!*" On coming to the isles of Britain, Douglass immediately enjoyed "respite" (*My Bondage and My Freedom* 226, 227). As William Wells Brown experienced it, his arrival in the port of Liverpool constituted in an enchanted flash the disappearance of chattelhood and the dawning of personhood, an epiphanic shift from invisibility to visibility: "No person of my complexion can visit *this* [my emphasis] country without being struck with the marked difference between the English and the Americans. The prejudice which I have experienced on all and every occasion in the United States, and to some extent on board the *Canada*, vanished as soon as I set foot on the soil of Britain . . . no sooner was I on British soil, than I was recognized as a man, and an equal. The very dogs in the streets appeared conscious of my manhood" (98). Likewise, setting foot on British soil proved an extraordinarily eye-opening experience for William P. Powell, a free black from New York, who was able to see more clearly the moral turpitude of a country notable for its republicanism. "I never knew I had a country until I crossed the Atlantic ocean," Powell declared in a letter to Maria Weston Chapman. "In old England Liberty is not an empty name, as the American democratic cradle robbers would have us believe." Once he "set [. . .] his foot upon British soil," Powell found the holy of holies, a country "consecrated to the genious [*sic*] of Universal Emancipation." For "in monarchical England," he found "asylum from the storms of American persecution & negro hate. In this strange country I am regarded as a *man*, and invested with all the rights of a British born subject, without even the *farce* of *naturalization*. Taxation & representation are together alike awarded to every subject who conforms to the provisions of the Reform Law of 1832" (Taylor 437). For Powell, England was a consecrated land where he and others like him could become humanly and fully invested in the life and rewards of a nation. England's freedom was real, America's a farce.

Just as surely as Britain worked its magic on African Americans, African Americans tended literally to work their magic on Britain. Antebellum black Americans spent the lion's share of their time lecturing before British audiences, "the more democratic element" of which, according to Bolt, "was forced," interestingly enough, "to express itself publicly through meetings and demonstrations" (xiii). Their speaking schedules were extremely demanding. As Blackett tallies it, Douglass, who drew large audiences (e.g., "twenty-five hundred at Edinburgh; twelve hundred at Dundee; crowds of three thousand and fifteen hundred at two Paisley meetings") "delivered fifty lectures in the first four months of his visit, the number rising by the end of his nineteen-month tour, to three hundred" (*Building an Antislavery Wall* 17, 18–19). No wonder that in 1846, a harried Douglass felt, as he expressed himself to the members of a sewing circle back home, "weighed down, oppressed, and almost overcome by constant effort—by engagements, public and private, growing out of immediate contact with deeply interested friends here—I find it very difficult to gain a moment of calm repose, during which to commune with dear friends on your side the Atlantic" (Foner 1: 186). William Wells Brown's schedule was no less harrowing. The fugitive and abolitionist "estimated that he had traveled twenty thousand miles and given over a thousand lectures in five years" (*Building an Antislavery Wall* 17). Indeed, in her biography of her father, Josephine Brown declares that during his residence abroad, her father William Wells Brown "travelled more than twenty-five thousand miles through Great Britain, addressed above one thousand public meetings, and lectured before twenty-three literary societies, besides speaking at religious and benevolent anniversaries" (94–95). During 1841, Charles Lenox Remond, Blackett determines, "spoke twenty-three nights out of thirty on slavery, prejudice, and colonization and lost his voice for his pains" (*Building an Antislavery Wall* 17). Remond must have experienced tremendous exhaustion given the fact that, as Quarles tells us, "his standard speech ran to two hours" (132). Dorothy Sterling reports that Remond's sister, Sarah spoke before "as many as two thousand people at a time" during her tour of the British Isles (178). In an 1859 letter to antislavery activist Maria W. Chapman, Sarah Remond herself indicated how demanding the lecture circuit in England could be: "I have lectured very frequently, in fact had more invitations recently than I could fill. Lectured on three successive evenings last week, which was rather too much for me and I am now with my friends . . . for a little rest, then go to York, to lecture there" (Sterling 179). Much later in the century, Ida B. Wells, it seems, would also find herself taxed as she "spent two weeks in Liverpool" where she "delivered by invitation ten addresses on 'Lynch Law in the United States'" at gatherings that "averaged a thousand persons each" (135).

In "'Negrophilism' and British Nationalism," Audrey Fisch argues that nineteenth-century British audiences may well have viewed the lectures of black abolitionists as a form of entertainment or "spectacle." Acknowledging and advancing beyond Fisch's critique of the British reception of black antislavery speakers, British scholar Sarah Meer points out that as early as 1840, the British were absorbing some of America's racial prejudices against blacks by attending among other things such "ethnic exhibitions" as those provided by a black face minstrel troupe such as the Ethiopian Serenaders: so that "at the very moment of Douglass's achievements in Britain, popular entertainments were offering simplistic or exploitative pictures of black people and evading the issue of slavery altogether" (142). Despite such subversive undercurrents, "the large number, frequency, and popularity" of antislavery appearances by blacks does, as Blackett observes, "suggest that they must have reached a large segment of the British population, bringing home to their audiences the horrors of slavery and discrimination" (*Building an Antislavery Wall* 18). Certainly during the last quarter of the nineteenth century, the conflicting representations of blacks persisted as, to use Douglass's words, "the battle at this point . . . [was] not yet fought out and the victory . . . not yet won" (Foner 4: 446). Thus, Douglass felt as late as 1886 that his presence in Europe could mitigate the negative representations of such entertainments as those provided by serenaders. In a letter to friends written during his last trip to Europe, Douglass averred, "I have felt however that my presence here even in silence, has a good influence in respect to the standing of the colored race before the world." He felt that by being in Europe he could deter "the leprous distilment of American prejudice" that flowed from America to Europe by way not only of performers but also of "malicious American writers" who "take pleasure in attacking us, as an inferior and good for nothing race" (Foner 4: 444, 445). Douglass more specifically noted, "America has her missionaries abroad in the Ethiopian singers, who disfigure and distort the features of the Negro and burlesque his language and manners in a way to make him appear to thousands as more akin to apes than to men." Admitting that "these influences are very hurtful" because they "avert from us the sympathy of civilized Europeans" and "bring us under the lash and sting of the world's contempt," Douglass who, while visiting Paris had "done little" to publicly gainsay these misrepresentations, having chosen instead to "bear my testimony . . . in private with pen and tongue," determined that when he returned to England he would "probably make a few speeches in that country in vindication of the cause and character of the colored race in America" (Foner 4: 444, 445).[6]

Whether laboring in the wake of blackface performances or not, the schedule of the black antislavery speaker in Europe often proved a grueling one as the physical presence of the black body served both to dispel lies and myths and disseminate realities about both enslaved and free blacks as no other agents could. Even though British writings and reports on the conditions of blacks in America raised awareness, nothing brought home the horrible fact of slavery, prejudice, and discrimination as forcefully as the physical person of the American black. Thus, as Isabel Jennings wrote to Maria Weston Chapman in 1843, "It is very hard for me to think that 'tis far short of two years since we first felt that Americans were our bretheren—and not the inhabitants of a world with which we had no feelings in common—for tho' Miss M's [British writer and abolitionist Harriet Martineau's] book [*The Martyr Age in the United States*] was *read* it was not *felt* until after [black abolitionist] C. L. Remond's visit" (Taylor 191). The physical body of the black American on British soil was the ultimate form of material evidence and authentication as Clare Taylor suggests when she remarks, "Especially after the passing of the Fugitive Slave Law, when many escaped slaves came to Britain, and when the success of *Uncle Tom's Cabin* was at its height, the presence of a Negro abolitionist on the anti-slavery platform was almost a popular necessity" (9).

Their presence in such high demand, black American abolitionists abroad were allowed little leisure, little time to sightsee and ramble. It was difficult to find time for study and for other projects for self-improvement. There was, however, as Fiona Spiers has indicated, the possibility of social interaction with the aristocracy, rich sponsors, British celebrities, politicians, and great writers (83, 84). The demands of racial performance and uplift were, nevertheless, always in place whether or not one was an abolitionist. Even when later in the century an African American such as Mary Church Terrell went overseas as a tourist, she nevertheless, as one critic points out, did double duty as a representative of the race. For Episcopalian and Cambridge-educated Alexander Crummell, the leisure of sightseeing could become a chore. He explained that "with constant charge, hospitality, continual daily, sometimes hourly, engagements; talking, speaking, and sight-seeing," he could not keep up with his correspondence. It became increasingly difficult to "bring myself more in evidence before the people" as Crummell puts it elsewhere, as relaxation tended to elude him: "I have been journeying from the East, in Lincolnshire to the West, in Somersetshire; going to and from London, on divers engagements and visits to friends; until I have become exhausted. One of the hardest things in life is sight-seeing, entertainment and visiting; for, not seldom, the exhaustion begins to overbalance the delight; which certainly, in our case, English hospitality has constantly given us." Although the hospitality of British friends and supporters who wished to see and be with the clergyman could prove physically punishing, Crummell was undoubtedly pleased when he found "very much interest in our cause in clerical and other circles" (*Destiny and Race* 86, 90). The visible presence of such African Americans as the articulate Mary Church Terrell and the priestly Alexander Crummell in Britain ratcheted up British awareness not only of American hypocrisy, but also of African American personhood and character; blacks abroad did not deport themselves as the beastly and depraved subhumans Americans made them out to be. The presence of black Americans tuned the British into black America as the British became sensitized to the messages African Americans communicated directly and indirectly. Thus in British newspapers and journals, reports on the manners of African American travelers, the timbre of their voices, the cut of the clothing, and the effectiveness of their speech gave them a civil body.

Being there, African Americans made a difference at the personal or domestic as well as at the public level. Irish abolitionist and publisher Richard D. Webb confessed a fondness and respect for the black woman abolitionist he had invited into his home. In 1859, he wrote of Sarah Remond, "Miss Remond writes beside me . . . She is really very clever." Describing Remond as "much more sensible & thoroughgoing" than Douglass whose intellectual prowess he conceded, Webb found that she was also "far less crotchety than Wright or Pillsbury. She has more common sense—& her devotion to the cause & its friends is thorough." He concluded, "We like her very much" (Taylor 440). Although Webb's reference to Sarah Remond provides insight into how blacks abroad could affect the European on an individual basis, Frederick Douglass proves one of the best examples of how blacks could stir the British public. Thus, on January 24, 1846, Mary Ireland wrote from Belfast to Maria Weston Chapman that such "an intense interest has been excited by the oratory of Frederick Douglass during his late visit to this town" that "in consequence a female AntiSlavery Society is about being formed just at present." Though not every one warmed to what he had to say at the time, especially about the Free Church of Scotland, Ireland could enthusiastically endorse his charismatic ability to mobilize a supportive contingent: "All who have listened to D—are warm in the cause of the slave many are earnest and energetic . . . I am convinced there is scarcely a lady in Belfast who would not be anxious to join in any means calculated to promote the enfranchisment [*sic*] of the deeply injured Africans" (Taylor 247). Mary A. Estlin of Bristol described Douglass's impact this way: "I have said nothing about F. Douglass, for there is but one opinion of him. Wherever he goes he arouses sympathy in your cause & love for himself. He is affecting a great work here, & the longer you can spare him to us the better it will be for us & I believe for you too in the end" (Taylor 282).

Black abolitionists must have been convinced that the grind of the lecture circuit was worth the effort as African American investment of time and person in the British Isles yielded some definite returns. Ultimately African Americans, at least during the first half of the nineteenth century, influenced the British to write letters; to reinforce antislavery societies; to establish women's sewing circles, fairs, and bazaars to support the abolitionist cause; to take a new and closer look at "ending conditions of near slavery in other British territories"; and to reexamine their own domestic oppressions such as those experienced by the British working class, the Irish, and women (Taylor 11). Finally, African American influence was such that some British subjects opened their purses to pay for the passage of some African Americans to Britain; to purchase occasionally the freedom of a slave, as in the case of Frederick Douglass; to underwrite antislavery societies and activities; to support individual black speakers and their families; and to finance the education of some black American at some of Great Britain's premier institutions of higher learning.

Having visited Europe and made their presence felt abroad, some black Americans, such as Alexander Crummell who emigrated to Africa, chose at some point not to return to the United States.[7] There were African Americans, however, who, instead of emigrating to Africa, literally became black Victorians by virtue of their decision to take up extended or permanent residence in Victorian England. It should come as no surprise that black Americans fleeing oppression in the United States sometimes went to England and ended up making it their home or spending a significant number of years among the English. Such is the case of William and Ellen Craft who, after their inventive and daring escape from slavery recorded in *Running a Thousand Miles for Freedom,* remained in England for twenty years before returning to the United States. In 1881, William Craft, Jr. would return to the country that had sheltered his parents to live out the rest of his days.

England may be said to have practically sent an engraved invitation to bondsman John Brown. Brown first heard of England as a place of freedom from a freeborn black seaman from Liverpool who had been seized, enslaved, and finally sold to the owner of the Georgia plantation where Brown—when he was not being cruelly worked or tortured—was for a period of nine months on loan to one Dr. Hamilton of Jones County who experimented upon Brown to discover, among other things, how deep the black of Brown's skin went. While Brown listened to the Englishman's talk about how black men and women were free in England, he solidified his perception of Britain as a land of salvation when John Morgan, a Scottish man who, having settled on a neighboring plantation, proceeded, unlike his fellow planters, to treat blacks with more regard and kindness, hiring both black and white free laborers instead of using slaves. No wonder then that in one of his first attempts to escape, Brown, whose thoughts were full of the old country, set off by a road he believed would take him directly to England. Inspired by the stories of Liverpudlian John Glasgow and by the fairness of the Scottish planter, John Brown eventually escaped by way of Canada to the very place that informed the substance of his emancipatory dreams. Brown, who in his narrative claimed he had no intention of remaining in England, ended up staying there because, as he himself acknowledged, the country afforded him a better chance of making and sustaining a decent living. As previously mentioned, Brown declared in the narrative he published in England in 1855 that although he had little education, he had some skills in carpentry and growing cotton that he could capitalize upon, if granted the real possibility of employment: "I am a strong man yet, in spite of the privations, hardships, and sufferings I have undergone . . . But I have just that sort of experience which I believe I could turn to account were the field open" (207–8). He continued in his narrative to assure readers, if not prospective employers that "with a fair field" he could make his own way, "earn my own living:" "I want to do it I want to rise. I do not want to stay in this country any longer than is necessary for me to get enough money to purchase some tools and to set me going in the world." He only needed, he persisted, a "fair chance" (208), which he apparently received and relished as he settled in England.

Francis Fedric, born a slave on a Virginia plantation, like John Brown, escaped his enslavers, fleeing first to Canada where he took a wife then continued on to England. He found life in England to be more synonymous with ideas of life and liberty than life in the United States or Canada. "When I issued forth from bondage to a land of freedom it was like stepping from death into life, from the deepest shades of night into the glorious sunny realms of liberty! liberty!" (10). Fedric, who eventually ran a lodging house in Manchester, could barely contain his "feelings at the kindness I have received since I landed in England from the English." From 1857 until his death, Fedric made England, primarily Plymouth his home.

Still other black Americans opted to become Queen Victoria's subjects independent of the threat and duress of slavery. When and where slavery was not an issue, sheer prejudice as well as professional and social obstruction proved inducements for African American allegiance to the British crown. William Wells Brown's daughter, Josephine Brown, for instance, understood that the prospect of return to America was not a particularly attractive one. As she observed in the biography she wrote on her father's life, "As it regards social position, any government is preferable to that of the United States for a colored person to live under. The prejudice which exists in most of the American States against people of color is unknown in any European country. This, therefore, is a great inducement to colored Americans to take up their residence abroad" (100). Josephine Brown and her sister Clarissa arrived in London in 1851, were enrolled in a seminary in Calais, and then completed their education at the Home and Colonial School in London where in December the sisters passed the examination for teacher certification. Josephine Brown, who at the age of fourteen became mistress of the East Plumstead School in Woolwich Kent, returned to the States only once to spend time with her father who had returned to American in 1854 and to complete his biography. By the end of 1856, Josephine Brown was back in England where she apparently lived out her life as a black Victorian.

One of the most famous examples of an African American who left the United States for England never to return was the actor who came to be known as the "African Roscius." Ira F. Aldridge quit the United States for England in 1824 when it became apparent to him that he would never have a successful or fulfilling career on the American stage.[8] Interestingly enough, when he made his debut in London, his reception there was not so completely divorced from his experience in America. Although the British audiences—which did not extend a unanimously warm welcome to the African American tragedian—could be said to have been more or less appreciative of his performances, the British press proved particularly hostile to Aldridge's color. The actor did not, however, turn his back on England to scurry back to the United States. Feeling, no doubt, that a mixed reception in England was better than the blatant exclusion and repudiation to which he was sure to be subjected back home, Aldridge persevered in great part by performing outside London. For a quarter of a century, he would tour the provinces, occasionally appearing at some of the smaller theaters in London. When renowned British actor Edmund Kean died in 1833, Aldridge was called upon to replace him at Covent Garden. After his brief stint at Covent Garden, he continued to tour London's provinces, winning more and more acclaim. Aldridge, who made his first continental tour in 1852, would have the honor of performing at the Lyceum in the fashionable west end of London in 1858. In 1863, he became a British subject.

Another American induced to stake his claim in Victorian England was Walter G. Allen, a free light-skinned black educated at Oneida College. In 1853, Allen, who edited the *National Watchman* and served as professor of rhetoric and belles letters at Central College in McGrawville, New York, dared to fall in love with and marry his white student, Mary King. Only nine days after the March nuptials, the couple beat a hasty retreat to England where Allen's British supporters eventually gained control of the Caledonia Training school and, by appointing Allen master there, made him the first black man to direct an educational establishment in England (Quarles 138–39).

Unlike Allen who settled in England to preserve his interracial marriage by circumventing a mob threatening tar and feathers, some of the African Americans who chose to live in Britain were enticed there, as was Josephine Brown, by the promise of a good education. Two black Americans who attended college in Britain and decided to remain in the country were Thomas Lewis Johnson and Isaac P. Dickerson both of Virginia. Johnson who had been a slave for twenty-eight years had lived in Chicago and Colorado after emancipation, but with the "lynching, violent repression, and political thievery" of the period and Johnson's desire to better himself in preparation for work in Africa, the forty-year old African American turned to Britain, arriving there with his wife in September 1876. He was trained as a nonconformist Christian minister at Pastor's College before he went to Africa as planned, but he was forced to leave that continent because of poor health. A resident of Britain in the 1890s, Johnson became a British subject in 1900, serving that same year as vice chairman of the organizational committee of the Pan-African Congress, which met in July (Lotz and Pegg 4, 10; Green 55–69). Isaac P. Dickerson, one of the original Jubilee Singers, also made Britain his home. Dickerson, who left the group after the 1873 tour, studied theology at the University of Edinburgh and did some work as an evangelist in France in 1878. According to Peter Fryer, Dickerson and another Jubilee Singer, Edmund Walker who studied music in London, were still in England by 1902. For Dickerson, the Scottish university, in particular the University of Edinburgh where Dickerson matriculated in 1874 at the age of 24, became a domestic foothold.[9] Described in 1858 by Victorian writer W. E. Aytoun as "institutions radically different in kind from Oxford and Cambridge," the University of Edinburgh and schools like it "were originally intended to afford, and they still do offer, the advantages of liberal education to a numerous class of young men, who, in England, could never have joined a university," thereby "extend[ing] the benefits of instruction to a far greater number in proportion to the relative population of the Kingdoms." Aytoun continues, "A stranger, on first visiting Edinburgh, must necessarily be much surprised by the very motley aspect of the crowd which issues from the College gates when the bell tolls . . . Boyhood, adolescence, manhood, and even age, are there represented." (77). Though Aytoun does not list race or color as one of the diversifying aspects of the motley crew pouring out of the college gates, black American students such as Dickerson must have experienced the university not only as a good fit but also as a good outfitter for life in Victorian Britain. In the process of qualifying these black foreigners, the university also domesticated them, as Lotz and Pegg suggest in their general observation that "those Black professionals who had adapted to student life in Britain would have considered settling in Britain" (8).

Once established upon British shores, these African-Americans-gone-Black-Victorians, joined the ranks of a population that until recently was considered negligible—the Black British bourgeoisie. Documented in such works as Peter Fryer's *Staying Power*, Jeffrey Green's *Black Edwardians*, and Gretchen Holbrook Gerzina's *Black Victorians/Black Victoriana*, this Black British middle class included such figures as composer Samuel Coleridge-

Taylor; Dr. George Rice, a superintendent of the Woolwich Union Infirmary in Kent who had studied medicine with the pioneer of antiseptic surgery, Lister; Queen Victoria's black goddaughter Victoria Davies; and Luranah and Amanda Aldridge, the British-bred daughters of American actor Ira Aldridge. The lives of such British-bred blacks were, if not exactly charmed, then notably more livable than those of blacks in America. As W. E. B. Du Bois would remark of Samuel Coleridge-Taylor whom he met in England around the time of the World's Fair at Paris in 1900, the Afro-British composer was "fortunate . . . to be born in Europe" as opposed to America, which would have stifled his "genius." America was given "to discourag[ing], chok[ing], and murder[ing] ability when it so far forgets itself as to choose a dark skin." But "England, thank God, is slightly more civilized than her colonies," though "even there the path of this young man was no way of roses and just a shade thornier than that of whiter men" (*Darkwater* 198–99). That slight degree more of civility and culture that England afforded the darker skin would be enough to entice some nineteenth- and twentieth-century African Americans away from the United States.

Even Frederick Douglass felt the pull of British citizenship, admitting that he "could have easily remained in England, for the same friends who had so generously purchased my freedom, would have assisted me establishing myself in that country." However, like other African Americans driven overseas to make a case for their humanity, he proved too deeply invested in America not to return. Douglass explained, "I will continue to pray, labor, and wait, believing that she [America] cannot always be insensible to the dictates of justice, or deaf to voice of humanity." His freedom purchased while he was abroad in England, Douglass still felt obligated to return to his brethren in the United States where "I had a duty to perform—and that was, to labor and suffer with the oppressed in my native land" (229, 225).

Friend of Frederick Douglass and William Wells Brown, black abolitionist James W. C. Pennington, who himself made three trips to Britain in 1843, 1849, and 1861 explained in a lecture before a Glaswegian audience that blacks ought to "*stand*" and "maintain our national rights" because "our destiny is bound up in that of America, her ship is ours, her pilot is ours, her storms are ours, her calms are ours. If she breaks upon any rock, we break with her. We love America and hate slavery the more; and thus, loving the one and hating the other, we are resolved that they shall NOT LONG DWELL TOGETHER" (17; also qtd. in Blackett, *Beating* 77). William Wells Brown, who spent five years in England and brought his daughters Clarissa and Josephine to France and England to be educated, also decided finally to go back to his native land. Abolitionists, such as Douglass, Pennington, and Brown, had, as Fiona Spears puts it in her essay on black Americans in

Britain, "absorbed enough of the American creed to wish to return there and make those ideals a reality" (89).

For a number of prominent African Americans, one of the roads to racial progress ran through Victorian Britain. To visit or to invoke Britain was to wield formidable international and cultural leverage. The British could and did make a difference in the lives of black Americans, especially in the first half of the nineteenth century. African Americans were not looking to reform Britain; they were looking to Britain to help them improve their position in America. African Americans who journeyed to Britain tended to go there so that they could take something back home—knowledge, attitude, perspective, support. The objective was not to leave the United States and remain in Britain but to find a way home through Britain.

By far most African Americans returned to the United States renewed, invigorated, and often more determined to press for human rights and democratic freedoms. A visit to Europe gave African Americans more clout and cachet back home, so that the European trip tended to translate for blacks into greater influence and visibility as leaders. As Alan J. Rice and Martin Crawford assert of Frederick Douglass and twentieth-century actor and activist Paul Robeson, "their leadership roles in the Africa American community were enhanced by their European sojourns" (6). Indeed, those sojourns abroad led for most black Americans right back to their communities where the homecomers were often transformed, according to Blackett, by a visit to Britain, which gave them "a new self-confidence" and enabled them "to dream of real freedom at home" (41)—these transformed homecomers worked with renewed and increased dedication and commitment to the idea of effecting change at home. Thus upon his return to the United States, Douglass, thanks to British supporters, was able to turn his attention to establishing his own paper, *The North Star.* Despite the opposition he experienced from American abolitionists who had heretofore directed much of his public activity and who felt that a paper would "interfere with [his] usefulness as a lecturer" and that he "was better fitted to speak than to write," Douglass, encouraged by British friends and backed by British funds, persisted, successfully establishing his paper. His time abroad had provided him with the resources, but especially with the confidence to break free of his "slavish adoration of my Boston friends" to realize a project that further enhanced "the development of my own mental and moral energies" (*My Bondage and My Freedom* 240, 241, 242).[10] This new mental and moral energy Douglass would in part expend in breaking with the Garrisonian abolitionists who sought to lock him into the lecture mill and revealed, according to historian Waldo E. Martin, Jr., "an unwillingness to allow Douglass, a black man, to speak his own mind" (27). Back home, Douglass would eventually work for African American recruitment into the

Union Army, agitate for the national voting rights act, serve as federal marshal and recorder of deeds for the District of Columbia, and as president, for a brief time, of the Freedman's Bureau Bank. Douglass, who would sail twice more to Europe—once in 1859 as a fugitive from the government that believed he had conspired with John Brown in his raid on Harper's Ferry and a last time in 1886 as a tourist with his second wife, a white woman named Helen Pitts—would also take the mission to liberate black people abroad to Haiti where he served as consul-general from 1889 to 1891 and as chargé d'affaires for Santo Domingo. European travel helped politicize Douglass.

Once his freedom was secured, William Wells Brown returned to the United States in 1854. His daughter explained, "Although recognised as a man, and treated with deference by all he met [in Europe], Mr. Brown wished to return to the United States. His feelings and inclinations were all with the slave and his friends, and his soul yearned to be where the great battle for freedom was being fought" (Josephine Brown 100). He fought that battle back home not only by lecturing and reading but also by using his pen to write literary historical compositions that presented black folk who "epitomized the ideals of aspiring black men and women of color." As scholar William L. Andrews contends, Brown's "pioneering" compositions aimed "to educate an American readership that saw mostly the defamation of African American character in newspapers, magazines, and books" (106, 107).

Unlike Douglass or Brown, Harriet Jacobs, whose 1845 visit to Europe overlapped by four months Douglass's European sojourn and who confesses to having received stronger religious impressions in England, returned not to a more public life in the United States but rather to domestic life in her community. No doubt, the less public life may be attributed partly to the fact that she was a single parent; however, the most obvious reason for this lower profile is that Jacobs was a fugitive slave returning just before the passing of the Fugitive Slave Law. Upon her return to the States, her efforts centered in securing an education and a home for her children. She did, however, support the antislavery cause, though she did not go on the lecture circuit. Her most notable venture into the public sphere was at the instigation of her brother who opened an antislavery reading room that ultimately failed for lack of funding. Meanwhile, England remained in her mind a saving place. Thus Jacobs tried in 1853 to get Harriet Beecher Stowe to take her daughter Louisa with her to England as a "representative of a Southern slave," but Stowe, who "was afraid' that Louisa would be subject to "much petting and patronizing . . . more pleasing to a young Girl than useful," was "much opposed" to such attention being given to "this class of people" (Sterling 76). In 1858, Jacobs herself would travel once more to England where she sought unsuccessfully to find a publisher for her book. A decade would pass before Jacobs along with her daughter Louisa would return to England this time to raise money for an orphanage and a home for the elderly.

For the nineteenth-century African American, time spent abroad, whether as a brief trip or longer sojourn, mattered deeply. In a country such as England, blacks were afforded the opportunity to take the measure of what it means to be treated as a human being even as they themselves participated in the phenomenon of what English professor Heike Raphael-Hernandez has called the "blackening" of Europe by spreading via personal and public contact their own influences, providing Europeans a chance to exercise and confirm their humanitarian ideals, and giving Europeans the opportunity not only to know firsthand something of blacks from America but also to work or become more involved with that population in the United States whose condition belied the touted enlightenment, progress, and humanity of one of the Western world's most democratic and Christian nations. At last, African Americans who sailed to Britain, especially during the first half the nineteenth century found an anodyne for the pain, if not the antidote to the poison of American slavery and prejudice. Black Americans who hailed Britannia could find in that country, if not a perfect and disinterested friend, then a serviceable one.

Whether as visitors to, subjects of, or dreamers about Britain, nineteenth- and early twentieth-century blacks in America were touched by Victorian Britain in all its glories, its possibilities, and even its shortcomings. For even though, as one fugitive slave confessed, there was prejudice in England too, that prejudice was somehow mitigated, especially in the first half of the nineteenth century, by a Victorian culture that approached more nearly than American culture did a sense of fairness when it came to dealings with blacks. As Lotz and Pegg have commented, "However much life in Britain fell below expectations, the experience of Black folk in the U.S.A. suggested that the British had higher standards" (10). Personally and politically black Americans tended to believe in the power of the mother country to set the younger state straight. After all, the Queen Mother herself showed some degree of tolerance. Still, as Joan Anim-Addo reminds us, where race is concerned, "it does not hold that [the Queen's attitude] influenced greater national tolerance of black people" (17). It does follow, however, that not only the queen's subjects but also and, in particular, African Americans themselves might perceive rightly or wrongly the country headed by this maternal monarch as a more compassionate one than the paternalistic, slavery-ridden democracy in America. Victoria's Britain could make a place for black Americans not only in Britain itself but also in the United States of America.

3. Thomas Carlyle

Case Study of a Dark Victorian

The presence of African Americans abroad advanced neither their emancipatory missions nor their human status in the hearts and minds of some British Victorians. Preeminent among those Victorians who proved unsympathetic to the condition and plight of blacks in England or the Americas was social and moral critic and prophet Thomas Carlyle, who critic Logan Pearsall Smith dubbed "the Rembrandt of English Prose." Over the course of his career, Carlyle was compelled, no doubt, by the force of such events as the emancipation of West Indian blacks in 1833, the American Civil War, the Jamaican Rebellion, and the Governor Eyre Controversy in 1865 to consider social and political issues surrounding nineteenth-century blacks. On both the public and private occasions Carlyle turned his attention to black people, he did so vigorously and violently, if not devastatingly. In an imperious, loud voice, he spoke, wrote, and performed in a manner and style that commanded the attention of audiences on both sides of the Atlantic. Carlyle provides a powerful, interesting, and influential example of British racist-imperialist thinking and of African American reaction to such thinking.

Thomas Carlyle's proclamations about blacks, definitively set forth in the December 1849 issue of *Fraser's Magazine* as "An Occasional Discourse on the Negro Question" (the essay was expanded and reprinted later as a pamphlet in 1853 with the title "An Occasional Discourse on the Nigger Question") could not be summarily dismissed because Carlyle's discourse, occasional or otherwise, was so undeniably and powerfully constitutive. Thus in 1850, one of Carlyle's friends, Edinburgh University regius professor and quondam editor of Macmillan, David Masson would declare in hyperbolic tones, "It is nearly half a generation since Mr. Carlyle became an intellectual power in this country; and certainly rarely, if ever, in the history of literature, has such a phenomenon been witnessed as that of his influence. Throughout the whole atmosphere of this island his spirit has diffused itself, so that there is probably not an educated man under forty years of age, from Caithness to Cornwall, that can honestly say he has not been more or less affected by it . . . one can hardly take up a book or a periodical without finding in every page some expression or some mode of thinking that bears the mint-mark of his genius" (2). Novelist George Eliot's famous, oft-quoted, pronouncement about Carlyle proved nearly as adulatory as Masson's: "there is hardly a superior or active mind of this generation that has not been modified by Carlyle's writings: there has hardly been an English book written for the last ten or twelve years that would not have been different if Carlyle had not lived" (344). Carlyle's influence was such that it boomed across the ocean to the United States with the help of transcendentalist and abolitionist Ralph Waldo Emerson who extended several invitations to Carlyle to travel to America. One such invitation urged the British sage to "come & found a new Academy that shall be church & school & parnassus, as a true Poet's house should be." Another invitation pressed Carlyle to "come here forthwith, and deliver in lectures to the solid men of Boston the *History of the French Revolution* before it is published . . . here. There is no doubt of the perfect success of such a course now that the *five hundred copies of the Sartor are all sold,* and read with great delight by many persons" (Slater, *Correspondence* 110, 149). According to Carlylean biographer Fred Kaplan, such correspondence from Emerson "assured him [Carlyle] quite correctly if with some exaggeration, that his American brothers were more eager than the English to recognize his genius and provide a supportive environment for his work" (230). Others seconded Emerson's assurances of welcome and support in the United States. Thus, George Ripley, a Unitarian minister from Boston and a young friend of Emerson's was "effusive" in his "transatlantic applause" for Carlyle, averring that "a letter of yours to my friend R. W. Emerson, has convinced me that you are an actual Incarnation, and not merely a Presence and a Force, sent to say, 'Let there be Light,' but invisible t[o the] fleshly eye" (Slater, "George Ripley" 341, 343, 344).[1] Another American, Arthur Buller, as Carlyle himself recalls, practically clamored for a Carlylean visit to America, "preach[ing] to me . . . that I, namely, am the most esteemed &c, and ought to go over and Lecture in all great towns of the union, and make &c &c.!" (Slater, *Correspondence* 222–23). White male Americans such as Emerson, Ripley, and Buller must have found in Carlyle's "rugged, emotional style," as Kaplan has proposed, "an embodiment of their own glorification of Romantic independence" (230).[2]

In "Occasional Discourse," the influential and prophetic voice of Carlyle bespeaks neither glory nor Romantic independence for the West Indian blacks upon whom Carlyle heaps harsh invective and insulting racial stereotypes, which an earlier devotee and friend of Carlyle's, John Stuart Mill, feared were scandalously damaging.[3] Even Mill, a staunch abolitionist who himself subscribed, as many enlightened white and black men of the age did, to the idea of civilized and barbarian races, believed Carlyle had struck a long discordant chord with the publication of the "nigger question." In an anonymous response to Carlyle's essay, Mill, who recognized that "the words of English writers of celebrity are words of power on the other side of the ocean," declared that Carlyle had launched a "missile . . . into the abolitionist camp." In his soberly but forcefully crafted essay "On the Negro Question," in which he disputes Carlylean ideas about the excess of philanthropy, the right of might, and the gospel of work, Mill worried that "circulated as his dissertation will probably be, by those whose interests profit by it, from one end of the American Union to the other, I [Mill] hardly know of an act by which one person could have done so much mischief as this may possibly do" (49–50).[4] Across the ocean, New England Quaker poet and abolitionist John Greenleaf Whittier also bemoaned the Carlylean mischief that abnegated black worth, will, and minds, relegating these, as it were, to the void of the everlasting no just as surely as the Southern planter relegated black bodies to the fields and auction blocks. Whittier, whose poetry Frederick Douglass had quoted in his slave narrative, declared in 1854 after he read "a late number of *Fraser's Magazine*" containing "Occasional Discourse" that Carlyle "vituperates the poor black man with a coarse brutality which would do credit to a Mississippi slave driver, or a renegade Yankee dealer in human cattle on the banks of the Potomac. His rhetoric has a flavor of the slave pen and auction block—vulgar, unmanly, indecent—a scandalous outrage upon good taste and refined feeling—which at once degrades the author and insults his readers" (34, 35–36). Carlyle had styled the West Indian blacks who opted to grow pumpkins for their own subsistence instead of working to harvest spices for British plantation owners pumpkin-eating Quashees, unwilling or incapable of realizing the gospel of work. To the exasperation of Carlyle, these lazy blacks had become the adoptees, if not the minions, the "beautiful Black darlings" of philanthropists and democratic reformers who were mistakenly intent upon abolishing all pain when, in Carlyle's opinion, the absence of pain led to improvidence and was likely to "issue as a universal 'Sluggard-and-Scoundrel Protection Society.'" As a man of letters and one of that group of priests or sacred men who bore the standard of truth and fought for the maintenance of the "civilised world," Carlyle felt compelled to assure his audience that although he truly "like[s] poor [i.e., weak, deficient] Quashee," Quashee remained a species of "two-legged cattle" and a "nigger" to be whipped into the service of white masters determined to harvest spices in the New World outposts of the British Empire (*CW* 29: 349, 350, 354, 357, 376).

Carlyle valued the "permanency" in relations between master and servant. "Happy [is] he," wrote Carlyle, "who has found a master . . . and . . . having found . . . him [will] well keep him." He disparaged what he deemed more superficial and evanescent relations such as "marriage by the month" which "has been tried, and is still extensively practised in spite of Law and Gospel; but is not found to do! The legislator, the preacher, all rational mortals, answer, 'No, no!' You must marry for longer than a month, and the contract not so easily revocable, even should mistakes occur, as they sometimes do" (*CW* 29: 367, 368). Carlyle thought there was too little stability, too much shifting and moving around in society, in marital relations, and in the relations of one man to another. The instability, the impermanence, the abbreviations, if not the quick fixes were all of a piece—a kind of "nomadism" he decried (*CW* 29: 368). In the opening pages of "Occasional Discourse," Carlyle warns readers about the dangers that are likely to come out of any concerted efforts by do-good philanthropists and social scientists to tamper with what he saw as the perfectly irrevocable relations between master and slave. In these same opening pages, Carlyle goes on to express metaphorically his belief that the emancipation of blacks that some of his fellow countrymen and women sought would result in abominations he describes—in his efforts to point out how the family, but especially civilization is at risk—in terms of one of the most sacred of Victorian institutions—marriage. The miscegenational mix of philanthropy, science, and blacks was an invitation not just to social but also to physical disintegration. "These two, Exeter-Hall Philanthropy and the Dismal Science, led by any sacred cause of Black Emancipation, or the like, to fall in love and make a wedding of it,—will give birth to progenies and prodigies; dark extensive moon-calves [daydreamers, imbeciles], unnameable abortions, wide-coiled monstrosities, such as the world has not seen hitherto!" (*CW* 29: 354). Comparing the achievement of black liberation to the corruption of the marriage-bed issue, Carlyle admonishes readers that to free those who are naturally slaves is freakish. According to Carlyle, the "unhappy wedlock of Philanthropic Liberalism and the Dismal Science" for the sake of freeing blacks will lead to "huge woe for us, and for the poor civilised world, in these days" (*CW* 29: 354).

As powerful as these wedding and marriage metaphors and analogies are, the most memorable metaphor in Carlyle's "Occasional Discourse on the Nigger Question" represents the black Quashee as an animal. More specifically, Carlyle's metaphor reduces West Indian blacks to mere beasts of burden:

"Sitting yonder with their beautiful muzzles up to the ears in pumpkins . . . the grinder and incisor teeth ready for ever new work, and the pumpkins cheap as grass" (*CW* 29: 350). The equine beings Carlyle describes are not even granted the intelligence of Swift's Houyhnhnms, but are rather dumb animals, having neither voice nor mind, just body—specifically, teeth and stomachs, the markers of lazy overconsumers whose "indolence," as critic Jude Nixon remarks, "is black recalcitrance to satisfy obligatory consumer demands of whites" (93). Interestingly enough, at an address delivered at an annual fair in Tennessee, Frederick Douglass asserts, "There is no denying that slavery had a direct and positive tendency to produce coarseness and brutality in the treatment and management of domestic animals, especially those most useful to agricultural industry. Not only the slave, but the horse, the ox and the mule shared the general indifference to rights engendered by a state of slavery" (Frederick Douglass Papers, Reel 14 12). Whereas Douglass recognizes how the mistreatment of animals could not only compromise agricultural production but also reveal something about the brutalization of humanity, Carlyle is only able to attribute the lack of production not to the mistreatment and brutalization of men but rather to the dullness of blacks he identified as horselike creatures not entitled to any human rights. In *Latter-Day Pamphlets,* where Carlyle draws an analogy between horses and men to make a point about emancipation, he seems initially to share Douglass's understanding of how the mistreatment of men and the mistreatment of animals correspond to each other. Writing of the "the Horse, poor dumb four-footed fellow" with its own "private feelings, . . . affections, gratitudes," Carlyle admits, "Him too you occasionally tyrannise over; and with bad result to yourselves, among others; using the leather in a tyrannous unnecessary manner; withholding, or scantily furnishing, the oats and ventilated stabling that are due" (*CW* 20: 26). The sympathy Carlyle seems to elicit here for these tyrannized horses and thereby for tyrannized peoples is mocked and undercut as Carlyle proceeds to suggest that the idea of emancipating the likes of the blacks and Irish is as asinine as that of Farmer Hodges emancipating his horse, Black Dobbin. "Rugged horse-subduers, one fears they are a little tyrannous at times. 'Am I not a horse, and *half*-brother?'—To remedy which . . .—the horses all 'emancipated'" (*CW* 20: 26). In his comparison of blacks to horses, Carlyle evokes ridicule instead of compassion.

Carlyle has no more compassion for African American slaves than he has for those newly freed slaves in the West Indies. When it comes to the question of American slavery, Carlyle's thoughts go out to the white masters. In "Occasional Discourse," one of his concerns is that white Americans not make the same mistake the British did in abolishing slavery. Carlyle does not wish to see white Americans replicate Britain's "sad failure." He instead proposes that the "abuses" of the institution not the institution itself should be eradicated. There was to Carlyle's way of thinking some precious nougat at the center of slavery, and where Britain had failed, America had the opportunity to "save the precious thing in it." His advice to the American Farmer Hodges and to the Hon. Hickory Buckskin, a Carolinian "senator in those Southern States" is to make slavery work in a way that Americans hitherto had not. "Forgive me for saying," observes Carlyle, "that I do not think you have yet got to that point of perfection with your Negro relations; that there is probably much in them *not* fair, nor agreeable to the Maker of us, and to the eternal laws of fact as written in the Negro's being and in ours." Rather than manumit its slaves as Britain had done, Southern slave states ought, in Carlyle's opinion, to clean up slavery by making it, "with all diligence," a "fair" and "just" enterprise. Thus, Carlyle offers, the slave states might consider "a fixed legal sum" black Americans can pay to purchase freedom. As he sees it, the legal system provides the best, if not the only way out of the morass. "Many laws," he warns, "and gradually a whole code of laws, on this matter could be made! And will have to be made; if you would avoid the ugly Demerara issue, or even uglier which may be in store. I can see no other road for you." The law could make it possible for black and white men to live together in such a way that whites could continue "to command Black men" who "decidedly . . . have to be servants to those that are born *wiser* . . . that are born lords of you; servants to the Whites, if they *are* (as what mortal can doubt they are?) born wiser than you" (*CW* 29: 368, 370, 371, 372, 379, 381). Carlyle's hubris, his egregious lack of compassion, his intolerance, and his conviction that blacks were cattlelike creatures born to do the bidding of whites—these prompted Whittier to remark the regrettable fact that in a "splenetic and discreditable production," Thomas Carlyle, a celebrated European "writer of genius [, had] lent the weight of his authority and his fame, if not of his power, to the perpetuation of a prejudice which Christianity was undermining" (35, 45).

Indeed, Carlyle's declarations about blacks carried as much weight as those proffered by British celebrities such as Charles Dickens and Harriet Martineau who had toured and actually seen something of the complexion of life for blacks in America. His words resounded authoritatively despite the fact that his immediate and real knowledge of Africans and their descendants, in general, and African Americans, in particular, was practically nonexistent. Carlyle, whose *Sartor Resartus* had been more favorably received in the United States, who had a great friend and promoter in Ralph Waldo Emerson, who "had investments in America" (Gohdes 1), and whose brother Alick ultimately took his big brother's advice to the British public to emigrate to the States, disseminated his decidedly unfavorable opinions about blacks although he had apparently little if any contact with black Britons and certainly may not be said to have numbered blacks among his circle of friends and acquaintances, which admittedly at some point included such Victorians as John Stuart Mill, Harriet Martineau, and American James Moncure—all three of whom were ardent and steadfast abolitionists. Furthermore, there is no indication that he even entertained the prospect of a black, such as Frederick Douglass, "distinguished by intellect" (Fielding and Campbell, *Reminiscences* 201), to borrow a phrase Carlyle uses in his *Reminiscences* (1881), or by heroism. Finally, there is also no evidence that Carlyle read Douglass's autobiography, which passed through several editions in England.

No lover of novels, Carlyle did, however, sit down with Harriet Beecher Stowe's novel about slavery, *Uncle Tom's Cabin*, a bestseller both in the United States and in England, but found he "fairly could not and would not read beyond the first 100 pages of it." *Uncle Tom's Cabin*, which Carlyle described in 1853 as "the mania of *this* season," to Carlyle, "seemed a pretty perfect sample of Yankee-Governess Romance" (*CL* 28: 15). The enthusiastically warm reception of Stowe's novel by the British public was to Carlyle much ado about nothing: "The Beecher-Stowe concern is tumbling along, I believe, amid the May Meetings, like the carcass of a big ass in a dunghill tank which many men are stirring with long poles," he wrote to A. H. Clough. He continued, "There was a big foolish meeting of quality people about it, last week again. . . . It is a fact, however, that the great body of rational people are indifferent to it or more; and only the weak-minded and strong-lunged are concerned in these phenomena" (*CL* 28: 134). The fact was that Carlyle put his own lungs to work, disparaging the novel and the public's reception of the novel in several of the letters he wrote during 1853. In these letters, he detects the "malodorous melancholy of *Uncle-Tommery*," "days of rampant *Uncletommery*," and describes "sad epochs" in which men are lost "amid their *Uncle-Tommeries*, Railway-Scriperies, and mad *Gadarenes-swineries* of many kinds" (*CL* 28: 137, 144, 132). When a proposal was made "to reprint just now, for the benefit of Uncle Tom and Co, that *Lecture on the Nigger Question*, which distressed the world . . . a couple of years ago," Carlyle was not adverse to using his essay to counter the ideas espoused in Stowe's novel. For "the Piece," as he saw it, "is heartily *true* in *its* way, and capable of being useful just now, tho' Uncle Tom and Co think it far otherwise!" (*CL* 28: 144). As far as Carlyle was concerned, "Uncle Tom's flat nose would really be much better for a seasonable fillip in these extravagant days: but I could wish any other than I had been appointed for that outpost duty!" (*CL* 28: 145). There was little, if anything Stowe's book could do to sensitize or educate Carlyle about a people at the farthest outposts of his world.

A native of Scotland where blacks have never been present in overwhelming, striking, or even modest numbers, Carlyle, upon moving to London in 1834, must have found himself in a world where the likelihood of contact with blacks increased considerably.[5] In a letter to his brother Alick, Carlyle, on an 1824 visit to London, betrayed a slight note of irritation with the multicultural mix in which he suddenly found himself, as he "was hurrying along Cheapside into Newgate-street amid a thousand bustling pigmies [*sic*], and the innumerable jinglings and rollings and crashings of manycoloured labour" (*CL* 3: 93). Carlyle sounded this same note of disdainful irritation in an 1853 letter to his mother, Margaret A. Carlyle, in which he is pleased to find that a black musical troupe outside his home in Chelsea have moved on: "The Nigger Songsters are off elsewhither with their clatterbones, some time ago" (*CL* 28: 74). Four years earlier in the summer of 1849, Carlyle, unbeknownst to himself, had ridden the tram with African American fugitive slave and abolitionist William Wells Brown who records in his autobiographical narrative that tram ride and his sighting of Carlyle for all posterity. Carlyle makes no mention of that tram ride in his papers or reminiscences because Brown did not approach Carlyle, who, though apparently aware of, did not attend the antislavery lectures men such as Brown were delivering throughout Great Britain. "As early as 1833 he had written to Mill, from Edinburgh, that 'we have two blustering Turkey-cocks lecturing here at present on the Negroes: one an Anti-Slaver; the other a Slaver that follows him Ibis-like to destroy his Crocodile-eggs . . .'" (Heffer 251). Blacks remained essentially invisible and insignificant to the great Victorian sage who ranked them very low indeed in his hierarchy of men. The point to be made here is that without ever sailing to the Americas, Carlyle still managed to reach American shores where he inflicted what wounds he could upon black humanity and threw up what barriers he could to black freedom.

Though Carlyle literally never set foot on U.S. soil, he did travel twice to Ireland where he found the best if not unproblematic foil to the black question—the Irish question. According to Carlyle, it was not black slaves abroad but white laborers at home, especially the Irish, who deserved British attention and sympathy. Carlyle's first trip to Ireland in 1846 was the prelude to the more extensive visit he paid the Irish three years later in 1849, only four months before *Fraser's* publication of his "Occasional Discourse on the Negro Question." The 1846 jaunt to Northern Ireland was indeed a quick affair, a detour undertaken in the company of young Irish revolutionary Charles Gavin Duffy as Carlyle made his way to Scotland. The more deliberate 1849 trip was undertaken by a Carlyle armed this time with letters of introduction, determined to observe not just Northern Ireland but as much of the country and its poor famine-stricken population as possible. In 1849, spurred on by his search for another French Revolution and thus seriously considering making Ireland the subject of his next book, Carlyle spent the whole month of July visiting the poor and workhouses of one of England's closest white colonies. In remembrances Carlyle recorded about three months after the second trip to Ireland, he remarked upon the dire straits in which the Irish people found themselves. Various places at which he stopped drew from him frequent comments on "beggars, beggars," "scarecrow figures . . . ragged all," "hideous crowds of beggars," "tattered people everywhere," "squalid hamlets, ditto cottages . . . with their lean goats and vermin," "pauperism in geometric progression" (*Irish Journey* 64, 65, 72, 102, 80, 184).

Carlyle who deplored the poverty and deprivation he witnessed nevertheless noted from time to time in the Irish conversation, demeanor, and "the Irish physiognomy" that which he was inclined to disdain (*Irish Journey* 90). Thus after only two or three days into his Irish journey, Carlyle recalls how "talk, in spite of my endeavors, took an Irish-versus-English character; wherein, as I really have no respect for Ireland as it now is and has been, it was impossible for me to be popular" (*Irish Journey* 47). Elsewhere he is met with "talk again [about] *England versus Ireland;* a sad, unreasonable humor pervading all the Irish population on this matter" (*Irish Journey* 50). Some of Carlyle's observations about the Irish suggest that for Carlyle the Irish fell tellingly short as a people. At one point during his Irish journey, Carlyle thinks to himself, "Yes, indeed: you govern yourself. He that would govern you well would probably surprise you much, my friend—laying a hearty horse-whip over that back of yours" (*Irish Journey* 74). He is also led to consider during his trip how some of the Irish "people won't work (in all, or, I fear, the majority of cases) a day's work for hire, if they have *potatoes* or other means of existing" (*Irish Journey* 214–15). Here is early evidence that Carlyle associates not just blacks but the Irish themselves with the movement toward a Niagara Falls or "the belly of Chaos" (*CW* 29: 353). For just as Carlyle criticized those Irish reluctant to work when potatoes were plentiful, he decried West Indian blacks who would not work when pumpkins were in supply. In "Occasional Discourse on the Nigger Question," he could, moreover, imagine no greater Kurtzian horror than the melding of the Irish and Black conditions:

> To have "emancipated" the West Indies into a *Black Ireland;* "free" indeed, but an Ireland, and Black! The world may yet see prodigies; and reality be stranger than a nightmare dream.
>
> Our own white or sallow Ireland, sluttishly starving from age to age on its act-of-parliament "freedom," was hitherto the flower of mismanagement among the nations: but what will this be to a Negro Ireland, with pumpkins themselves fallen scarce like potatoes! Imagination cannot fathom such an object; the belly

of Chaos never held the like. The human mind, in its wide wanderings, has not dreamt. . . ." (*CW* 29: 353)

If Carlyle found blacks equine, he found the Irish no less porcine. So that for Carlyle, the heart of darkness would prove the juncture of pumpkin and potato, of black and Irish. Carlyle trembles to think what one might expect if blacks were accorded the same mismanaged freedom as the Irish—a fate more horrible than that of slavery or servitude, the fate of the unemployed, starving Irish.

Interestingly enough, by the time Carlyle published his *Latter-Day Pamphlets* in 1850, the year in America of the Fugitive Slave Law, he clearly excoriated not just blacks but the Irish too. Speaking in the guise of a British prime-minister addressing the "floods of Irish Beggars, Able-bodied Paupers, and nomadic Lackalls, now stagnating," Carlyle more stridently accused the Irish and the poor British of being just as incapable of self-government as the Blacks he often associates with horses: "glorious self-government is a glory not for you,—not for Hodge's emancipated horses, nor you" (*CW* 20: 38, 40). The Irish poor and the British are damned, much like the lazy, pumpkin-glutted West India Quashees, by their own "imperfect energy and redundant appetite," for "by doing too little work and drinking too much beer," the Irish with their "perpetual staggerings and sprawlings," according to Carlyle, have gotten themselves "plainly in the ditch" (*CW* 20: 40). As with the West Indian blacks, these poor whites, as Carlyle put it, "demand . . . that some genuine command be taken of you" (*CW* 20: 40). Using the black man as a yardstick to gauge the depth to which the "foolish," "criminal," "miserable," and "vagrant [Irish and British] Lackalls" have fallen, Carlyle finds that they "are of the nature of *slaves*": "Algiers, Brazil or Dahomey," he avers, "hold nothing in them so authentically *slave* as you are, my indigent incompetent friends!" (*CW* 20: 38, 42, 41).

Even as Carlyle skewers in his *Latter-Day Pamphlets* the shiftless Irish and the poor British as black approximations, he is careful to maintain the distinction "between our Black West Indies and our White Ireland, between these two extremes of lazy refusal to work, and of famishing inability to find any work" (*CW* 20: 27). White Ireland has "imperfect energy"; black West Indians are lazy. White Ireland has a "redundant appetite" for beer; black West Indians "imbib[e] sweet pulps and juices" while "sitting yonder with their beautiful muzzles up to the ears in pumpkins" (*CW* 29: 350). White Ireland stands slavelike here, while black West Indians sit horselike "yonder." The literal and figurative chains that fetter blacks restrict only blacks even as they promote white civilization; however, the figurative chains that fetter the

Irish and the British pauper are the particular concern of British Victorians because they impede white progress. Carlyle, in the persona of the chief governor who wrangles with "the question, What to do with you? especially since the potato died," observes, "one thing, after much meditating, I have at last discovered, and now know for some time back: That you cannot be left to roam abroad in this unguided manner, stumbling over the precipices, and loading ever heavier the fatal *chain* upon those who might be able to stand" (*CW* 20: 39). The chain the Irish wear is more than a manacle of economic depression and oppression but one of connectedness to other whites. Carlyle fears that the Irish and the poor will "load the fatal *chain* . . . till we all lie sprawling" (*CW* 20: 40). This is to say, that even when Carlyle compares the condition of the Irish to that of blacks he never loses sight of the Celtic or Gaelic, if not Anglo-Saxon people at home versus the black others abroad. This distinction informs Carlyle's thoughts in 1849 as he travels among the poor Irish and as he pens his "Occasional Discourse." For even as Carlyle observed firsthand how in parts of Ireland "human swinery . . . [had] here reached its *acme*," he was still able to detect instances in which "their poverty gave them even a kind of dignity," which he did not concede to blacks (*Irish Journey* 175, 183). If he declared the Irish rough and rather Neanderthal, he could glimpse redemption for them in the fact that "they are, in brief, dark barbarians not intrinsically of ill dispositions" (*Irish Journey* 211).

Clearly unable to rise above the prejudice against Irish who were in the minds of many Euro-Americans white niggers, Carlyle, nevertheless, found the members of the "savage poor republic" more pathetic figures than black Dahomey and his descendants. One of the things Carlyle sought to do in "Occasional Discourse" was to inscribe a binary, which, in effect, tended to disrupt, if not to obliterate sympathy for blacks. So that the opening salvo Carlyle fired in his essay on the black question consisted of a reminder to the British public that it would do best to consider the plight of whites at home. Carlyle determined that his fellow Victorians should not perceive the condition of blacks to be particularly special or important in the greater scheme of things. The suffering of blacks, he averred, was in no way singular. "Frightful things are continually told us of Negro slavery, of the hardships, bodily and spiritual, suffered by slaves. Much exaggerated, and mere exceptional cases, say the opponents. Exceptional cases, I answer; yes, and universal ones! On the whole, hardships, and even oppressions and injustices are not unknown in this world." Without having traveled to the West Indies or the United States, Carlyle would reduce the bondage and injustices blacks experienced to ones not so unlike his own or any man's. "I myself," he offers, "have suffered such, and have not you? It is said, Man, of whatever colour, is born to such, even as the sparks fly upwards" (*CW* 29: 358). Carlyle's pragmatic instruction about taking care of home before looking to address ills abroad was predicated on the notion that the British owned the Irish problem in a way that they did not own the West Indian problem. This idea of Ireland as a special case was not without currency as historian D. G. Boyce suggests when he dates English "recognition of Ireland as a special area, with a particular character, which required special treatment" from a speech made in parliament by Lord John Russell on February 13, 1844 (1). As Carlyle declared, "at home too, the British Whites are rather badly off; several millions of them hanging on the verge of continual famine." The suffering of these whites he argued was "extremely extensive and important" and as poignant as that of any black in the throes of slavery (*CW* 29: 349, 350). As critic John Ernest, referring to David R. Roediger's *The Wages of Whiteness*, has observed, such a comparison could serve double duty, for "though the comparison between the white hireling and the black slave could encourage analyses of wage labor as bondage, the emphasis on visible social contrasts also could reassure wage workers that they belonged to the ranks of 'free white labor'" (431). The point to be made here is that economically, Carlyle could identify with the Irish. Unfortunately, race rendered him incapable of a similar identification with West Indian blacks who were because of their color even more victimized by the capitalistic system.

Carlylean scholar and biographer Ian Campbell explains the thinking of Carlyle and by extension those who agreed with Carlyle's reassertion in "Shooting Niagara" nearly twenty years after the publication of "Occasional Discourse" that "To me individually the Nigger's case was not the most pressing in the world, but among the least so" (*CW* 30: 6): "English and Irish poverty, and the chaos following the American Civil War, seem to him more immediate questions. Practical, as distinct from abstractly moral[,] questions are much more important to Carlyle's treatment of the slavery question. He brushes aside the rights and wrongs of slavery in order to reach the *realities* of suffering, which he knew from living in London, and touring in the industrial Midlands and in Ireland" (Campbell 280).[6] Carlyle and those of a like mind who had not traveled abroad to witness firsthand the condition of black West Indians or American slaves more readily embraced reports similar to the one that follows by *Blackwood's* contributor Charles Mackay: "As regards his [the black slave's] physical condition, he was far better provided for than the agricultural labourer of Russia, Poland, Germany, and some parts of the south of England. He lived in a good hut or cottage, received medical treatment in infancy, old age, and ill health, at the expense of his master; saw his children provided for, without an extra tax on his own exertions, or any diminution of his usual comforts. . . ." Mackay argues that the black slave benefited from slavery, which was no more than one big welfare system: "Slavery, it should be remembered, contained [not Penal laws but] a Poor Law within itself." So what if the slave was not free? He reaped the advantages of European contact. Contrary to Frederick Douglass's recounting of how a man was made a brute by slavery, this writer suggests that the real gift of the peculiar institution was to make a savage a slave (588).

The condition of the Irish and the blacks apparently bore a special relation in that these two groups raised issues that went straight into the heart of imperialist imperative—freedom, emancipation, reform, and accountability. The Irish who tended to be identified by the English as wild, improvident, drunken, papist, and poor experienced no small measure of an oppression that had roots in the Penal Laws under which Irish Catholics had lived during the same century that the American colonies rebelled against British rule. Irish Catholics were essentially colonized under laws that forbade them to vote, hold municipal, parliamentary, military or civil posts, or practice law. In the eighteenth century, they had been

> forbidden to open or teach in a school, serve as private tutors, attend university, or educate their sons abroad. They were forbidden to take part in the manufacture or sale of arms, newspapers, or books, or possess or carry arms. No Catholic might own a horse worth more than five pounds. Except in the linen trade, they might take on no more than two apprentices, and Protestants might not take on Catholic apprentices. Catholics might not buy, inherit, or receive gifts of land from Protestants, nor rent land worth more than thirty shillings a year, nor lease land for longer than thirty-one years, nor make a profit from land of more than one-third of the rent paid; no Catholic estate could be entailed but instead had to be divided at death among all the children. By converting to Protestantism a Catholic son could dispossess his father and disinherit all his brothers. A Protestant landowner lost his civil rights if he married a Catholic, a Protestant heiress her inheritance. All bishops of the Catholic Church were ordered to leave the country under penalty of death if they remained or returned; no priest might enter the country from anywhere, and only one priest was permitted per parish, forbidden to set foot outside it without special permission. Like all Irish, Catholics paid taxes to support the Protestant Church of Ireland. Catholic orphans were to be brought up as Protestants. (Ignatiev 34–35)

Although the list of restrictions is impressively long, even in the eighteenth century, Irish freedom was never denied though it was severely curtailed. No one owned an Irishman or woman's body; sold the Irish child; controlled the hours of waking and sleeping, work and leisure; prohibited knowledge of reading; managed sexuality and reproduction. Even though the religious, political, and economic strictures listed clearly underscored "the conviction that Englishmen and Irishmen were separated from one another by irreconcilable differences . . . of religion and culture . . . [and] of temperament" (Curtis 1), they did not evince the virulent segregation and alienation predicated upon the color of skin. As Mackay indicates in his 1866 article, "The Negro and the Negrophilists," even in the deep-seated animosity between the Anglo-Saxon and Celtic races, the color of the skin is not the divisive factor: "There *is* an antipathy of race, against which all argument is powerless. Even in our own little isles, where we are all white, there is a repugnance between the Irish and the Anglo-Saxon, and *vice versa,* which defies analysis and logic, and which prevails among the same races when transplanted to America" (590).

The reality is that by the nineteenth century with its political unrest and the potato famine, the diminished life of the poor Irish became a factor in the lives of those blacks who had had generations of servitude and racism thrust upon them. The idea that blacks were the lucky beneficiaries of slavery, while poor British and Irish were suffering a fate worse than slavery was one nineteenth-century blacks felt compelled to address. Consequently, in *Incidents in the Life of a Slave Girl* (1861), Harriet Jacobs declared in the opening lines of one of the narrative's autobiographical chapters, "I would ten thousand times rather that my children should be the half-starved paupers of Ireland than to be the most pampered among the slaves of America." Personal experience, furthermore, taught her that Irish poverty, work on a cotton plantation, or life in a penitentiary were more negotiable positions than that of the black female who must "live with an unprincipled master and a jealous mistress" empowered by an institution that legalizes the rape of the black female slave (31). In a similarly pointed, if brief response "to those who insisted that the lot of the free white laborer was worse than that of the slave," Noel Ignatiev writes, that Frederick Douglass, whose *Narrative* was published during the years of the Irish potato famine, "liked to point out that his old position on the plantation had been vacant since his departure, and encouraged them to apply" (107).

Fugitive slave William Wells Brown would comment even more extensively on Irish paupers and British laborers in his 1852 sketches of Europe. Like Thomas Carlyle, William Wells Brown arrived in Ireland during the month of July in 1849. He would spend three weeks in this country where he, too, witnessed "in and about the market-place . . . throngs of beggars fighting for rotten fruit, cabbage-stock, and even the very trimmings of vegetables." Like Carlyle, he saw "sickly and emaciated looking creatures, half naked . . . at our heels at every turn" (100). Unlike Carlyle, however, who traveled to Ireland in 1849 to study Ireland's poverty, Brown, who spent most of his time in Dublin which was all astir with a royal visit from Queen Victoria, though fully aware of the unremitting destitution in the land, tried to fit his observation of that poverty into a larger picture of Ireland—a picture more textured and complex than the one Carlyle presents in *Reminiscences of My Irish Journey in 1849*. Brown gathered from his Irish sojourn a sense of the Irish as a "strange people" who were "varied [in] their aspect . . . [and] contradictory [in] their character." The Ireland he discovered was one of tensions and extremes: a "land of genius and degradation, of great resources and unparalleled poverty, noble deeds and the most revolting crimes, the land of distinguished poets, splendid orators, and the bravest of soldiers, the land of ignorance and beggary!" (103).

Unlike Carlyle, Brown had not gone into the Irish cottage to investigate conditions there; however, as he continued his European travels, he would enter English cottages to learn for himself whether the lot of the poor British was indeed as dire as that of the African American slave. For having been "taught in America that the English laborer was no better off than the slave upon a Carolina rice-field," Brown made a point of visiting and examining "several of the cottages of the work-people," only to have confirmed his suspicion that "the people of the United States know nothing of the real condition of the laboring classes of England." For when he "looked upon the home of the laborer," his "thoughts were with . . . [his] enslaved countrymen" who were certainly not on the same plane as British workers: "What a difference, thought I, there is between the tillers of the soil in England and America! There could not be a more complete refutation of the assertion that the English laborer is no better off than the American slave, then [*sic*] the scenes that were then before me." Brown concluded, "Whatever may be the disadvantages that the British peasant labors under, he is free; and if he is not satisfied with his employer, he can make choice of another. He also has the right to educate his children; and he is the equal of the most wealthy person before an English court of justice." These rights and privileges locate the nineteenth-century British laborer in a place starkly different from the black American's as Brown's subsequent question and answer indicate: "But how is it with the American slave? He has no right to himself; no right to protect his wife, his child, or his own person. He is nothing more than a living tool. Beyond his field or work-shop he knows nothing. There is no amount of ignorance he is not capable of. He has not the least idea of the face of this earth, nor of the history or constitution of the country in which he dwells. To him the literature, science and art, the progressive history and the accumulated discoveries of by-gone ages, are as if they had never been."

With no past, no monuments, no voice, "his condition," Brown determines, is "that of the leopard of his own native Africa. It lives, it propagates its kind; but never does it indicate a movement towards that all but angelic intelligence of man. The slave eats, drinks and sleeps, all for the benefit of the man who claims his body as his property . . . He has no higher appeal than the mere will of his owner. He knows nothing of the inspired Apostles through their writings. He has no Sabbath, no church, no Bible, no means of grace,—and yet we are told that he is as well off as the laboring classes of England" (125–26, 139, 140). W. E. B. Du Bois echoes these ideas nearly a century later in 1935: "No matter how degraded the factory hand, he is not real estate." Slaves, as Du Bois points out in *Black Reconstruction in America*, "could own nothing; they could make no contracts; they could hold no property, nor traffic in property; they could not hire out; they could not legally marry nor constitute families; they could not control their children; they could not appeal from their master; they could be punished at will. They could not testify in court; they could be imprisoned by their owners, and the criminal offense of assault and battery could not be committed on the person of a slave" (10). Challenged, disadvantaged, and beleaguered as they were, neither Irish paupers nor British peasants actually experienced what Carlyle implied they experienced—the bondage of slavery.

Carlyle, who stayed at home and wrote so powerfully and detrimentally about the black question, would seem readily and easily identifiable as a dark Victorian, an enemy to be routed at every single turn by freedom-seeking blacks abroad. Certainly by 1865, Carlyle had become more actively and aggressively authoritarian taking up as chair of the Defence Committee the cause of Governor Edward Eyre who, in response to a black uprising during which about a score of Englishmen were killed, had slaughtered over four hundred blacks. There were African Americans, however, who did not peremptorily dismiss Carlyle. When African American writer and escaped slave, William Wells Brown, for example, found himself riding a London omnibus that Carlyle had boarded, Brown, whose reaction to the "Sage of Chelsea" was shaped by all that he had read by Carlyle, recalls how he, having "read his [Carlyle's] 'Hero-worship,' and 'Past and Present,' . . . had formed a high opinion of his literary abilities" (167). Brown's opinion of Carlyle is adversely affected, however, by the "Occasional Discourse on the Nigger Question." Confessing that Carlyle's "recent attack upon the emancipated people of the West Indies, and his laborious article in favor of the reëstablishment of the lash and slavery, had created in my mind a dislike for the man," Brown, who "almost regretted that we were in the same omnibus," revises his high opinion of Carlyle's literary abilities, finding them "often monotonous and extravagant" as Carlyle "generally takes commonplace thoughts and events, and tries to express them in stronger and statelier language than others" (167). Brown declared of Carlyle, "He cares little what he says, so as he can say it differently from others" (167). Brown came to see Carlyle as a fallen, alienated, and alienating writer: "He holds no communion with his kind, but stands alone, without mate or fellow. He is like a solitary peak, all access to which is cut off. He exists not by sympathy, but by antipathy" (167). Viewing Carlyle through the lens of the essay on West Indian blacks, Brown detected a number of contradictions in Carlyle the writer and the man:

> He writes one page in favor of reform, and ten against it. He would hang all prisoners to get rid of them; yet the inmates of the prisons and "workhouses are better off than the poor." His heart is with the poor; yet the blacks of the West Indies should be taught that if they will not raise sugar and cotton by their own free will, "Quashy should have the whip applied to him." He frowns upon the reformatory speakers upon the boards of Exeter Hall; yet he is the prince of reformers. He hates heroes and assassins; yet Cromwell was an angel, and Charlotte Corday a saint. He scorns everything, and seems to be tired of what he is by nature, and tries to be what he is not. (167)

Brown's most definitive statement about Carlyle—in whom he recognizes a notable literary ability, yet a style that is often "not to be understood" and a sympathy keeping company with antipathy—is that "in some things Mr. Carlyle is right: but in many he is entirely wrong" (167).

Interestingly enough, in 1851, William Wells Brown in a letter he wrote to Frederick Douglass from Oxford, England, referred that great black autobiographer, orator, and abolitionist to some Carlylean wisdom on the topic of obstacles. "A young man once asked Carlyle," Brown informed Douglass, "what was the secret of success. His reply was, 'Energy: whatever you undertake, do it with all your might'" (Ripley 303). It turns out that Douglass himself was not adverse to marking the authority of Carlyle as he does in a speech about, among other things, President Lincoln's manner of presenting "his propositions [about emancipation] with many qualifications." At one point, Douglass brings the weight of Carlyle to bear on his critique of the president's comments, observing, "It is the first utterance, and first utterances are not according to Carlyle the most articulate and perfect" (Blassingame 3: 518). Douglass acknowledged Carlyle as "one of the latest and most potent European prophets" and conceded that "warning and advice from any quarter are not to be despised, and especially not from one so eminent as Mr. Carlyle"; however, ultimately perceiving Carlyle to be neither infallible nor unassailable, Douglass believed "Americans will find it hard to heed even men like him, while the animus is so apparent, bitter and perverse" (Blassingame and McKivigan 4: 243). Although Douglass had not, like Brown, ridden a car with Carlyle, he was familiar with and had taken the measure of Carlyle's discourse and deemed that portion of it on blacks, freedom, and democracy unacceptable. In 1869, Douglass described Thomas Carlyle himself as

> A man to whom despotism is the saviour and liberty the destroyer of society, who, during the last twenty years, in every contest between liberty and oppression, uniformally and promptly took sides with the oppressor; who regarded every extension of the right of suffrage, even to white men in his own country, as shooting Niagara; who gloated over deeds of cruelty, and talked of applying to the backs of men the beneficent whip, to the great delight of many of the slaveholders of America in particular. . . ." (Blassingame and McKivigan 4: 243)

Douglass felt that a man such as Carlyle "could have but little sympathy with our emancipated and progressive Republic, or with the triumph of liberty any where" (Blassingame and McKivigan 4: 243). Indeed, Douglass decreed that Carlyle was out of touch with the times as he deftly set Carlyle aside elsewhere as one of the "old time people" who subscribed to the belief that the common man or the masses had no place in the political world. "The crowned heads and privileged classes in the Old World take political affairs under their exclusive jurisdiction," Douglass explained, "—and such men as Mr. Thomas Carlyle magnify the wisdom of this arrangement." As Douglass saw it, Carlyle's outdated ideas about government were enlisted in efforts to stymie black progress; Carlyle's shot at democracy constituted a particularly menacing shot at black Americans as well. "Thus, it will be seen that the substantial ground of objection to the active participation of colored men in American politics has ancient authority and example for its origin and support. Those who urge it here against the black man, only take up the worn out lament of the fading aristocracy of the old world." Aristocracies of any form or fashion were objectionable. Douglass expostulated, "For ourselves, it is scarcely necessary to say that we are opposed to all aristocracy, whether of wealth, power, or learning" (Foner 4: 271) The time had come, Douglass indicated, for a more progressive kind of thinking that, in the final analysis, put him at odds with the man Williams Wells Brown called sometimes right and sometimes wrong.

Later in the nineteenth century, black Presbyterian minister and emigrationist Alexander Crummell, in a speech delivered in 1870 before the Common Council and the citizens of Monrovia, Liberia, also found Carlyle to be right in some things but wrong in others. Unlike Douglass, Crummell tended to agree with Carlyle's ideas about force and authority, observing,

"All historic fact shows that force, that is authority, *must* be used in the exercise of guardianship over heathen tribes." Crummell, in fact, praises that "brilliant writer" who avers that "Force and right . . . are the governors of this world; *force till right is ready.*" Yet in this same speech, Crummell takes exception to Carlyle's characterization of black workers as lazy. "The native man," Crummell declared, "has not only physical capacity, but he has also the habit of labour. He is a WORKER; notwithstanding all that Mr. Carlyle and all his brother Anthropologists, may say to the contrary" (185, 175).

Around the turn of the century, young William Edward Burghardt Du Bois had read Carlyle's *Sartor Resartus* as well as his work on heroes and hero worship. For Du Bois, Carlyle's writings proved highly influential. "His immersion in the works of Carlyle had yielded a rhythm and prose ideal," observes Du Bois's biographer, David Levering Lewis, "for expressing insights and outrage. *The French Revolution,* Carlyle's dazzling, Calvinist history of divine chastisement and human agency, would remain near at hand" (*Biography* 115–16). Even before his immersion in Carlyle at Harvard, Du Bois had raised the presence of Carlyle before his Fisk University peers in an editorial warning that if Carlyle were to visit the campus, he would find ample opportunity to admonish students who were not working and planning for the future (Lewis, *Biography* 74–75). According to Lewis, "the High Tory prejudices Carlyle expressed through effulgent adjectives and magnificent invective" strongly impressed Du Bois who, unlike Brown, "was undoubtedly ignorant of Carlyle's infamous fulminations against blacks in 'The Nigger Question' as incapable of surviving outside slavery" (*Biography* 75).

Interestingly enough, Carlyle's rhetorical style would impress twentieth-century African American novelist and folklorist Zora Neale Hurston differently as she found Carlyle's adjectives neither effulgent nor his invective magnificent. In an essay characterizing black expression, Hurston identified Victorian Thomas Carlyle as a white writer whose prose bore little relation to "the characteristics of negro expression." Describing black expression as "highly dramatized," "impromptu," adorned, vibrant, pictorial, and "hieroglyphic [. . .]," that is to say ornamentally rich in metaphor and simile and strongly invested in action, Hurston found in the expression of writers such as Carlyle and Milton language that eschews drama in that it has left behind its relation to action, having become, as it were, detached, if not abstract. "So we can say the white man thinks in a written language and the Negro thinks in hieroglyphics" (49, 50). Illustrating her point about the distinctiveness of "negro expression" with the idea that "language is like money," Hurston traces a move from bartering with real goods to use of "cheques": "In primitive communities actual goods, however bulky, are bartered for what one wants.

This finally evolves into coin, the coin being not real wealth but a symbol of wealth. Still later, even coin is abandoned for legal tender, and still later cheques for certain usages" (49). The real thing, bulky as it is, is replaced by a simulacrum. Substitution after substitution leads to symbol and thereby to a distancing and detachment from the "actual goods," rhetorically speaking, from vibrancy, action, drama. "Perhaps we might say," writes Hurston, "that *Paradise Lost* and *Sartor Resartus* are written in cheque words," those furthest removed from "real wealth" and detached from action and thus furthest from the highly descriptive and dramatic verbal exchanges of the "Negro [who] even with detached words in his vocabulary—not evolved in him but transplanted on his tongue by contact—must add action to it to make it do" (49).[7]

Despite the gulf Hurston detects between Carlyle's rhetoric and that of black folk, she, like the other black writers and thinkers mentioned here, feels compelled to remark upon Carlyle and his work, no doubt recognizing how Carlyle, much like the black preacher in America, proved to be what Henry Louis Gates, Jr., would term a "point of consciousness, or superconsciousness, of his . . . people" (176). Carlyle was, as George P. Landow has identified him, a Victorian Jeremiah and a sage. As such, it would have been odd indeed if prominent blacks had not taken some note of and responded to Carlyle in their efforts to come to terms with a society that excluded their dignified and equal participation in the social, political, and economic polity.

The divergent responses of Brown, Crummell, Du Bois, and Hurston to Carlyle as a writer raise questions and open up new possibilities for understanding the impact of imperialist and racist writings such as Carlyle's on the disenfranchised and the colonized. Are there other ways, for example, to account for Brown's initial approval of and later ambivalence toward Carlyle's writing? Are there ways to understand Du Bois's attraction to Carlyle's style and Hurston's alienation from it? How is it that a great black thinker and leader such Du Bois can lay claim to Carlyle? As Judith Butler so cleverly queries: "How is it that the apparently injurious effects of discourse become the painful resources by which a resignifying practice is wrought? . . . it is not only a question of how discourse injures bodies, but how certain injuries establish certain bodies at the limits of available ontologies, available schemes of intelligibility. And further, how is it that the abjected come to make their claim through and against the discourses that have sought their repudiation?" (571).

It would appear that enslaved, freedom-hungry blacks had little in common with the authoritarian Carlyle who "had become the embodiment of the reactionary movement in England against parliamentary and social reform" (Heffer 3). Race, politics, and literature (there is no evidence that Carlyle read much of anything by or about the Africans and African Americans who wrote and lived during the nineteenth century) appear to create an impassable divide. Certainly Thomas Carlyle did not think highly of black folk, though he professed some affection for the "swift, supple . . . merry-hearted, grinning, dancing, singing, affectionate kind of creature" who "with a pennyworth of oil, you can make a handsome glossy thing of . . . when the soul is not killed in him" (*CW* 29: 357–58). He most probably did not credit poor Quashee with enough intelligence to evince any rhetorical skills.

Despite Carlyle's attempt to revisit and perhaps to put to rest the Negro question that, in his opinion, siphoned off some of the public's attention to the more relevant Irish question, the truths he sought to convey in "Occasional Discourse" not only articulated the imperialism and racialism of his time but also marked the beginning of a shift "of public opinion away from anti-slavery . . . towards more overt racism" (C. Hall 182). Carlyle's would prove "commonplace assumptions of racists in the nineteenth century," the assumptions of a dark Victorian (I. Jones 189); "Occasional Discourse" is arguably one of the most pernicious expressions of a man who, according to Henry Crabb Robinson, "declared the tyranny of the Anglo-Americans to be a natural and just aristocracy, that of race indicated by colour," a man who "hoped this slavery would last for ever" (542). Because Carlyle was one of the most influential, representative voices invested in the promotion of second-class status of blacks, African Americans responses to Carlyle and to his entrenched conservative and racist preachments are indicative not only of African Americans' awareness of the forces ranged against them in England where their cause was initially, at least, more successfully advanced, but indicative also of the ability and willingness of black Americans to take from even the most recalcitrant of Victorian men, letters and ideas that were usable.

4. W. E. B. Du Bois and the Victorian Soul of Black Folk

If Thomas Carlyle may be aptly described as one of Britain's preeminent dark Victorians, then African American historian, sociologist, editor, and race man William Edward Burghardt Du Bois may fairly be characterized as one of America's consummate black Victorians. Nineteenth-century England and Europe were powerful points of social and cultural reference for W. E. B. Du Bois who took as one of his role models for his early thoughts Thomas Carlyle. Du Bois, who was exposed to Carlyle's work as an undergraduate at Fisk University, would become, like the stern Victorian, a respected and influential prophet for his age. Interestingly enough, one of the things that attracted young Du Bois to Carlyle was the Scotsman's style. Du Bois was aware of a fierce passion and unexampled conviction in Carlyle's writing for which he felt great affinity; he found in Carlyle's works "a rhythm and a prose ideal for expressing insights and outrage" to which he could relate (Lewis, *Biography* 115–16). According to biographer David Levering Lewis, Carlyle's "effulgent adjectives" and "magnificent invective" appealed to Du Bois who, like Carlyle, would become a sage with a keen eye for the signs of the time (*Biography* 75). Perhaps no black thinker has been better able to appreciate Thomas Carlyle than W. E. B. Du Bois who not only produced, as critics have noted, a performative prose informed as Carlyle's was by sermonic tradition but who also espoused some of Carlyle's positions and approaches.[1] Thus, Carlyle and Du Bois, who were both deeply concerned about the spirituality of their societies, write books of cultural quests that probe compellingly the zeitgeist as well as the national and racial psyche of their people in *Sartor Resartus* (1838, as a book) and *The Souls of Black Folk* (1903), respectively. Both of these works are, to borrow Kerry McSweeney's and Peter Sabor's terminology, "seminal expressions" in that they visit and revisit issues and ideas germane to each man's philosophy and thinking about the status and the phenomenon of culture and civilization, the condition of mankind. *Sartor Resartus,* by Carlyle's own admission, "contains more of my opinions on Art, Politics, Religion, Heaven Earth [*sic*] and Air, than all the things I have yet written" (McSweeney and Sabor vii, 227–28), and Du Bois's *Souls of Black Folks* gathers, in Du Bois's own words, "thoughts of mine" about "work, culture, liberty" that "have seen the light before in other guise" as efforts to make some sense of what it means to be black "here in the dawning of the Twentieth Century" (3, 14). Although *Sartor Resartus* is fictional and, therefore, properly a more imaginative and "playful" (McSweeney and Sabor xiv) account of the conversion of one Herr Diogenes Teufelsdrockh from the spiritual negation of what Carlyle names "everlasting no" to the affirmation of "the everlasting yea," *Resartus* resembles *Souls* in its multigenred but mainly biographical and messianic striving after a truth that transcends the individual (*CW* 1: 128, 146).[2] On the one hand, Carlyle uses essay, history, biography, and drama in his "whimsical" effort to reveal the falsehoods, quackery, puffery, and shams that obstruct and beset the likes of Teufelsdrockh and his society. On the other hand, Du Bois wields the forms of history, sociology, biography, essay, and even, as Eric Sundquist suggests, opera to render truths about a race written out of history (577). Both writers employ singular narrative strategies to draw readers into works that are simultaneously personal and cultural manifestos. Thus, Carlyle creates two narrative voices in *Sartor Resartus*—that of Diogenes Teufelsdrockh, the central character who rambles through a world of materialism and unbelief, and that of an editor who talks directly to the audience commenting on Teufelsdrockh's condition. Similarly, Du Bois's narrative voice is doubled as readers experience the first person narration of Du Bois himself who offers personal examples from and commentaries on his life ("I remember well when the shadow swept across me. I was a little thing, away up in the hills" [*Souls* 7]) and a more distant, if not objective, voice that speaks generally about the Negro ("Men call the shadow prejudice, and learnedly explain it as the natural defence of culture against barbarism . . . To which the Negro cries Amen! [*Souls* 12–13]). These two narrative voices are born of Du Bois's efforts, according to Hazel Carby, "to integrate *his* voice with the voice of the wider black community . . . to situate himself as both an exceptional and a representative individual: to be different from and maintain a distance between his experience and that of the masses of black people" (30). Whereas Du Bois's narration seeks to bridge and integrate, that of Carlyle's Teufelsdrockh remains a narration of isolation. Both narratives, however, are commensurate in their deployment of reiterative or bifurcated voice.

Both writers describe in their narratives a nadir during which they, to borrow Cornel West's phrasing, "delve into the depths . . . of despair and dread" (*Race Matters* 12). Indeed this compelling point of anguish or hopelessness threatens not only the individual soul but also society itself. The pangs of despair culminate in a chapter of Carlyle's *Sartor Resartus* appropriately titled "The Everlasting No." Here, the pilgrimaging Teufelsdrockh, homeless, destitute, friendless, betrayed, is represented as being "shut-out from Hope, in a deeper sense than we yet dream of"; as having "lost all tidings of another and higher"; as being "a prey incessantly to . . . corrosions," "a feeble unit in the middle of a threatening Infinitude," and a wretched and solitary wanderer in a universe that resembled "one huge, dead, immeasurable Steam-engine, rolling on, in its dead indifference, to grind me limb from limb" (*CW* 1: 129, 132, 133). The only thing that keeps Carlyle's Teufelsdrockh from succumbing to despair is truth and courage. For Teufelsdrockh, "after all the nameless woe . . . nevertheless still loved Truth," and in the end he "shook base Fear away from me for ever," thereby changing "the temper of my misery" and becoming indignant and defiant (*CW* 1: 131, 135). Du Bois's rendering of one of his darkest moments is set forth in the chapter "Of the Passing of the First Born." In this account of the death of his child, Du Bois faces his own "everlasting no" as the "wild phantasm of the world" (*Souls* 152) is poignantly brought home to Du Bois who feels one of the few affirmations he is allowed as a black man—fatherhood—slip away. Similar to Victorian poet laureate and master of lamentation, Alfred Lord Tennyson, who in *In Memoriam* mourned at length and with meticulous if not obsessive imagery the death of his friend Arthur Hallam, Du Bois plumbs the depths of his own painful bereavement, marking it with as much passion and poetry if with far fewer words than Tennyson. Wretched, Du Bois wonders how a life such as his own, already so starkly limited, can sustain such unremitting loss: "Is not this my life hard enough,—is not that dull land that stretches its sneering web about me cold enough,—is not all the world beyond these four little walls pitiless enough" (*Souls* 153). In a world divided by the Veil, that is to say, in a world which requires that he "*forego*" (*Souls* 154) the rights, privileges, treasures and pleasures of white citizens, Du Bois, walking along the street to bury his son, finds that even in his grief there is still no reprieve as he is verbally assaulted and ground down by "those pale-faced hurrying men and women" who "only glanced [at the funeral procession] and said, 'Niggers!'" (*Souls* 153). Yet at this lowest point in his life, he takes comfort in the fact that his dead child is beyond the reach of the hatred and prejudice he most surely would have suffered had he lived. "All that day and all that night there sat an awful gladness in my heart . . . 'Not dead, not dead, but escaped; not bond but free' . . . Well sped, my boy, before the world had dubbed your ambition insolence, had held your ideals unattainable, and taught you to cringe and bow" (*Souls* 154). As with Carlyle's beleaguered Teufelsdrockh, the grieving Du Bois reveals his will to overcome the loss, pain, and adversity that would oppress his spirit, declaring, "I shirk not. I long for work. I pant for a life full of striving. I am no coward, to shrink before the rugged rush of the storm, nor even quail before the awful shadow of the Veil" (*Souls* 152). The will and courage Carlyle and Du Bois showcase in *Sartor* and in *Souls* are the very will and courage they call upon in all their efforts to unlock the "secret of . . . [their] convulsed era[s]" (*CW* 29: 154).

Some twenty years before the birth of Du Bois, the Victorian Carlyle had long since turned his admiration for will and courage into a doctrine of hero worship. In a series of six lectures on heroes and hero worship Carlyle delivered in May of 1840, he explored "the many different names, in different times and places . . . we give to Great Men" (*CW* 5: 78). Be he poet, priest, prophet, king, or man of letters, the hero is endowed with the lion's share of intellect, sincerity, and vision (*CW* 5: 84). Although scientific knowledge casts the age-old concept of the hero and heroism in a rather crude light—science being inimical to talk of a "fellow-man either [as] a god or one speaking with the voice of a god" (*CW* 5: 78)—Carlyle attests in his lectures to "our indestructible reverence for heroism" (*CW* 5: 85). Carlyle avers, "The man of intellect at the top of affairs: this is the aim of all constitutions and revolutions." He continues, "For the man of true intellect . . . is the noblehearted man withal, the true, just, humane and valiant man" (*CW* 5: 169). Du Bois subscribes to Carlyle's hero worship arguing, "To the unraveling of human tangles we would gladly believe that God sends special men—chosen vessels which come to the world's deliverance" (Paschal 9). Du Bois's belief that "The Negro race, like all races, is going to be saved by its exceptional men" (Paschal 31) approximates Carlyle's conviction that the "history of what man has accomplished in this world, is at bottom the History of the Great Men who have worked here" (*CW* 5: 1).

Just as striking as Carlyle's and Du Bois's faith in the hero or exceptional man is their dedication to the credo of work, which, Carlyle thundered, was salvation, the raison d'être of mankind. In preacherlike tones, he admonished fellow Victorians to "know thy work and do it" because "a man perfects himself by working," because "labour is Life," because "there is a perennial nobleness, and even sacredness, in Work," because "he who has found his work" is indeed "blessed" (*CW* 10: 196, 197). Time and again, Du Bois corroborates these Carlylean dictums, remarking upon work's efficacy and necessity. "Education and work are the levers to uplift a people," he declares (Paschal 50). In a 1920 credo that echoes Carlyle's declarations about the nobility and blessedness of work, Du Bois invokes in Carlylean fashion the sanctity of work, announcing, "I believe in Service—humble, reverent service, from the blackening of boots to the whitening of souls; for Work is Heaven, Idleness Hell, and Wage is the 'Well done!'" (Paschal 125; see also Du Bois's *Darkwater* 3). The dithyrambic cadences of Carlyle are again evident in Du Bois's insistence that "work, continuous and intensive; work, although it be menial and poorly rewarded; work, though done in the travail of soul and sweat of brow, must be impressed upon Negro children as the road to salvation" (Paschal 195). Elsewhere Du Bois more fervently touts the Victorian work ethic: "The ideal of *Work*—not idleness, not dawdling, but hard continuous effort at something worth doing, by a man supremely interested in doing it, who knows how it ought to be done and is willing to take infinite pains doing it" (Paschal 321).

The work ethic Du Bois represents so straightforwardly in *The Souls of Black Folk* receives its most imaginative treatment in the political romance, *Dark Princess* (1928). In this, Du Bois's "favorite book" (*Dusk of Dawn* 270), the African American protagonist Matthew Towns struggles to find among other things what he must do in life and to work at it. The former medical student, Pullman porter, and Chicago politician finally engages in physical labor—first building a subway and finally working in a stockyard—which ultimately informs the political vision of racial uplift to which he is introduced during an earlier trip to Europe. As his fellow workers and he literally dig a hole, a subway tunnel, Towns gains "a sense of reality in this work such as I have never had before—neither in medicine nor travel, neither as porter, prisoner, nor law-maker" (*Dark Princess* 264). Born in a cabin in segregated and racist Virginia, blocked because of his color from obtaining a medical degree, imprisoned for protecting the identity of a dead revolutionary, involved in a highly charged emotional, political, and sexual relationship with an Indian princess, Kautilya, who seems socially beyond his reach—so situated, the troubled Matthew finds mooring and purpose in his manual labor that proves reinspiriting as it offers him "a singular sense of physical power and spiritual freedom" (266).[3] As a laborer, Matthew cultivates his identity, his manhood. It was a kind of cultivation Carlyle well understood when he wrote figuratively about the yields of labor: "Foul jungles are cleared away, fair seedfields rise instead, and stately cities; and withal the man himself first ceases to be a jungle and foul unwholesome desert thereby. Consider how, even in the meanest sorts of Labour, the whole soul of a man is composed into a kind of real harmony, the instant he sets himself to work!" (*CW* 10: 196). Much as Carlyle represents it here, Towns not only develops his body, but he also secures his soul. Thus, at one point Towns revels in the sheer physicality of what he does, feeling himself "bare, sweating, and untrammeled," feeling like one of the "hard-limbed Grecian athletes" (265), he never subscribes to Booker T. Washington's idea of the accommodating, if not lobotomized, industrial black worker but rather to Carlyle's idea of the antiutilitarian and the antimercenary gratifications of labor. Once work and the kinds of jobs and vocations he had pursued were a means to various Philistinian and materialistic ends—"knowledge and fame . . . wealth . . . comfort" (287). When Towns joins the ranks of the proletariat, he decides to commit to work for its own sake: "Now he would seek nothing but work, and work for work's own sake" (287). What Towns proposes is an "intelligent digging" as "the fulcrum" by which "to uplift our world and roll it forward" (269). Physical work is "indispensable" (264) but intelligence is essential. "The first step is to reunite thought and physical work. Their divorce has been a primal cause of disaster. They that do the world's work must do it thinking. The thinkers, dreamers, poets of the world must be its workers," declares the character Matthew Towns who at one point concludes what Carlyle all but announces, "Work is God" (*Dark Princess* 266). However, in reality Towns cannot simply settle for the notion that God is work or that work should be undertaken for its own sake because work, for him, is ultimately a means to an end: "it was the physical work of the world that had to be done as prelude to its thought and beauty. And then beyond and above all this was the ultimate emancipation of the world by the uplift of the darker races" (287). Work, after all, paves the way for thought, beauty, and ascension to a finer culture. Du Bois's protagonists confirm Carlyle's assertion that "there is a perennial nobleness . . . in Work" (*CW* 10: 196); however, Du Bois ultimately proposes that while work can and may indeed constitute an end in and of itself, greater cultural imperatives may be achieved by virtue of work. Carlyle had bemoaned the "tragic spectacle" of "industrial work, still under bondage to Mammon, the rational soul of it not yet awakened" (*CW* 10: 207). In *Dark Princess*, Du Bois imagines the great awakening of that soul. To put it another way, Du Bois apparently takes stock in Carlyle's contention that if you "show me a People energetically busy; heaving, struggling, all shoulders at the wheel; their heart pulsing, every muscle swelling, with man's energy and will;—I show you a People of whom great good is already predicable [*sic*]; to whom all manner of good is yet certain, if their energy endure. By very working, they will learn . . ." (*CW* 10: 207). In the character of Matthew Towns, Du Bois extends Carlyle's faith in people who work energetically to a faith in that people's ability not only to learn but also to rise. By creating Matthew Towns who has worked hard at various métiers to become someone worthy and capable of leading his people, Du Bois goes a long way toward realizing a version of

Carlyle's "Industrial Hero" who is "recognisable and known . . . as developing himself, and as an opulent and dignified kind of man" (*CW* 30: 30). Carlyle, who further observes that this kind of hero "is already by intermarriage and otherwise coming into contact with the Aristocracy by title," advised that the industrial hero could do no "better than unite with . . . [the] naturally noble kind of Aristocrat by title" (*CW* 30: 30–31). In *Dark Princess,* Du Bois follows Carlyle's dictum by making Towns first the worshipper then the lover of an Indian princess upon whom he fathers a child who will become the maharajah of Bwodpur. The correspondence between Carlyle's ideas about heroism and work and Du Bois's imaginative construction of these ideas in *Dark Princess* is finally so pronounced that one might expect an inscription to Carlyle to precede the text.

Du Bois's debt to Carlyle is further evident in commentary that recapitulates the Victorian's expressions or amounts to direct quotation. Thus, oddly enough, Du Bois invokes the words of Carlyle who scorned "Nigger-emancipating" (*CW* 30: 30) to oppose segregation: "Surely then, in this period of frustration and disappointment, we must turn from negation to affirmation, from the ever-lasting 'No' to the ever-lasting 'Yes'" (Paschal 142). Du Bois also owed much to Carlyle who denounced the cash nexus, claiming in his "Gospel of Mammonism" that "we have profoundly forgotten everywhere that *Cash-payment* is not the sole relation of human beings" (*CW* 10: 146). In *The Souls of Black Folk,* Du Bois worried that the ideals of black people would succumb to the national urge toward greed and "suddenly sink to a question of cash and a lust for gold" (*Souls* 63). More specifically, he feared that black Americans would become the worshippers of that Mammon Carlyle had decried sixty years earlier in a chapter on the modern worker that appeared in *Past and Present* (1843). "What if the Negro people be wooed from a strife for righteousness, from a love of knowing, to regard dollars as the be-all and end-all of life? What if to the Mammonism of America be added the rising Mammonism of the re-born South, and the Mammonism of this South be reinforced by the budding Mammonism of its half-awakened black millions?" worried Du Bois (*Souls* 63). The emphatic and repeated use of the term "Mammonism" in this passage from *Souls*'s "Atalanta" clearly demonstrates Du Bois knew of and sympathized with Carlyle's rejection of crass materialism. Du Bois's chapter "The Sons of Master and Man" affords an even better example of how Du Bois not only read and heeded Carlyle but sometimes also adapted the Victorian's ideas to suit the predicament of the black race. Thus, in "The Sons of Master and Man," Du Bois, in drawing a parallel between the South's economic system and the preindustrial England of the early nineteenth century, literally invokes the Victorian sage when he refers to "the England that wrung pity from thinkers and fired the wrath of Carlyle" (*Souls* 123). As Du Bois goes on to explore the "economic relations of the races" in the United States (122), he relies heavily on the Carlylean notion of the "captains of industry." Du Bois, for example, observes that "there is in these new captains of industry neither love nor hate, neither sympathy nor romance; it is a cold question of dollars and dividends" (123). After deploring the motives and focus of the exploiting captains, Du Bois calls for leaders among blacks—"men of skill, men of light and leading, college-bred men, black captains of industry, and missionaries of culture" (125). Although it is clear that Du Bois finds Carlyle's belief in the captains of industry useful and appropriate, it is also clear that Du Bois is not nearly as axiomatic in his admiration of such men. Du Bois "freely acknowledge[s] that it is possible, and sometimes best, that a partially undeveloped people should be ruled by the best of their stronger and better neighbors for their own good," but such rule should last only "until such time as they can start and fight the world's battles alone" (*Souls* 128). Here, Du Bois who shows himself to be amenable to the idea of temporary guardianship, indicates that he does not totally accept, as Carlyle did, the right of might or the inevitability or permanence of natural aristocracies.

Du Bois's borrowings from Carlyle indicate that, like another important Victorian thinker, Matthew Arnold, Du Bois recognized in Carlyle "a man of genius to whom we have all at one time or other been indebted for refreshment and stimulus," and he recognized in Europe a cultural standard (Arnold 435). He also, however, understood how one size does not always fit all, how the Arnoldian call for the "*study of perfection*" means that no one society or culture has attained it, how each people must ultimately discover its own "*best self*" by developing and extending the intricacies of its own gifts (Arnold 409, 443). The linkages between Carlyle and Du Bois are manifest if not always complete. Like Carlyle, Du Bois subscribed to the idea of the strong man, but he tended to qualify that strength with moral sense and compassion. Thus, during an 1890 Harvard commencement address, Du Bois does not hesitate, in describing Confederate General Jefferson Davis as a strong man, to point out Jefferson's weaknesses. Although giving the concept of the strong man Carlyle so highly prized its due, Du Bois felt that the principle of the strong man in and of itself was not enough. Thus, as a representative of the Teutonic civilization, Davis was to be commended for "his stalwart manhood and heroic character"; however, he was, according to Du Bois, incomplete because he was plagued by "moral obtuseness and refined brutality" (Lewis, *Reader* 18). Jefferson Davis, a man much like Carlyle's hero, is "not wholly evil or fruitless," Du Bois concludes, and "the world has needed and will need its Jefferson Davises; but such a type is incomplete and can never serve its best purpose until checked by its complementary ideas," which will come from black men and women who have "made . . . [their] beauty, patience, and . . . grandeur, law" (Lewis, *Reader* 18, 19). This is to say that, while Carlyle numbered among his heroes the likes of Cromwell, Napoleon, and Governor Eyre, Du Bois's heroes included not only Bismarck and Jefferson Davis, but also such men as the martyr John Brown and Toussaint L'Ouverture, the savior. Carlyle exhorted men to work and remain in their places, and Du Bois encouraged men and women to work at uplifting a race from its lowly place. Du Bois advocated a work that could be rewarded by a master who would mark "no distinction between the black, sweating cotton hands of Georgia and the first families of Virginia, since all distinction not based on deed is devilish and not divine" (Paschal 125). Du Bois would also require that work be conjoined with education, for "work will not do it [uplift] unless inspired by the right ideals and guided by intelligence" (Paschal 50). In an even more definitive statement that aligns him as much with that other cultural prophet of the Victorian Age, Matthew Arnold, as it does with Carlyle, Du Bois declares that "education must not simply teach work—it must teach life" (Paschal 50).

Finally, one of the most interesting points of continuity and discontinuity in the ideas of Victorian Thomas Carlyle and black Victorian W. E. B. Du Bois centers on the themes of democracy and liberation, a point with spectacular resonance in the thought and life of Du Bois whose ancestors were not only European but also black slaves. Carlyle set little store by what he saw as a "rush into Democracy" (*CW* 10: 216) and liberation. As Carlyle saw it, democracy was a paltry and misbegotten attempt to reestablish a genuine but collapsed order. He defined democracy as the "despair of finding any Heroes to govern you, and contented putting-up with the want of them" (*CW* 10: 215). For Carlyle, the real solution to the problem of governance was the discovery of "your Real-Superiors" (*CW* 10: 220). Believing as he did that there were men who "*deserved* to be . . . master" and that there were men meant to wear well the "rude brass-collar," believing as he did in a natural hierarchy of "superiors, inferiors, equals," Carlyle more readily accommodated tyranny and slavery in his thinking (*CW* 10: 212). According to Carlyle, "true liberty were that a wiser man, that any and every wiser man, could, by brass collars, or in whatever milder or sharper way, lay hold of him when he was going wrong, and order and compel him to go a little righter" (*CW* 10: 212). Advocating the right of force, the appropriateness of "brass collars, whips and handcuffs" as legitimate instruments of just societies and civilized order, Carlyle, unsurprisingly, condemned the emancipation of West Indian blacks and sympathized with the South during the Civil War (*CW* 10: 213).

Although there is no evidence that young Du Bois read Carlyle's crude racial denigration of West Indian blacks in "Discourse on the Nigger Question" (1849, 1850), a more mature Du Bois, who as late as 1935 numbered Thomas Carlyle among nineteenth-century philanthropists Lord Shaftsbury, Buxton, and Gladstone (*Black Reconstruction* 88), was certainly aware of Carlyle's adherence to the Southern cause and of what Du Bois himself referred to as "the Carlyle [*sic*] contempt of levelling democracy" (*Autobiography* 165). Du Bois himself, though early on a proponent of the concept of an elitist talented tenth that corresponds to Carlyle's "Real-Superiors" had a more complicated, if not equivocal engagement with ideas of democracy and liberty. After all, Du Bois submits, "had it not been for the race problem early thrust upon me and enveloping me, I should have probably been an unquestioning worshipper at the shrine of the established social order . . . into which I was born" (*Autobiography* 155). Race and the social order into which he was born located Du Bois near the bottom of the American pyramid. Yet because America was a democracy, the color of Du Bois's skin should not ideally have left Du Bois so situated. The ideas of liberty and equality inherent in American democracy were antithetical to the tyranny and slavery Carlyle's thought accommodated, but only if those democratic ideas were truly realized. Initially Du Bois was convinced of the rightness and the value of the democratic idea. He argued that emancipated blacks needed democracy and "the power of the ballot . . . in sheer self-defence [*sic*],—else what shall save us from a second slavery?" (*Souls* 14). In fact, Du Bois understood how democracy had been so integral to the African American condition that, as he commented, between 1854 and 1876, "democracy died save in the hearts of black folk" (*Black Reconstruction* 30). After World War I, Du Bois became increasingly critical of democracy in the United States. It was not the real thing: "so-called democracy today was allowing the mass of people to have only limited voice in government" (*Dusk of Dawn* 285). He felt that, unfortunately, "the democracy which the white world seeks to defend does not exist. It has been splendidly conceived and discussed, but not realized" (*Dusk of Dawn* 169). Whereas Thomas Carlyle remained very much a reactionary, by the end of his career, Du Bois had completed a trajectory toward Pan-Africanism and socialism.[4] It had not only been the repeated failure of America to achieve for all of its citizens the democracy it professed to champion and "the phantasmagoria of war" (*Dusk of Dawn* 258) fought by Americans just as guilty as Germans of brutal oppression but also Du Bois's travels and subsequent repeated exposure to Europe, the site of the several race congresses in which Du Bois participated—it had been all of these which prompted Du Bois to a more critical assessment of the democratic process Victorian Thomas Carlyle mocked as "Shooting Niagara."

Du Bois's European and Victorian sensibilities, but especially his relation to Thomas Carlyle, if largely and systematically unexplored, have not gone unnoted. Thus, Du Bois's biographer David Levering Lewis describes a young Du Bois as "almost giddy" at finding himself among Europeans and unhesitant in recommending to those he wished to lead that they embrace "the late-Victorian Zeitgeist" (131, 173). British cultural critic Paul Gilroy, who contends in his book *The Black Atlantic* that "striving to be both European and black requires some specific forms of double consciousness," eventually and unsurprisingly comments on Du Bois's Europeanized African American consciousness by pointing to "W. E. B. Du Bois's childhood interest in Bismarck, his investment in modelling his dress and moustache on that of Kaiser Wilhelm II, his likely thoughts while sitting in Heinrich Von Treitschke's seminars, and the use his tragic heroes make of European culture" (1, 17). Calling for further and deeper investigation and reconsideration of this hybridization, Gilroy is more speculative in his observations on Du Bois than scholar Orlando Paterson who defines Du Bois's Victorianism as the cultural appropriations of a rebel. "What, after all," argues Patterson, "was W. E. B. Du Bois but an Afro-Saxon? Can anyone intimately acquainted with his life and words doubt this? Nor did he even try to conceal the fact: His aristocratic bearing is attested by all who knew him. He admired Thomas Carlyle, the nineteenth-century racial elitist; and his call for the promotion of a vanguard elite of Afro-American people as a precondition of progress was in keeping with his aristocratic view of change" (104). Du Bois's aristocratic views and his decision not to conceal his Afro-Saxonism earned him, Eric Sundquist notes, the disapprobation of a younger generation of Harlem Renaissance intellectuals who "sometimes perceived Du Bois as the embodiment of a reactionary, Victorian cultural ethos" (543). As Sundquist puts it elsewhere in his massive work *To Wake the Nations*, "At times Du Bois's double consciousness left him open to accusations of Eurocentrism and blinded him to important elements of African life and the colonial situation" (462). Black philosopher Cornel West looks more closely at Du Bois's Victorian bearing, ethos, and view of change. West, who points to Du Bois's "Victorian three-piece suit—with a clock and chain in the vest" not only as a signifier of dignity and intellectuality but also as a symbol of "the age that shaped and molded him" (*Race Matters* 40), identifies Du Bois as an adherent to the "rich tradition of Victorian critics"—among whom he includes Thomas Carlyle, John Ruskin, Matthew Arnold, and others (Gates and West 70). West then takes to task Du Bois's enlightened "*Victorian strategies*" for realizing "an *American optimism*" (Gates and West 57). He contends that these strategies, which amount essentially to an elitism aimed at molding the masses with an eye to attaining "material and spiritual progress," ought to undergo "wholesale reconstruction" by today's public intellectual (Gates and West 65, 71). For although the Victorian strategies Du Bois adopted are laudably rooted in the real, they are not, according to West, democratic enough. More recently, Hazel Carby, who begins her study of how Du Bois excluded women from his paradigm for black leadership with a comment on Du Bois's "grand Victorian gesture of self-sacrifice," returns briefly to the Victorian idea when she refers to Cornel West's mention of Du Bois's Victorian three-piece suit, finding in a comparison of the physical appearance of West and Du Bois an example of how the male body can be fashioned or represented as the model intellectual (9, 21).

The sum of remarks such as those of Lewis, Gilroy, Patterson, Sundquist, West, and Carby is that Du Bois, a powerful and influential race man born around the height of the Victorian era, did not repudiate Victorian England or Europe but rather embraced it and its ideas, sometimes deliberately and sometimes unconsciously. Yet "what is Europe to me" is curiously a question the Afro-Saxon Du Bois, subject as he was to those accusations of Eurocentrism, never literally posed, choosing as he did instead to consider, in the spirit of Countee Cullen's poem, what Africa was to him. Africa was the missing piece of the national cultural puzzle, the maligned fatherland, a powerful but historically occulted source of his being, a place to which he came to feel himself inextricably bound by the historical fact of bondage: "The real essence of this kinship is its social heritage of slavery; the discrimination and insult; and this heritage binds together not simply the children of Africa, but extends through yellow Asia and into the South Seas. It is this unity that draws me to Africa" (*Dusk of Dawn* 117).

One black Victorian who probably not only drew Du Bois to Africa but also influenced his appreciation for Europe and England as well was Episcopalian clergyman and founder of the American Negro Academy, Alexander Crummell. Crummell's own attraction to Africa began as he himself observes during his childhood: "From my early childhood my mind was filled with facts and thoughts about Africa and my imagination literally glowed with visions of its people, its scenery, and its native life. In my boyhood I read the 'Arabian Nights Tales,' and all you who have read them know how they stimulate the youthful mind. It was just thus with me with regard to Africa." Crummell's father, an African abducted from the kingdom of Timanee, also quickened Crummell's interest in Africa: "By listening to his tales of African life, I became deeply interested in the land of our fathers; and early in my life resolved, at some future day, to go to Africa" (*Destiny and Race* 61). As an adult, although Crummell's "principal concern," as biographer and historian Wilson Jeremiah Moses observes, "up to the year of his departure for Liberia had been to support the cause of the free black population in the United States," Crummell's thoughts ultimately turned to the continent of Africa, but more specifically to Liberia as an epicenter for the great good work of evangelizing and elevating what he himself described as his "deprived," "debarred," "cut off," "shut out," and "brutalised" race (*Alexander Crummell* 86; *Destiny and Race* 159). It was after his sojourn in England, where he earned a degree from Cambridge, that Crummell went to live in Africa where he worked among the Liberians for the betterment of the African race. In his efforts to uplift Africans and secure their place among the great civilizations of the world, Crummell looked more often than not to the English and their institutions for examples and models of what could be achieved. Thus, he had nothing but praise for the English university that granted him a degree when American institutions of higher learning had turned him away and praise for men the English university turned out. Pointing out how "many of the greatest minds of England were trained and nurtured under her [Cambridge's] fostering care and lofty erudition," Crummell in a eulogium to Cambridge-educated abolitionist Thomas Clarkson identifies Cambridge as a wellspring of "human liberty and human well-being" that has produced such thinkers and abolitionists as "Latimer, Cranmer, George Herbert, Ridley, Wilberforce, and Clarkson" (*Africa and America* 208). Understandably, Crummell advised the Africans among whom he chose to live and work to learn from the English people, to take a page from the English character. The English had the soundness and security that comes with experience and maturity. They were not to be numbered among those people who "must always be petted and flattered, and made to believe they are the greatest nation in existence." In fact, England, as Crummell went on to remark, "is one of the oldest and greatest of European nations; and yet there is no people on the earth who so continually find fault with themselves as the English." This tendency to feel "constant dissatisfaction with an imperfect state" and to "aim after an ideal perfection" is one Crummell encouraged Liberians to cultivate. The English had "that quality which *we* are yet to attain, namely *prescience*—the disposition to work for the future. We have but little of it in Liberia" (*Africa and America* 195–96). Another "one of the most remarkable traits of English character" that Crummell suggested black folk emulate involved the English predilection for "statistical information." This particular scientific proclivity set them apart from other European nations in Crummell's opinion. "What is done in Germany by profound and massive learning, in France by acute and subtle reasoning, and in our own country [the United States], by popular address and splendid eloquence, is effected in England by FACTS." Crummell was convinced that "for favor and success in any cause, it is absolutely necessary that this national propensity should be satisfied to the utmost" (*Africa and America* 236). The Victorians ultimately afforded blacks in America and Liberia powerful lessons that literary critic and comparatist scholar Simon Gikandi terms the "racial exceptionalism" that was "the essence of nationhood" (175). For Crummell, "Victorianism was," Gikandi further explains, "the Afro-Victorian's mode of imagining institutions of society beyond the harsh realities of imperialism" (176). In chapter 12 of *The Souls of Black Folk*, Du Bois identifies Crummell as priest, prophet, and mentor. Indeed, in his biography of Crummell, Wilson Jeremiah Moses declares that "Du Bois was clearly the intellectual heir of Crummell, Eurocentric yet Pan-Africanistic, chauvinistic yet cosmopolitan" (264). Like Crummell, who embraced Africa and respected England, Du Bois admired one place without precluding esteem for the other.

By the time Du Bois completed the writing of the last of the three autobiographies he would compose, having his day in the Western metropolis did not necessarily surpass having his day in the marginalized African state. So Du Bois recalls: "Once before the assembled races of the world I was called to speak in London in place of the suddenly sick Sir Harry Johnston. It was a great hour. But it was not greater than the day when I was presented to the President of the Negro Republic of Liberia" (*Dusk of Dawn* 122). By the beginning of the twentieth century, Du Bois would have fallen under the "mystic spell of Africa," to which Du Bois determined the United States itself owed a great deal of inspiration as "it has guided her [America's] hardest work, inspired her finest literature, and sung her sweetest songs" (Paschal 7). Nevertheless, this older Du Bois, like the younger acolyte of Victorian masculinist and intellectual muscularity, did not dismiss England and Europe even after he had moved well beyond the allure of "that sort of etherial [*sic*] sheen which, to the fresh American, envelopes everything European" (*Against Racism* 29). As Du Bois announced first in *Dusk of Dawn* (1920) and later in the *Autobiography of W. E. B. Du Bois* (1968), "I know Western Europe through a repeated series of visits covering the years 1892 until the present." He details the extent of his knowledge cataloging the places to which he traveled. "I knew Germany as a student and traveler before the world wars, and as a traveler since. I had lived at times in various places in England and Scotland, in France, and in Holland and Belgium. I have been more briefly in Switzerland, Italy, Spain and Portugal; in Greece, Turkey and in the old Austro-Hungarian empire" (*Autobiography* 14). Elsewhere he could boast, "Fifteen times I have crossed the Atlantic and once the Pacific. I have seen the world" (*Autobiography* 53, see also 286). These Atlantic crossings provided him a better political and international perspective as Du Bois himself recognized. "My attitude toward current problems arose from my long habit of keeping in touch with world affairs by repeated trips to Europe and other parts of the world" (*Autobiography* 286). These transatlantic crossings also provided him with a wider window onto his race and his people. Indeed, as Paul Gilroy intimates, Europe could play an important role in how a thinker such as Du Bois arrived at his "understanding of racial identities" (17). Early on, it was Europe more than Africa that factored into the shaping of Du Bois's identity. Thus, Europe, which Du Bois first visited in 1892 as a graduate student in Carlyle's beloved Germany, gave Du Bois a greater will to strive. He declares, "Europe modified profoundly my outlook on life and my thought and feeling toward it, even though I was there but two short years." He credits Europe with the formation of his tastes, his style, his values, and his very acculturation. He remembers with fervor how the two years he spent in Europe introduced him to "something of the possible beauty and elegance of life," which "permeated my soul; I gained a respect for manners . . . I came to know Beethoven's symphonies and Wagner's *Ring*. I looked long at the colors of Rembrandt and Titian. I saw in arch and stone and steeple the history and striving of men and also their taste and expression. Form, color and words took new combinations and meaning" (*Autobiography* 156). He returned home around 1896 to extol Europe as the repository of "the Good, the True and the Beautiful," declaring in an address before a Wilberforce University audience, "Only in Europe can we study the art of the world" (*Against Racism* 34, 36). His admiration for European art and music would announce itself powerfully in *Dark Princess* where African American Matthew Towns and his Indian princess lover, Kaudylia, take frequent if brief respites from their physical, social, and political struggles to uplift the colored masses. They are liable at any given moment to seek healing and restoration by immersing themselves in European art and music. It so happens that in one of Matthew's meetings in Europe with the princess and some of her retinue, discussion turns momentarily away from the pressing issue of Pan-African and Pan-Asian relations to the art of Kandinsky, Picasso, and Matisse—artists about whom Matthew knows nothing (20). By the time Matthew goes back to America and again encounters the princess it is clear that Matthew's trip to England has brought about not only the awakening of his political consciousness but also the quickening of his cultural and artistic sensibilities. At one point in the novel, a more cultured Matthew visits a Chicago art gallery where the paintings of Monet, Pisano, Gauguin, Picasso, Cézanne, Renoir, and Van Gogh stir his soul to various rhythms (280). He soon rents a little room, an inner sanctum for himself, where he goes to be alone and draw comfort and sustenance from his Turkish and Chinese rugs, his "genuine

Matisse," his "copy of a Picasso," but more often than not from European music (192, 193). Thus, as Matthew makes a big decision about his political career, he sits and "listen[s] to the luscious thrill of the 'Spanish Fandango'" (193). Later in the novel, after making love with Matthew, Kautylia awakens to Matthew's Victor record recording of the "the andante from Beethoven's Fifth Symphony, infinite in tenderness, triumph, and beauty" (219). As the couple eat breakfast, "the music was changed to that largo of Dvorák built on the echoing pain of the Negro folksong" (220). Elsewhere in the novel, Matthew and Kautylia "had their benediction of music—the overture to *Wilhelm Tell*, which seemed to picture their lives" (235). At the end of the day, Matthew's idea of uplifting physical work calls not for the accompaniment of sorrow songs but rather of European music: "If only I could work and work wildly, unstintingly, hilariously for six full, long hours; after that, while I lie in a warm bath, I should like to hear Tschaikowsky's Fourth Symphony. You know the lilt and cry of it. There must be much other music like it" (271). From Shakespeare's *Hamlet*, which Towns reads as one of "a hundred master-thoughts," to Tschaikowsky's Fourth Symphony, European art stirs Matthew Towns's soul just as surely as it stirred Du Bois's (270). Ultimately, both character and author sought the flowering of the "finer culture"; they both valued and aspired to "that fine old accumulation of the courtesies of life with its gracious delicacy" that was still much in evidence in Europe (284).

Perhaps one of the most powerful representatives of that fine old accumulation of the courtesies of life with its gracious delicacy was Queen Victoria herself. Queen over millions and mother of nine, Victoria Regina had shown herself to be relatively progressive in her relations with some members of the black race. According to British scholar Joan Anim-Addo, she had accepted several blacks into her domestic sphere, the first of whom in 1850 was a young Dahomean captive given the name Sally Bonetta Forbes. However, the queen, who demonstrated such open-mindedness where these black individuals were concerned ultimately proved not to be especially "philanthropic," as writer, editor, and commentator Andrew Ward has put it, toward the race as a whole. She after all "during the American Civil War . . . supported Prime Minster Palmerston's early decision to de-emphasize Britain's opposition to slavery and support the South in the name of protecting the cotton supply of Lancashire's textile industry" (212). Then, too, for this same queen, reported, if not proven to be "part African—her grandmother Queen Charlotte was directly descended from a black wing of the Portuguese royal house—the dilemma of American freedmen was not one of Her Majesty's burning concerns" (212).[5] Be that as it may, for Du Bois, this regal old-world personage served as a marker of his life's progression. Du Bois, thus, recalls that shortly after he was born, "in England, Victoria opened her eighth parliament" (*Dusk of Dawn* 9). He likewise refers to his eighth year of life as the year "Victoria of England became Empress of India" (*Dusk of Dawn* 18). He contextualizes his university education by observing how "the Queen's Jubilee in June, 1887, while I was still at Fisk, set the pattern of our thinking" (*Dusk of Dawn* 41; *Autobiography* 142). In this way, the queen of England proved as great a signifier as any American president whose term in office might frame the events of the life Du Bois recorded in his autobiographies. Du Bois could certainly be numbered among those Americans of whom Andrew Carnegie wrote in 1882, "At the mere mention of 'the Queen' every American hat is off in a moment. I only say '*the* Queen.' It is not necessary to add Victoria, for to the American there is but one Queen in the world, and she has not within her own dominions a more devoted constituency than she has here" (164). The queen provided a matrix not only for Du Bois's life but also for that of his people. Thus, "the little old woman at Windsor [Queen Victoria] became a magnificent symbol of Empire. Here was England with her flag draped around the world, ruling more black folk than white and leading the colored peoples of the earth to Christian baptism, to civilization and eventual self-rule" (*Dusk of Dawn* 41; see also *Autobiography* 142). This respect for and awareness of the queen underscores a tendency Du Bois shared with many Victorian Americans to look to England for some of its icons. As Du Bois commented in his final autobiography, "Even I was a little startled to realize how much that I had regarded as white American, was white European and not American at all" (157).

Europe via its art, music, literature, even its rulers and heads of state did more than knock at the door of Du Bois's consciousness; it entered his very soul. By his own admission, Du Bois first "crossed the ocean in a trance. Always I seemed to be saying, 'It is not real; I must be dreaming!'" (*Autobiography* 156). Two years later he would find himself, as he put it, "dropped suddenly back into 'nigger'-hating America" (183) and consequently even more firmly under the spell of Europe, which had rendered the veil—which he described later in *The Souls of Black Folk* as that which separated him and fellow blacks from whites—more translucent. In Europe, Du Bois had experienced "unhampered social intermingling with Europeans of education and manners," which enabled him to transcend his "racial provincialism" (*Autobiography* 160). He lavishes praise upon the Europeans when he credits them not just with tolerance but indeed with the promotion of his very own humanity: "I became more human . . . I ceased to hate or suspect people simply because they belonged to one race or color" (*Autobiography* 160). Humanity, art, manners, interracial fellowship, and manhood were

Europe's gifts to Du Bois. Here was, to borrow Mary Pratt's clever expression, a "contact zone" that put the "greater, finer world at my back," that offered him most especially insights into the workings of culture that would become his life's work (*Autobiography* 157). Ultimately, Europe afforded Du Bois an understanding of the transformative and radicalizing power of cultural capital, which he would seek to define and develop for the black community back home in the United States. He would become as much an arbiter of culture for his people as Victorians Thomas Carlyle and Matthew Arnold were for the British. Du Bois's regard for Europe's cultural capital would never wane. Instead, it would pave the way to Africa and beyond.

For indeed, it is fair to say that Du Bois came circumlocutorily to Africa by way of Europe. He began not only with a college student's idealism, but more significantly also with a Victorian belief in progress, with a robust sense that the time into which he was born was in some ways, to borrow one of Charles Dickens's most memorable phrases, "the best of times." Du Bois recalls how "it was to my mind and the minds of most of my teachers a day of Progress with a capital P. Population in all the cultured lands was increasing swiftly . . . cities everywhere were growing . . . transportation . . . was drawing the nations near . . . Commerce was madly seeking markets all around the earth; colonies were being seized and countries integrated into European civilization in Asia, Africa, South America and the islands" (*Autobiography* 154–55). Never mind that this progress came at the expense of people of color; Du Bois felt as Victorian poet Robert Browning—"that colored Robert Browning, who died just after I [Du Bois] received my first bachelor's degree"—did, that "'God's in His Heaven; All's right with the world'" (*Autobiography* 155). As Du Bois himself honestly and succinctly explains, "I was blithely European and imperialist in outlook" (*Autobiography* 126). At Harvard, he had accepted the idea of an English and European culture that served all. He believed, as indicated earlier, that Queen Victoria had at heart the best interests of the darker people over whom she extended her empire and that her rule was preparing colored people for self-governance (*Autobiography* 142). The mature Du Bois admits he "did not question" and took no exception to "the Berlin Conference of 1885," during which Europeans carved up Africa for exploitation of its people and resources. The conference was represented to him as "an act of civilization against the slave trade and liquor" (*Autobiography* 143). Du Bois who latched onto the concept of progress quickly enough, apparently came more slowly to the recognition of how England and Europe were implicated in the problem of the color line. His realization would begin during his "*Wanderjahre* in Europe," where he started to note the global dimensions of racism and Europe's role in the problems of blacks

(*Autobiography* 159). In the European classroom, "under these teachers and in this social setting, I began to see the race problem in America, the problem of the peoples of Africa and Asia, and the political development of Europe as one" (*Autobiography* 162).

In the end, Du Bois did not blindly and indiscriminately embrace European ideals; in fact, he disapproved of Europe's role in the underdevelopment of darker peoples—the Teutonic or the European, however, remained for him a cultural "touchstone," to borrow Matthew Arnold's expression. Nowhere is this function of things European as a cultural standard so clearly evident as in the headings of the chapters in his landmark work, *Souls of Black Folk*, where Du Bois tends to pair—again in the spirit of Victorian cultural critic, Matthew Arnold—the best that has been thought and said in England and Europe with the best and most soulful creations of African Americans. At the opening of twelve of the fourteen chapters of *The Souls of Black Folk*, lines of poetry by white authors are followed by bars of black folk music that Du Bois reverently identifies in his final chapter as "sorrow songs." Of the writers whose lines of poetry head Du Bois's chapters, three are Americans—James Russell Lowell, John Greenleaf Whittier, and William Vaughn Moody; one is German—Friedrich Schiller; and seven are British—Arthur Symons, Lord Byron, Edward FitzGerald, Elizabeth Barrett Browning, William Sharp (pseudonym Fiona MacCleod), Charles Swinburne, and Alfred Lord Tennyson. In only two of the chapters are the poetic selections not attributed to a specific white writer, as Du Bois takes the lines that frame chapter 7 from the Song of Solomon and those that frame chapter 14 from a Negro song. Du Bois collimates the works from which the white and black inscriptive texts are taken as follows:

Chapter 1
Arthur Symons's "The Crying of Water"
"Nobody Knows the Trouble I've Seen"

Chapter 2
James Russell Lowell's "The Present Crisis"
"My Lord, What a Mourning, When the Stars Begin to Fall"

Chapter 3
Lord Byron's "Childe Harold's Pilgrimage"
"A Great Camp-Meeting in the Promised Land"

Chapter 4
Friedrich Schiller's *Die Jungfrau von Orleans*
"My Way's Cloudy"

Chapter 5
John Greenleaf Whittier's "Howard at Atlanta"
"The Rocks and the Mountains"

Chapter 6
Edward FitzGerald's translation of "The Rubáiyát of Omar Khayyám"
"March On"

Chapter 8
William Vaughn Moody's "The Brute"
"Children, You'll Be Called On"

Chapter 9
Elizabeth Barrett Browning's "A Vision of Poets"
"I'm a Rolling"

Chapter 10
Fiona McCleod's [William Sharp's] "Dim Face of Beauty"
"Steal Away"

Chapter 11
Algernon Swinburne's "Itylus"
"I Hope My Mother Will Be There in that Beautiful World on High"

Chapter 12
Alfred Lord Tennyson's *Idylls of the King*
"Swing Low, Sweet Chariot"

Chapter 13
Elizabeth Barrett Browning's "A Romance of the Ganges"
"I'll Hear the Trumpet Sound" (or "You May Bury Me in the East").

As this list suggests, the preponderance of European, especially British texts with which the spirituals are paired is further indicative of Du Bois's familiarity with and respect for Victorian literature and European culture from which he drew no little cultural sustenance. For Du Bois had sat down at the table of European culture and found a "breadth and broadening of . . . reason" and a "catholicity of taste" (*Souls* 69) that would enable him to lead his people across red seas into Canaan. "I sit," he wrote, "with Shakespeare and he winces not. Across the color line I move arm in arm with Balzac and Dumas, where smiling men and welcoming women glide in gilded halls. . . . I summon Aristotle and Aurelius and what soul I will, and they come all graciously with no scorn nor condescension. So, wed with Truth, I dwell above the Veil. Is this the life you grudge us, O knightly America? . . . Are you so afraid lest peering from this high Pisgah . . . we sight the Promised Land?" (*Souls* 82).

Critics such as Eric Sundsquist and Hazel Carby offer astute analyses of the relation between the bars of music and Du Bois's chapters, but the architectonics of the scraps of poetry and fragments of songs and the relation between the predominantly European poetic and the African American musical "epigraphs," as Sundquist calls them, bear further consideration. Thus, Du Bois's physical and spatial treatment of the lines of the European poems and the strains of African American music reveals something of the nature of Du Bois's own culturally reversible consciousness. In the prefatory space heading each chapter, the excerpts of what may be loosely characterized as European poetry typically come before strains of black music, mirroring perhaps the fact that for Du Bois, as for many educated African Americans then and now, formal knowledge of Anglo-American culture precedes formal knowledge of African and African American culture. Interestingly enough, the lines of poetry are readily identifiable in the sense that the words of the poetry are generally more immediately comprehended than musical notation, and each poetic selection is clearly attributed to a single individual writer. Even though poetry and music are recorded differently, it is worth noting, as does Dena J. Epstein in *Sinful Tunes and Spirituals* (1977), that "nineteenth-century transcriptions of the music display few distinctive features that would differentiate it from white nineteenth-century music" (217). Still, the measures of black music, however recognizable as music, are not so easily apprehended, assuming most readers do not, as Du Bois conceded of himself, have the technical knowledge to read it. Homi Bhabha might identify the lines of poetry or the English text as the "text of authority" because it is more visibly articulated and because it is more thoroughly identified and thus recognized (32, 33). In this postcolonial scheme of things, the fragments of music resist the "articulacy of authority" ultimately by blurring the lines between poetry and music and calling into question "the rules of recognition" (35, 33). Positioned between the printed lines of poetry and the printed text of Du Bois's own essay, the bars of music "hover [. . .]," to borrow an expression of Du Bois's, in physical singularity that may seem "oppositional," if not "agonistic" (*Souls* 184; Bhabha 32). However, as Bhabha explains, "resistance is not necessarily an oppositional act of political intention, nor is it the simple negation or exclusion of the 'content' of another culture. . . . It is the effect of an ambivalence produced within the rules of recognition of the dominating discourses as they articulate the signs of cultural difference and reimplicate them . . ." (33). The bars of music articulate the signs of cultural difference and reimplicate those differences through hybridity—music is a kind of poetry—and through music's "disavowal" of the individual, in this case, individual white authors (33). Placed in the company of poetry owned by specific writers, the musical measures have no specified authors or accompanying words. The music, Du Bois intimates, is neither the property nor the creation of any one individual. It belongs instead to the community and is a product, as it were, of the folk.

In the final chapter, where Du Bois focuses on and finally names several of the songs whose measures have, along with snippets of Euro-poetry, prefaced his chapters, Du Bois explains why he has chosen not to put the lyrics with the music. The words are missing because they, aside from being often improvised by the original singers, have been "forgotten," "caricatured," "imitated," and sometimes "debased" (*Souls* 181, 182). The music alone, Du Bois's arrangement indicates, is just as beautiful as any of the poetic words that precede it on the opening page of each chapter. This music informs some of the songs whose power and beauty have met European culture on its own turf, this music having, thanks to the Fisk Jubilee singers, Du Bois tells us, traveled "across the land and across the sea" to be heard by "Queen and Kaiser, in Scotland and Ireland, Holland and Switzerland" (*Souls* 182). Besides, Du Bois, who is keen to have us focus on the "message" of the music as opposed to the technicalities of the notes, implies, by pairing it with lines of poetry, that music has its own verbal qualities: it articulates, tells, witnesses (even historicizes as the "music is far more ancient that the words" [*Souls* 182]). Melodies signify as mightily as lyrics; however, in the spiritual, the melody is so wed to the lyrics that the two are nigh inseparable. As Arthur C. Jones points out, "in the spirituals, we normally hear (or sing) both lyrics and melodies together, making it impossible to sort out the impact of melodies versus lyrics. This is as it should be; it is the combination of inspired poetry *and* inspired music" (19). Du Bois must have understood as much, for despite the pattern he establishes in *Souls* of rendering the music of the sorrow songs without the lyrics, in the final chapter he is compelled to address the absence of lyrics that silently but no less effectively inform the lines of poetry.

In fact, the lines of poetry and the lyrics that implicitly accompany the bars of music, if not exactly cultural simulacra that replicate each other, prove cultural correlatives as they cohere around concerted if not identical messages and themes. Delving into the "cultural archives" of the Europeans and the African Americans, Du Bois set up what Edward Said calls "an organized interplay that derives from the themes" (51). Arthur Symons's poem, for instance, which lends its title, "Our Spiritual Strivings," to the first chapter of Du Bois's *Souls of Black Folk* is paired with the sorrow song "Nobody Knows the Trouble I've Seen" as mutual expressions of solitude, forlornness, and mournfulness. Symons's dominant image of a restless water that is the "voice of my heart" that cries long, "for rest," and "without avail" (ll. 1, 5, 11) captures the ceaseless anguish and the bone-deep weariness of the black song about a life so hard, so beleaguered that it is nigh incomprehensible to other men: "Nobody knows the trouble I've seen but Jesus."[6]

In chapter 2, the excerpt from James Russell Lowell's "The Present Crisis" and the missing lyrics to "My Lord, What a Mourning, When the Stars Begin to Fall" both deal with a moment of upheaval and change. Russell's poem, which goes on to describe slavery as a monstrous "earthborn Cyclops," declares that "Once to every man and nation comes the moment to decide" between "right" and "wrong," "Truth" and "Falsehood" (ll. 46, 21, 17, 22). Having arrived at the crossroads of the present crisis, Russell would remind readers to choose in the knowledge that "In the gain or loss of one race all the rest have equal claim" (l. 20). This sense of urgency is present in the music and lyrics of "My Lord, What a Mourning," which also posits the sense of being brought to the brink, to the very edge of awakening. For, according to the words of the song, "when the stars begin to fall," if you listen "you'll hear resurrection the trumpet sound / To wake the nations underground." Both poetic and musical fragments are oracular wake-up calls to nations, black and white, above ground and below.

In the chapter on Booker T. Washington, Du Bois couples three lines from the second canto of British Romantic poet Lord Byron's "Childe Harold's Pilgrimage" with the spiritual "A Great Camp-Meeting in the Promised Land." The traveling and self-exiled persona of Byron's long poem speaks directly of "enslaved" and "hereditary bondsmen," punctuating his lines of Spenserian stanza with exclamation points that ultimately lead up to a rhetorical exhortation to arms: "From birth till death enslaved; in word, in deed, unmanned! / . . . / Hereditary Bondsmen! know ye not / *Who* would be free *themselves* must strike the blow? (canto 2, stanzas 74–76, ll. 710, 720–21). Although the spiritual is not a call to arms, per se, it does call for those living in this troubled world to join hands and press forward to a place of concerted action—a camp-meeting: "Oh walk togedder, children / Don't yer get weary / Walk together children / . . . Dire's a great camp-meeting in de Promised Land." Both Byron's challenge to "strike the blow" and the spiritual's eschewal of weariness ("Mourn an' nebber tire") rehearse the courage and fortitude that are necessary for, what Du Bois identifies in the essay that follows the two texts as, "a determined effort at self-realization and self-development despite environing opinion" (*Souls* 40).

The lines from Friedrich Schiller's five-act drama, *Die Jungfrau von Orleans*, and the sorrow song "My Way's Cloudy," which head chapter 4, address in complementary ways the difficulty humans have making headway in the world. That is to say, both works speak to the fact of human frailty. Schiller's version of Joan of Arc, Johanna, concedes the weakness inherent in simply being human after she, finding herself attracted to her English enemy Lionel, releases him instead of killing him or taking him prisoner. In the lines of the drama that open chapter 4 of *Souls*, Johanna implores the Virgin Mary to choose some other, some higher being to work her will as Johanna herself admits to being mortal, "tender virgin," and "a herdmaid . . . frail." She suggests that the Virgin Mother may want to call on an angel—a spirit blameless, pure, immortal: "Thine own spirits send to roam, / Who is pure, who will not die, / Who feels not, who doth not cry!" Similarly, the lyrics of the sorrow song posit a person whose weakness is announced in the inability to either find or to clear a pathway: "My way, my way is cloudy." What is needed are stronger, more capable beings to disperse the clouds: "Go send them angels down." Prefacing Du Bois's chapter on "the Meaning of Progress," lines from the drama and the song adumbrate Du Bois's conviction that the progress that is so difficult for humankind to achieve, comes even harder to those who have the "Veil . . . hung between . . .[them] and Opportunity" (*Souls* 54).

Northern Quaker abolitionist John Greenleaf Whittier's "Howard at Atlanta" is the source of the poetic lines that accompany the sorrow song "The Rocks and Mountains" in chapter 5. This pairing, much like the pairing in chapter 2, refers to a turning point, to some possible future. More specifically, both the black song, with its reference to rocks and mountains that get up and run away, and the poem, with its promise (half of which is made by a little black boy) that in the wake of emancipation blacks and whites shall rise together, are centered in change and transformation, the hope of something better to come, even if that something is only, as the song puts it, "a new hiding place, " or as the poem suggests, the willingness to "Meet Fate half-way, and make it / A joy and blessing" (ll. 55–56).

Fragments of the second edition of Edward FitzGerald's translation of "The Rubáiyát of Omar Khayyám" and the spiritual "On the March" open Du Bois's chapter "Of the Training of Men." Du Bois brings together stanza 69 of FitzGerald's translation of the Persian poet's poem with this particular sorrow song because both poem and song are about ascension. In lines from the "Rubáiyát," the soul can put aside the cumbersome flesh—"this clay carcase crippled"—that binds it and weighs it down and rise "naked on the air of heave [to] ride." In the lyrics of "March On," those who live "Way over in the E-gypt land," the place of bondage, will also rise like the soul in "The Rubáiyát": "you shall gain the vic-to-ry." The movement in the poem and the song lifts the reader into the realm of possibilities for overcoming the heaviness of clay and the shackles of Egypt land. These fragments are about not being held down or back; they are about leaving behind or getting free of the physical, material, and spiritual burdens that thwart and oppress. Finally they are about gaining, winning, and abiding—the very things "heavily handicapped" black men will do, Du Bois tells us in the chapter that follows these fragments, if they aspire to a training and to an education that does not preclude "the loftiest of ideals" and "finer spirits" (*Souls* 71, 72, 82).

Du Bois's choice of William Vaughn Moody's poem "The Brute" and the song "Children, You'll Be Called On" as epigraphs for chapter 8 seems odd, because the poem and song do not readily yield their complementarities or associations. "The Brute" is a poem about labor, industry, and machines for which men "have boweled out the hills / For food to keep him toiling in the cages they have wrought / And they fling him, hour by hour, / Limbs of men to give him power; / Brains of men to give him cunning . . ." (ll. 2–6). The spiritual "Children, You'll Be Called On" is another resurrectional song to rally "soldier[s] of the cross." Unrelated as they appear to be, the poem and the song both develop the notion of warfare. The spiritual does so explicitly, calling upon the children "to march in the field of battle." The song, the lyrics of which could very well have been favored by blacks during the Civil War, anticipates the moment when the battle will be over and the soldier of the cross may become "a soldier of the ju-bi-lee": "When this war-fare'll be ended Hal-le-lu [chor.] When this war-fare'll be ended / I'm a soldier of the ju-bi-lee." Unlike the song that directly presents the idea of war, Moody's poem advances the notion of a more insidious siege. "The Brute" represents a beleaguered world strewn with the "limbs of men" (l. 5) and scarred by "boweled out . . . hills," (l. 2) and "streams . . . choked with clay" (l. 21). The men, women, and children the poet describes have succumbed to a brute of a power they had thought to reign in and control: "We will use this lusty knave: / No more need for men to slave" (ll. 28–29). However, the Brute plans its countermoves:

> "On the strong and cunning few
> Cynic favors I will strew;
> I will stuff their maw with overplus until their spirit dies;
> From the patient and the low
> I will take the joys they know;
> They shall hunger after vanities and still an-hungered go.
> Madness shall be on the people, ghastly jealousies arise;
> Brother's blood shall cry on brother up the dead and empty skies. (ll. 33–40)

In these lines, the Brute plans to launch an attack upon the spirits and souls of a people too invested in getting and spending. The result of the Brute's counterattack will be civil strife, if not indeed a civil war in which "brother's blood shall cry on brother." When the poetry fragment, the bars of music, and Du Bois's essay on the Golden Fleece are all taken into account, the idea of waging war on vanity, surfeit, greed, and economic subjugation emerges. Ultimately Du Bois uses the poem and song to preview the contention he advances in the essay proper: "The rise of a nation, the pressing forward of a social class, means a bitter struggle, a hard and soul-sickening battle" (*Souls* 118).

In chapters 9 and 13, Du Bois borrows lines of poetry from the only woman featured in the headings, British poet Elizabeth Barrett Browning. From the 1,005 lines of Barrett Browning's "A Vision of Poets," Du Bois excerpts three of the concluding lines to match up with the sorrow song "I'm a Rolling" in chapter 9. The refrain of the sorrow song strikes the dominant chords of brotherhood, sacrifice, suffering, and sympathy: "I'm rolling through an unfriendly world / O brothers, won't you help me . . . / O brothers, won't you help me, / Won't you help me. . . ." Although these themes of brotherhood and sympathy are obviously borne out in the essay itself where Du Bois argues for a "union of intelligence and sympathy across the color-line" (*Souls* 136) if the sons of masters and men are to continue to prosper and improve, these themes are not so readily apparent in the lines from Elizabeth Barrett's poem about a poet who falls asleep in a forest and has a vision of an angelic, muselike figure that reveals to him the great poets from Homer to Coleridge. What ties this poem to the sorrow song about suffering and sacrifice is Browning's rendering of a great brotherhood of poets who have not only been wounded and therefore suffer ("But where the heart of each should beat, / There seemed a wound instead of it, / From whence the blood dropped to their feet" [ll. 427–29]) but who have also sacrificed themselves for Beauty and for Truth ("these were poets true, / Who died for Beauty as martyrs do / For Truth—the ends being scarcely two" [ll. 289–91]). Du Bois chose lines from Browning's poem that touch upon the hurt and suffering we cause each other as "life treads on life, and heart on heart" (l. 820). In choosing the poetic and musical fragments he did for this chapter, Du Bois also wanted to demonstrate our connectedness. We are "brothers," the bar of music proclaims; we cannot be separated declares the poet for "we press too close in church and mart / To keep a dream or grave apart" (ll. 821–22).

Du Bois turns again to British poet Elizabeth Barrett Browning in "Of the Coming of John" where he pairs lines from her poem "A Romance of the Ganges" with six measures from "I'll Hear the Trumpet Sound" (or "You May Bury Me in the East"). Browning's poem centers in a midnight ritual whereby maidens learn whether or not "love will endure" (l. 34). During the ritual one of the maidens, Luti, who has been betrayed by her lover, persuades the lover's new flame, Nuleeni, to avenge the wrong Luti has suffered. Nuleeni vows to whisper of Luti's suffering in the ear of her bridegroom and spoils her own wedding day. Nuleeni also promises to reveal to the son she will have how his father mistreated Luti. A verse from this ballad of vengeance accompanies a black song that is apparently, as are a number of the spirituals Du Bois selected, about resurrection: "You may bury me in the East / You may bury me in the West, / But I'll hear that trumpet sound in that morning." When Du Bois joins the fragments of poetry and song together at the beginning of chapter 13, the differences prove striking. Not only is one about revenge and the other about resurrection, but one is also about a broken heart and the other treats a life stilled momentarily in death and burial. What becomes apparent upon closer examination is that both the poem and the song present the idea of a human heart that always beats with awareness, a heart that, like the river in Browning's poem, "floweth on" (l. 9). Browning's verse pictures a heart that is restless, if not broken, a "human heart wherein / No nightly calm can be" (ll. 12–13), but the sorrow song prefigures a heart or soul that cannot be stopped. For even if the human heart is buried underground, it will still hear the trumpet sound. Both poetic and musical verses point to, if not indomitability, then to persistence and endurance that "floweth on."

In chapter 10, lines from William Sharp's poem "Dim Face of Beauty" and a bar of music from the spiritual "Steal Away" constitute a cosmic yearning for a peaceful place in the universe. To put it another way, both fragments are about the here and the there. "Here" in both the poem and the song is a problematic place. "Here" is the home of "foolish babbling men . . . who cry with little noises 'neath the thunder" (ll. 12–13). It is the place where "all the dreams of men are whirled / Like sere torn leaves of autumn to and fro" (ll. 6–7). For the slaves, "here" is a place where there is no peace, no rest, and no justice. In the spiritual, the implication is that "there"—the place to which the trumpet of the Lord calls the singer—is a better place. "My Lord he calls me, he calls me by the thunder, the trumpet sounds within my soul I hain't got long to stay here." Though neither the poet nor the singer can offer details about this other glorious place, this "there" or this "home," faith exists that "there, there alone for thee / May white peace be" (ll. 4–5).

Peace proves almost as elusive in the epigraphs to chapter 11 where Du Bois prefaces his elegiac essay on the death of his son with lines from British poet Algernon Swinburne's "Itylus" and music from "I Hope My Mother Will Be There in that Beautiful World on High" (or "The Mayo Boys' Song"). These are particularly interesting selections because Du Bois initially uses words that foreground the mother to set up a chapter that dwells on paternal grief and loss. Swinburne's poem harkens back to the Greek myth about two sisters who avenge the rape and mutilation of one sister by killing, cooking, and serving up the son of the rapist for the rapist's own horrible delectation. According to the myth, the gods turn Procne, mother of Itylus and wife of Tereus, the offending king of Thrace, into a swallow, and her violated sister is turned into a nightingale. Swinburne's poem takes up where the myth leaves off, imagining how the transformed sisters come to terms with the awful events that have transpired. The swallow and her sister each deal with the tragedy of loss and grief in different ways. The swallow wants to move forward into the spring to simply sing and forget. The nightingale, however, cannot forget and marvels that the swallow is able to do so. "I know not how thou hast heart to sing. / Hast thou the heart? is it all past over?" (ll. 32–33). She, who once felt solidarity with and conspired with her sister to wreak revenge, now feels separated from that sister by the very weight of her memory:

> O sweet stray sister, O shifting swallow,
> The heart's division divideth us.
> Thy heart is light as a leaf of a tree;
> But mine goes forth among sea-gulfs hollow
> To the place of the slaying of Itylus
> The feast of Daulis, the Thracian sea. (ll. 43–48)

Though her sister is one of the first individuals she has ever loved, the Nightingale cannot forget the ignominious death of the first-begotten, the child Itylus.

Similarly, the lyrics of the music to the sorrow song also bespeak the power of memory. In this case, it is the mother who is remembered and longed for, in successive verses, the sister and the brother. As with the lines of Swinburne's poem, the lyrics treat the idea of separation and loss; however, in the plantation song, memory is no burden but rather the agent by which the lyricist hopes to recover the mother, sister, brother—the relatives who "used to join with me in prayer." Interestingly enough, while the singer hopes to be with his or her mother in that beautiful world on high, the singer can only be certain of two things: that he or she will arrive at that special place ("Oh, I will be there") and that the presence of the Savior is assured ("I know my Saviour will be there").

Finally, in chapter 12—a tribute to the anglophile and Cambridge-educated Alexander Crummell who influenced Du Bois's thinking about the talented tenth—the poetry fragment comes from the end of the final book of a work by of one of Britain's most famous Victorian poets Alfred Lord Tennyson, and the five measures of the sorrow song are taken from one of the best-known spirituals, "Swing Low, Sweet Chariot." Du Bois chooses lines from

Tennyson's Arthurian epic *Idylls of the King* that point simultaneously to the idea of endings and beginnings. In the last book of *Idylls,* "The Passing of Arthur," a war has concluded, as the image of "a king returning from the wars" (l. 461) suggests. There is mention of "the last" not the first "echo," and the very mention of Arthur's "passing" as opposed to his "coming" in Book I figures as a sort of death, cessation, or end. Yet the presence of such words as "dawn," "beyond," and "born" indicate, however faintly, the possibility of beginning anew: "as if some fair city were one voice / Around a King" who did not die, but survived and brought an end to that which causes destruction and endings—war (ll. 457–61). The spiritual also presents the idea of passing away into another world: "Swing low, sweet chariot, Coming for to carry me Home . . . If you get there before I do . . . Tell all my friends I'm coming to." The sweet chariot that will transport the singer away from life here to a place beyond that is truly home is reminiscent of that of Tennyson's King Arthur who in *Idylls* leaves Camelot and is charioted in a ship back to a purer place called Avilion. Just as the singer asks his friend to bear witness that "I am coming after you," in Tennyson's poem, Sir Bedivere bears witness to Arthur's passing. Both poem and song are poems of resurrection.

Du Bois has paired the epigraphs at the head of his chapters so that for every Anglo-American poetic call there is a corresponding African American response. Cultural meaning manifests itself in the folk music of African Americans as powerfully as it does in the poetic words of the Europeans. As John Lovell Jr. has remarked in the preface to *Black Song: The Forge and the Flame,* "If a folk song ever grew to epic stature, it is the American Negro spiritual" (xiii). In the African American songs and the mainly Victorian poems, Du Bois seeks ultimately to convey that inexpressible something that testified to the shared humanity of black and white folk—soul. This was a concept that had appealed to Thomas Carlyle who also found himself settling upon the notion of "soul" to explore the relation between poetry, speech, and song. Like Du Bois, Carlyle located poetry and song on the same page. "For my own part," remarked Carlyle, "I find considerable meaning in the old vulgar distinction of Poetry being *metrical,* having music in it, being a Song" (*CW* 5: 83). Just as Du Bois offers the sorrow songs as evidence of black culture, black depths, and black humanity, Carlyle also speaks more generally about song's connectedness to human depths. "The meaning of Song goes deep. Who is there that, in logical words, can express the effect music has on us? A kind of inarticulate unfathomable speech, which leads us to the edge of the Infinite, and lets us for moments gaze into that!" (*CW* 5: 83). Here Carlyle's words can be enlisted to support Du Bois's efforts to use the sorrow songs to take his readers deep into the heart and souls of black folk. The inner place toward which Du Bois seeks to steer us is strikingly similar to that interior space at which poetry itself, according to Carlyle, aims. Both poetry and song, Carlyle indicates, are achieved "by a mind that has penetrated into the inmost heart of the thing; detected the inmost mystery of it, namely, the *melody* that lies hidden in it; the inward harmony of coherence which is its soul, whereby it exists, and has a right to be, here in this world" (*CW* 5: 83). In his references to penetration, detection, inmost mystery, and the melody that lies hidden, Carlyle not only presents ideas that prefigure Du Bois's central idea of soul, but he also makes statements that correspond to Du Bois's own problematic references to the veil and to the complications of seeing. The point is that Du Bois could and would have done well had he used Carlyle's observations to further establish the reciprocity of Afro-music and Euro-poems. For as Carlyle attested, "all passionate language does of itself becomes musical" and "all deep things are Song" (*CW* 5: 83). A more recent formulation of this idea comes from postcolonial critic Edward Said who contends, "Cultural experience or indeed every cultural form is radically, quintessentially hybrid" (58).

By the last chapter of *The Souls of Black Folk,* Du Bois pairs the bars of black music with a Negro song instead of the fragment of a white poem to signal that this chapter will work to identify and name the music that has throughout *Souls* stood powerfully but anonymously with the likes of Byron, Tennyson, Swinburne, and Schiller. This shift in the pairing also suggests how the black gift of "soft, stirring melody in an ill-harmonized and unmelodious land" may be acknowledged and enriched when talented folk such as Du Bois take the time, as he does in his final chapter, to catalog "master songs," to recover and bear witness to music and songs that have been like the bars of music at the head of each chapter powerful, influential but veiled cultural forces (*Souls* 189, 183). By the end of *The Souls of Black Folk,* Du Bois's pairing of black music with a black song constitutes an uncloaking that reveals the important role Du Bois himself plays in *Souls* both as the articulator of a message that has been for too long veiled and half articulate and as the harbinger of a beautiful expression of human experience that he intuitively valued as much as any Victorian poem he had studied.

In describing his own condition and position as well as that of his people, Du Bois discovered in the example of the Victorians much more than aggressive imperialism. He also discovered a more vital spirit of progress, a sense of reform and greatness, and a belief in culture he greatly valued. In a writer such as Victorian Thomas Carlyle, Du Bois found early on a passion for the ungilded word, for the efficacy of strong leaders, and for the power of work with which he strongly identified. He claimed for himself some of the qualities most prized by Carlyle and his fellow Victorians. "My redeeming feature," wrote Du Bois, "was infinite capacity for work and terrible earnestness, with appalling and tactless frankness" (*Autobiography* 188). In light of the criticism he eventually leveled at the British and at Europe, it is unfair to say that Du Bois, though steeped in a Victorian ethos and credentialed in Europe, sold out to the empire. However, one could argue, he spent enough time in England and abroad to learn that being black does not preclude the benefits of a Victorian soul.

Conclusion

Reconsidering Victorian Britain and African America

In the nineteenth century, neither Britain's soil nor its soul was as hardened by slavery as America's was, or at least not hardened in the same ways. Victorian England radiated a morality, a confidence, a commitment to reform and to social responsibility that a number of African Americans found appealing and inspiring. From England to Ireland, from the highest ranking noble to the lowliest worker, the British comprised a people to be courted, respected, even emulated because the British were a people whom early nineteenth-century African Americans perceived to be open. This is to say that when it came to black Americans, the British were more likely than white Americans to open their minds, their front doors, and their purses. The Victorianism, which appealed to white Americans, was twice as seductive for some of the more prominent African Americans who sought to advance their own people and culture. Britain may be said to have owned the nineteenth century, and a black leader such as Frederick Douglass was not adverse to British hegemony as African Americans could look to Britain for some measure of moral if not political intervention in plantation-minded America.

The twentieth century would see a shift in the position of Britain as the United States laid claim to the century. Indeed, as the twentieth century progressed and the United States became the dominant world power, Victorian Britain, its culture, ideals, values, and beliefs, in short the Victorianism that served throughout the nineteenth century as a model for black and white America, certainly had its share of critics who denounced the Victorians and their ideas as puritanical, prudish, and hypocritical. As ascendancy shifted from Britain to the United States, conditions for blacks in America worsened as lynching, segregation, and disenfranchisement became the order of the day (the most notable high point for black folk during this period proving to be the literary flowering called the Harlem renaissance that took place between the two world wars). It would take the civil rights, black power, and black studies movements of the 1960s to establish African Americans as a political and cultural force around the world, "influenc[ing] all post-slavery societies," as Steve Fenton, referencing Manning Marable's *Race, Reform, and Rebellion,* observes (Fenton 42). The black arts movement that complemented the black power movement turned to Africa instead of England and Europe for its inspiration. Not all, but many blacks, as a result of the new black aesthetic, eschewed things Eurocentric. In this rejection of Eurocentrism, the participants of the black arts movement of the 1960s differed from the artists of the Harlem Renaissance who tended "to adopt the critical standards of Euro-American culture" and to take as their "ultimate point of reference . . . 'the great tradition' of Western European literary culture"—one of the main tributaries of which was the Victorian Age of Britain (Mitchell 4). The artists associated with the black aesthetic movement were more interested in exploring the distinctiveness of black sensibilities, art, and culture.

In the 1960s, playwright Adrienne Kennedy proved to be one artist who, while exploring the distinctiveness of black sensibilities, culture, and identity, insisted on its rootedness not only in Africa but also in Victorian England. In her 1964 one-act drama, *Funnyhouse of a Negro,* the fragmented persona of Sarah, the black female around whom the play centers, appears on the stage not only as Patrice Lumumba, Jesus, and the duchess of Hapsburg but also as Queen Victoria who is, Sarah declares, "my idol." In the play, Queen Victoria with her alopecic head of kinky hair "always wants me [Sarah] to tell her of whiteness. She wants me to tell her of a royal world where everything and everyone is white and there are not unfortunate black ones" (*In One Act* 5). What Kennedy manages to convey to her audience in her "autobiographically inspired" drama is how Queen Victoria and Victorian culture are an important part of her identity as a black woman (Sollors vii).

Among the list of fairy tale characters, movie stars, family members, and assortment of national, international, and local people who influenced the creation of plays such as *Funnyhouse,* Kennedy would include the Victorian novelist Charlotte Brontë. In her experimental autobiography, *People Who Led to My Plays* (1987), Kennedy recalls how she "read *Jane Eyre* and learned that life was to be a great journey and it was a journey that would be spelled out with love, loyalty, devotion, loneliness, madness, sacrifice and happiness, and that very life had been experienced by an English girl one century before" (14). Of the many English writers and characters she mentions in her autobiographical work—from Shakespeare to Queen Victoria—she makes repeated reference to Charlotte Brontë's Jane Eyre who was sent away to boarding school just as Kennedy's mother had been as a five-year-old (36). Kennedy recounts how thrilled she herself was when she fulfilled the requirements of a drama class assignment by delivering a "ten-minute . . . monologue from *Jane Eyre* (the novel)." Kennedy reminisces, "It was the only time in my life I publicly had a chance to become Jane Eyre. Even I could feel the passion I evoked in the class" (63). Near the end of *People Who Led to My Plays,* Kennedy, who later in life understood how powerfully she had connected to Jane Eyre the child, writes about "*reread*[ing] *Charlotte (again).*" She confesses that the Victorian novelist "imbued in me a curiosity and love of the English moors which I would finally see twenty years later on a rainy, misty July afternoon when I would tour Haworth and the Brontë's house with the English poet Adrian Mitchell. No place had ever quite captured my imagination as wildly as Yorkshire, as the winding streets of Haworth" (84, 110). Earlier on in her life, during trips down south to Montezuma, Georgia, Kennedy had discovered that her white ancestors "had come from England," and she subsequently "became very interested in 'England'" and in Charlotte Brontë's *Jane Eyre* (*People Who* 22). Her appreciation not only for such individuals as Haile Selassie, Tennessee Williams, and Richard Wright, but also for Percy Shelley, Winston Churchill, and especially Charlotte Brontë lends further support to the contention that Kennedy was interested in examining what Lovalerie King terms "multi-ethnic origins," and that she did so "at a time when other African American playwrights were making profound assertions of black pride in their works" (418). Clearly, in the work of a writer such as Kennedy, Victorian heritage was not eschewed. Still, during the period of the black arts movement, most African Americans committed to celebrating the uniqueness and beauty of blackness may be said to have, like Nigerian writer Chinua Achebe, "dropped the tribute to Victorian England" (Achebe, "Named for Victoria" 33).

If, in the 1960s, a number of blacks, unlike playwright Adrienne Kennedy, dropped the tribute to Victorian England, in the 1980s white neoconservatives would pick it up as part of a backlash that ushered in massive political reversals for people of color. Thus during the 1980s, when, as poet, essayist, and journalist Kevin Powell put it, "Ronald Reagan then George Bush (the daddy, not the 'W') made things unsafe, spiritually, physically, psychologically, for the Negro everywhere" (1), Reagan's political counterpart in England, Margaret Thatcher, began, during an interview with British television journalist Brian Walden, to enlist the idea of Victorian values in her 1983 campaign for reelection.[1] In the United States, Thatcher's references to "Victorian" and "perennial" values would find their expression in the phrase "family values" and in, as cultural commentator Nelson George points out in *Post-Soul Nation* (2004), "conservative calls for a return to 'traditional values' (a phrase sure to worry any black person with a memory of America's racist traditions)" (13). Federal cuts in spending for domestic programs, attacks on civil rights legislation and affirmative action indicated that the government in its Victorianesque call for family values was no valuer of black families. As George remarks, "accelerated erosion of government protections and a growing civic insensitivity to poverty; the enforcement of rigid rules governing programs and government spending would replace treatment of social ills," signaling that the government had indeed "abandoned the struggle for equality for blacks" (14, 12). Although, as historian Robin D. G. Kelley reminds us in his foreword to Eric Mann's *Dispatches from Durban,* the 1980s also saw "movements that emerged in opposition [and] created real challenges for the Right," it remained a "period of tremendous right-wing drift, capital flight, monopolization, unemployment, decline of urban communities, and state terror" (xviii).

Although the neoconservative co-optation of Victorian values did not serve blacks well in the 1980s, by the 1990s, historian Gertrude Himmelfarb would, to her dismay, detect a new brand of Victorianism and a new breed of Victorians who seemed to serve blacks all too well. In what literary and cultural scholar Simon Joyce has described as a "tendentiously Thatcherite diatribe," Himmelfarb expressed her fear that Victorianism was going awry, that it had fallen into the wrong hands (5). Thus, according to Himmelfarb, the so-called "'New Victorians' . . . [were] a travesty of Victorianism," especially in their practice of a new "moralistic paternalism" that sought the "shift of responsibility from one individual to another" (260, 259, 262). So that, as she contends, "in cases of rape or racial disputes, the New Victorian almost invariably places the burden of guilt upon the 'privileged' or 'hegemonic' person—the man rather than the woman, the white rather than the black. . . . The individual thus functions not as an independent, responsible moral agent but as a surrogate for gender or race" (262). Clearly, Himmelfarb may be numbered among those "conservative behaviorists" whose "projects," according to black cultural critic Cornel West in *Race Matters* (1993), "rest largely upon a cultural revival of the Protestant [or Victorian work] ethic in black America" (11, 12). Like the behaviorists West describes, Himmelfarb believes that blacks should not refer to their victimization (West 14). She also, in keeping with the behaviorist's approach, is given to "talk[ing] about values and attitudes as if political and economic structures hardly exist . . . rarely, if ever, examin[ing] the innumerable cases in which black people do act on the Protestant ethic and still remain at the bottom of the social ladder"

(West 13). That which is egregiously new and disturbing for Himmelfarb is the blackening of Victorianism, which had evolved in such a way that blackness and femaleness had been put at its center. The New Victorians, she was convinced, were mounting a counterattack against the white male, misconstruing "Victorian virtues" for "modern values," and thereby contributing to the "demoralization of society."

More recently, black journalist Randall Robinson has also bemoaned the demoralization of society, or what he calls "the unremarked disintegration of American democracy" (73). More specifically, he characterizes America as hypocritical, materialistic, and callous, dismissive of "the cultural lifecraft of others" and incapable of providing "spiritual sustenance" (98, 23). Life for him as an African American has deteriorated to such a point that he has been forced, as with some of his Victorian Age forebears, to quit America, but not, as it were, for Britain. For, instead of wishing to reclaim, as Himmelfarb does, Victoria and the virtues of the age that bears her name, Robinson maintains that it is people like Queen Victoria who are the originators of the messes and crises that abound in the lives of many of the world's dark-skinned peoples. Robinson contends that "the tortured black and brown of the earth have Queen Victoria, the Spanish conquistador, King Leopold, and all the other white-skinned heirs to Columbus to thank for the bloody turmoil that is Kashmir, the unsolvable dilemma that is the Middle East, the suffering that is Haiti, the political instability that is Africa, the lethal poverty that is Latin America, and the sickness of splintered identity that is black America" (44). Because Queen Victoria heads this list of perpetrators, it is fair to assume that Robinson views Victoria and Victorian Britain as powerful agents in the disempowerment and disadvantaging of brown and black peoples.

Robinson's concern about an America that is becoming increasingly unlivable is anticipated in scholar Cornel West's identification of "the most basic issue now facing black America: *the nihilistic threat to its very existence*" (*Race Matters* 12). Like Robinson, West attributes a portion of this nihilistic threat not only to the juggernaut of American materialism and greed but also to the weakening, if not the absolute breakdown of those "cultural structures of meaning and feeling" that sustained black folk and enabled them to cast out "the demons of hopelessness, meaninglessness, and lovelessness" (15). Even though West does not denounce Queen Victoria as one of the conjurers of the demons that have beset blacks in America, he does not exactly discount the queen or the constellation of values and ideas that have been attached to her name. West's reference to the role of Victoria and Victorian ideas in the lives of black Americans, however, proves more nuanced. Thus, he recognizes, for example, the ways in which not only Victorian ideas but even Victorian dress empowered the great black thinker W. E. B. Du Bois, "dignify[ing] his sense of intellectual vocation," at the same time that he concedes how some of the ideas, values, and ethics that come out of Victorian Britain have militated against blacks in America (40). Thus, in commenting on white American "disgust" with black sexuality, West observes, "Victorian morality and racist perceptions die hard" (85).

Now in this, the first decade of the twenty-first century when events such as the September 11, 2001, terrorist attacks on the twin towers of New York's World Trade Center and the Pentagon in Washington, the wars in Afghanistan and Iraq, the extreme polarization of political parties, and the failure of President George W. Bush and his administration to respond with anything resembling a sense of urgency to the mainly poor black victims of hurricane Katrina, which devastated New Orleans in August 2005, herald exceptional tumult and upheaval, the relevance of the Victorians, who lived themselves in an age of turbulent change, abides. Given the fact that, as critic Mary A. Gervin reminds us, "the Victorian world was [itself] violently disruptive" and "divided sharply between two factions: the 'haves' and the 'have-nots,'" the new millennial upheavals only strengthen identification of the millennial present with the Victorian past (276). There is so little divarication that, as scholar J. O. Tate observes in a 1993 review of one of A. S. Byatt's neo-Victorian novels, "the spirit of Ruskin, the ghost of the younger Arnold, the shade of Dickens—these and many others hover about our heads when we think of the contradictions of capitalism, the disintegration of culture, and our responsibilities at home and abroad" (60). One critic, who also recognizes how events such as the terrorist attacks of September 11 "brought into popular consciousness the long—and largely Victorian—history of the 'great game' of empire," advises that "we may . . . begin to suspect how far we haven't come in one hundred years, that we appeal to Victorian culture in order to think about problems and needs that are not wholly unprecedented" (Krueger xi, xii). The Victorians have by no means been left behind.[2]

A growing chorus of cultural critics argue that the world can hardly divagate from, let alone dispense with, Victorian Britain. Thus, scholars John Kucich and Dianne F. Sadoff in *Victorian Afterlife* (2002) contend that the "explosion of postmodern Victoriana" coincides with what scholar Nancy Armstrong in her postscript to the volume calls "the Victorian boom in culture criticism." Postmodernism, which, the editors of *Victorian Afterlife* assert, "fetishizes notions of cultural emergence" has "identified the nineteenth century as a site of origin and rupture, a moment of emergence" (x, xv, xx, 312). In *Functions of Victorian Culture at the Present Time* (2002), editor Christina Krueger claims, "In our society at large Victorian culture has probably never been more popular and influential" (xiii). In the preface to yet another edition on both the recuperative value and, to borrow Peter Fryer's expression, the "staying power" of the Victorians, scholar Silvia Caporale-Bizzini declares in *We, the "Other Victorians"* (2003), "The end of the last century and the beginning of the new one have not brought with them a 'new' way of looking at the world; instead they have *re*interpreted [*sic*] and proposed the most conservative values of Victorianism" (14). Caporale-Bizzini goes on to explain how the volume she has edited "demonstrates how the heritage of Victorian thought is still alive" and furthermore shows "how we 'the other Victorians' have used" that thought "not only to forge hegemony, but also to construct counterhegemonic discourses and discourses of resistance" (16). Cultural critics such as Kucich and Sadoff, Krueger, and Caporale-Bizzini acknowledge the various ways in which Victorian culture continues to inform our world—our "ethics, politics, psychology, and art" (Krueger xi). The works of these critics indicate that in the twenty-first century, the heritage and the legacy of Victorian Britain remains essential and constitutive.

Victorian-infused politics, social policies, psychology, hegemony, and counterhegemony affect blacks, a historically devalued group living in a nation the anglophilia of which is largely predicated upon England and its Victorian era. As black cultural critic Michael Eric Dyson comments in his *Reader* (2004), England remains "a place America still cowers before intellectually" (507). The point to be made here is that England, especially the England of the Victorians—whether for good or for bad—still matters for black folk in America. Victorian England, its culture, and its values are contemporized in the lives of African Americans whether as contested family values or as an ethos of moral responsibility that places the burden of modern social ills on the white paternalistic structures that directly or indirectly engineered them. The struggle for blacks remains the very struggle black arts movement leader Addison Gayle, Jr., described when he admonished black folk, as African American Studies Professor Nathaniel Norment, Jr., restates it, not "to allow themselves to be degraded, dismissed, and devalued as black persons—shedding dignity and cultural identity in an effort to forge themselves into the round, gaping abyss of [an] Americanization" that is, I should add, the successor to British imperialism (372). Part of the continued efforts of blacks to fend off the forces of denigration will hinge on an understanding of the Victorian age—of how it is implicated in both hegemonic and counterhegemonic discourse and of how it may provide insight, for instance, into some of the persistent and negatively racialized ideas about black sexuality and black criminality. For, as cultural scholar Gary Day argues, "Victorian values have never ceased to be a shaping force throughout the twentieth century" because "Victorian values have never gone away; different ones have merely been emphasised [*sic*] at different times" (2). These values show no signs of waning in the twenty-first century.

For that matter, neither has the African American culture W. E. B. Dubois showcased alongside British Victorian culture in the last chapter of *The Souls of Black Folk* gone away. Even though the Victorians and their culture have remained a shifting and changing force in the lives of African Americans, African Americans have also been having their cultural say. In fact, certain aspects of African American culture have become as formidable a shaping force as that of Victorian Britain, especially among today's youth. Thus, in "Frontlines and Backyards," black British cultural critic Stuart Hall explains that "a distinctive feature of the new Black British identity is the extent to which it has been Americanized. Its ideal images, its stylistic reference are very powerfully Black American. Even though the style may have been indigenized, given a British home-grown stamp, all the leads come from Afro-America" (129). In a similar vein, black cultural journalist Greg Tate in *Everything but the Burden* (2003) notes, "The impact of African-American music and musical culture on white British and American notions of masculinity and style plays no small role in accounting for the largely white male and Japanese fandoms of jazz, blues, rock and roll, soul, funk, reggae, and now hip-hop" (9). Indeed as Tate goes on to comment, "the Black body, and subsequently Black culture, has become a hungered-after taboo item" not only "in the badlands of the American racial imagination" (4), but in Britain and, I daresay at the risk of making what Paul Gilroy calls one of those "easy claims of African American exceptionalism" (Gilroy 4), in the world. Still as widely influential as African American culture has become, its dissemination is problematic because it remains the culture of a people envied but reviled. The hungered-after taboo item is also, we are informed, a "nightmarish bugbear" (G. Tate 4). The story of the spread of African American culture, particularly African American popular culture, is the story, according to black historian Manning Marable, of cultural "'interaction without understanding" or semiacculturation. Marable writes, "With the legal desegregation of America's cultural and social institutions after the 1960s, white Americans absorbed critical elements of African-American music, dance, literature, language, and artistic expression. They accepted black participation in professional athletics, and extended acclaim to African-American film stars and entertainers. But their affinity and tolerance for blackness were almost always cultural and ethnic, rather than racial. Young whites have learned to mimic African-American music and singing styles, but they might vote against a black candidate for public office solely on racial grounds" (190).

What Marable does here is describe how, in effect, America has skinned, if not filleted African American culture and then, in the words of Tate, "sold [it] to the world as uniquely American in character" (3). African American culture today is commodified, exported, and consumed and in a way that Victorian culture never was. Be that as it may, the correspondence between Victorian Britain and African America remains viable; the two cultures are no more separate than they were a century ago. For, regardless of whether the culture and ideas associated with Victorian Britain and African America are pitted against one another as they have been since the 1980s or whether they are paired as they were by Du Bois at the turn of the twentieth century, the two still survive as "assemblages," to borrow Gilroy's expression, that continue to speak to each other and to resonate in the world (1). In doing so, Victorian Britain and African America continue to share a bond forged in the desires, efforts, and thoughts of individual British Victorians and African Americans who dreamed of a world that could be.

Notes

Introduction

1. For a discussion of the narrative's authorship see Robert Desrochers, Jr.'s "'Surprizing Deliverance'?: Slavery and Freedom, Language and Identity in the *Narrative* of Briton Hammon, 'A Negro Man.'" Desrochers, who also notes "the subtle transformation of Hammon into an Englishman with rights protected, at least aboard ship, by other 'true' Englishmen," remarks that "Hammon's tale captured the ultra-patriotic mood of the moment, evincing and encouraging a strong sense of English nationalism among whites and blacks" who did not allow slavery to "stop them from basking in the triumphant glory of being British, of being integral members of the most powerful empire in the world" (154, 165).

2. One could argue that the trip to London only served to further objectify Wheatley, making her even more of a curiosity back home. However, the fact that so many important Bostonians came out to officially authenticate her authorial claim—a practice that would become more common in the marketing of slave narratives—raises the stakes.

3. For studies of British and Europe's scientific racialization of the other, see George W. Stocking, Jr.'s *Victorian Anthropology* and Douglas A. Lorimer's "Nature, Racism, and Late Victorian Science."

For a discussion of Victorian travelers' confused use of the terms "English" and "British," see chapter 6 of Majorie Morgan's *National Identities and Travel in Victorian Britain*, "The Discourse of National Identity among Victorian Travellers," 195–216.

4. The act of writing is, intrinsically speaking, itself a voyage. One begins with a pencil in hand that traces the paper, one pauses to rest and to reflect, one begins again, one stops one more time, always with pen in hand, as if completing the various stages of some peregrination which, like writing, involves moving from A to go toward Z, crossing different letters of an alphabet simultaneously real and imaginary, zigzagging across them, making great detours, or taking short cuts . . . [my translation].

Chapter 1: On Coming to America

1. In the introduction to Charles Dickens's *American Notes,* Whitley and Goldman note that "during the period 1815–60 there were over 200 such books [accounts of travels across the Atlantic] and they were very popular" (11).

See Rapson's *Britons View America,* which reports that "by 1870 American shores swarmed with Britons who came to hunt, to fish, or, most commonly, simply to see sights. Individuals still came on special journalistic, agricultural, diplomatic, labor, and government missions, and many eminent personalities readily accepted lucrative offers to lecture . . . But tourism replaced all these as the leading motivation for the British to venture into the wilds of the New World" (26).

See also Dorothy Middleton's *Victorian Lady Travellers.* In the first chapter of her book, Middleton, who is interested in characterizing the women who '[f]rom about 1870 onwards . . . took journeys to remote and savage countries," remarks that "Fundamentally . . . the strongest impetus was the growing desire of the nineteenth-century woman for independence and opportunity, a desire which crystallized in the great movements for women's emancipation and the fight for women's suffrage" (3, 7).

2. The safety Cunard Lines worked to secure did not extend to protection from racial harassment as Frederick Douglass learned. See the letter he wrote to the London *Times* on April 6, 1847, protesting racist treatment and the response of an American agent for Cunard, Charles M. Burrop of Virginia. A portion of Burrop's response, which appeared in the *Times* on April 13, 1847, follows:

> When the sight and smell of the majority of your countrymen are so much altered as that their noses agreeably imbibe the odour of a Negro, we shall gladly welcome the change. Until then we are compelled by our own interest as a commercial company to place upon the issue of tickets to blacks such restrictions and conditions as were specifically stated to Mr. Douglass.

3. For telling nineteenth-century European commentary upon the Native American, the African American, and their relation to each other see chapter 6, "Black and Red Americans," in William J. Baker's *America Perceived* (107–37).

4. This change in the British attitude about race relations is also apparent in Dickens, who also visited the United States again some twenty-five years after his 1842 reading tour.

5. See Deborah Thomas's discussion of Thackeray and slaves in the United States (116–21).

6. See Simon Gikandi's "The Embarrassment of Victorianism: Colonial Subjects and the Lure of Englishness" (157–85) in Kucich and Sadoff's *Victorian Afterlife.* Gikandi provides an excellent examination of how colonial subjects such as C. L. R. James and Alexander Crummell "had been working hard to transform colonial Victorianism into a discourse of their own liberation from imperialism" (168).

7. For a discussion of black ancestry in the Barrett and Browning families, see Julia Markus's *Dared and Done,* 106, 112, 335, 348n. See also W. E. B. Du Bois's reference to Robert Browning as a "colored" poet in his *Autobiography* (155) and in *Dusk of Dawn* (27). See also *No Green Pastures* in which, Roi Ottley comments, "The fact that Robert

Browning's grandmother was a Creole from the West Indies was never considered to distract from the poet's standing, even though his father's skin was so dark that the beadle of a St. Kitts church ousted him from a seat among white people and ordered him to sit with Negroes" (19).

8. The title of Bay's book is *The White Image in the Black Mind: African-American Ideas about White People, 1830–1925.*

Chapter 2: Hail Britannia

1. For more on Washington's second trip overseas, see Booker T. Washington, *The Man Farthest Down: A Record of Observations and Study in Europe* (1911, 1912; (New Brunswick: Transaction Books, 1984).

2. I am here indebted to Paul Gilroy for whom the words "roots" and "routes" are a major trope in his book, *Black Atlantic.*

3. See also Mary G. Mason's essay on the metaphor and the reality of travel in African American women's autobiography from 1850 to 1972.

4. I have culled most of these names from Benjamin Quarles's useful study of black abolitionists. I am greatly indebted to this excellent work.

5. I am indebted to my colleague David Gellman for helping me pinpoint the time that the antislavery movement in the United States may be said to have ended.

6. For a fuller treatment of Douglass, the rising tide of British racial prejudice, and the role of minstrel troupes, see R. J. M. Blackett's "Cracks in the Antislavery Wall: Frederick Douglass's Second Visit to England (1859–1860) and the Coming of the Civil War," in *Liberating Sojourn: Frederick Douglass and Transatlantic Reform.* Ed. Alan J. Rice and Martin Crawford.

7. Crummell did finally go back to the United States to live, visiting England once more in 1897.

8. According to biographers Herbert Marshall and Mildred Stock, "the exact date of Aldridge's arrival in England is not known. The year 1825 appears to be generally accepted, but the evidence points to 1824, when he was seventeen years old" (48).

9. I would like to thank Mrs. Irene Ferguson, assistant to university archivist at Edinburgh for locating the entry identifying Dickerson's age and date of matriculation at the university. Ferguson did not find Dickerson in the graduate listing.

10. Douglass broke away from the Garrisonians who believed that abolitionists should not resort to or consider political action to promote abolition and that the constitution was a proslavery document.

Chapter 3: Thomas Carlyle

1. Although Ripley tempered his second letter to Carlyle and, as Slater suggests, ultimately cooled in his worship of Carlyle, Ripley's first letter practically gushes with a devotion that "embarrassed" Carlyle. Ripley declared, "I cannot address you as a stranger for the revelations of your mind have long been to me a source of the highest inspiration and joy. I have communed with your spirit in the utterance of its deep wisdom, and when I have felt the significance of your mystic sayings, my heart has leaped up with the

response, 'This unknown Being is my Brother.' The sentiment of reverence and awe has filled my soul when Idea after Idea from the Primal Fountain of Truth has flashed upon me from your kindling page, and I have felt that I would traverse forests and cross the ocean to express my gratitude to such a gifted Teacher of Humanity" (Slater, "George Ripley" 342).

2. Later, when Carlyle attacked America in *Latter-Day Pamphlets* and "Shooting Niagara," some of these American disciples would feel, according to Slater, "betrayed." Carlyle reports that one American man who visited Chelsea was "shocked by . . . [, among other things, Carlyle's] views upon the Nigger Question." Another held Carlyle accountable for the atrocities typical of a system that condoned the brutal whipping of a young slave woman for refusing to have sexual relations with her old master. As far as this young man, who Slater identifies as D. A. Wasson, was concerned, Carlyle did not understand America or its slavery: "Your eyes, though of wondrous efficacy in their way, blink in our atmosphere like those of an owl in broad sunlight; and if you come flying here, it is the privilege of the smallest birds—of which you are quite at liberty to esteem me one—to pester you back into your mediaeval twilight" (Slater, *Correspondence* 47, 49).

3. Although, as Edward Spivey asserts, it may well be that Carlyle's 1833 essay on Diderot became the occasion for "Mill's first open acknowledgement of dissent from Carlyle's views" (60), the earliest public, that is, published, indicator of troubled, if not beleaguered relations was Mill's publication in *Fraser's Magazine* in 1850 of "On the Negro Question" as a response to Carlyle's 1849 essay in *Fraser's* on the Negro question.

4. Carlyle's essay on the Negro question was printed in December 1849. Mill got his essay to *Fraser's* quickly enough for it to appear in the January 1850 issue (the next one).

5. While attending a conference on "The Carlyles in Scotland and Europe" in Edinburgh in April 2001, I was hard pressed to discover in that city materials documenting the presence of blacks in Scotland. Some of the individuals overseeing the exhibit I visited actually believed that blacks did not enter Scotland until after World War II. Such was not the case, as there exists research that places Africans in Scotland as early as the sixteenth century (see Mary E. Robbins, "Black Africans at the Court of James IV," in *Review of Scottish Culture* 12, ed. Alexander Fenton with Hugh Cheaps and Rosalind K. Marshall [Edinburgh: Tuckwell, 1999] 34–45). I also located a Scottish portrait (*Arab Princess* [with black maid], fl. 1628, wife of Sir John Henderson of Fordell by Walter Frier after an unknown artist, Scottish National Portrait Gallery, Edinburgh. Canvas 66 _ 123.2 cm, 1731) that includes a black female, featured as prominently in the painting as her Scots mistress. My happiest find was the brochure for an exhibition that had been mounted at the City Art Centre in Edinburgh May 24–July 12, 1997, called "Roots: The African Inheritance in Scotland."

6. Campbell tries to understand and contextualize, if not humanize Carlyle's Victorian brand of racism. Biographer Fred Kaplan denies Carlyle's racism: "His position [on blacks and the Governor Eyre incident] was based," Kaplan argues, "neither on personal cruelty nor on virulent racial prejudice. That blacks were innately inferior to whites seemed to him probable but irrelevant . . ." (489).

7. For a fuller treatment of the relation between Carlylean and black expressionism, see Vanessa D. Dickerson's "Performing Blackness: Carlyle and 'The Nigger Question.'" *The Carlyles at Home and Abroad*. Ed. David Sorenson and Roger Thorr. Hampshire, England: Ashgate, 2004. 151–58.

Chapter 4: W. E. B. Du Bois and the Victorian Soul of Black Folk

1. See Hazel Carby's *Race Men* in which she refers to Du Bois's *The Souls of Black Folk* as a possibly "performative text" (89). More specifically, Carby contends that in *Souls,* which is "unquestionably structured through a pattern of call and response . . . Du Bois does adopt and adapt the pattern of black sermonic performance" (90). In *To Wake the Nations,* Eric Sundquist, who is less comfortable identifying Du Bois's rhetorical style too closely with that of "the cadences of the black preacher," concedes that "if black religion did not provide him a language . . . it did provide the central matrix of his reconstruction of African American culture' (458–59).

2. Sundquist describes *Souls* as "a text of many dimensions—a first-rate, if unorthodox, history of post–Civil War race relations in the South; a trenchant essay in sociological and economic analysis; a brief for black education; and a study in comparative European American and African American cultures" (458).

3. The princess Kautilya also temporarily relinquishes her royal status to become a worker and thus come more meaningfully into contact with the masses Matthew and she would uplift.

4. His life having spanned nearly a century, "Du Bois's shifts, changes and intellectual permutations" were quite understandably the mark of growth and development that led him to become "linked up with the Communist Leftwing," which, in Cruse's opinion propounded a philosophy and had an influence "which added nothing to *his* historical stature—but abused and disoriented the thinking of countless other Negroes whose potential for positive achievements in society, were negated by the intrusion of Communist machinations" (Harold Cruse, *The Crises of the Negro Intellectual: A Historical Analysis of the Failure of Black Leadership* [New York: Quill, 1984] 334, 325).

5. This report about Queen Victoria's African ancestry is based on the authority of one Mario de Valdes y Cocom who asserts that "Queen Elizabeth II once startled a Commonwealth audience by alluding to her African (and India) forebears" (Ward, *Dark Midnight When I Rise* 443 n. 41).

6. With the exception of "I Hope My Mother Will Be There in that Beautiful World on High," all the lyrics to the sorrow songs listed are taken from J. B. T. Marsh's *The Story of the Jubilee Singers; with Their Songs,* rev. ed. (Boston: Houghton, Osgood, and Co., 1880). Lyrics to "I Hope My Mother Will Be There" are taken from M. F. Armstrong's and Helen W. Ludlow's *Hampton and Its Students: With Fifty Cabin and Plantation Songs Arranged by Thomas P. Fenner* (New York: G. P. Putnam's Sons, 1875).

Conclusion

1. It was actually Brian Walden who steered Thatcher toward the notion of Victorian values as the following excerpt for the interview makes clear:

> Walden: . . . Now obviously Britain is a very different country from the one it was in Victorian times when there was great poverty, great wealth, etc., but you've really outlined an approval of what I would call Victorian values. The sort of values, if you like, that helped to build the country throughout the 19th Century. Now is that right?

Thatcher: Oh exactly. Very much so. Those were the values when our country became great, but not only did our country become great internationally, also so much advance was made in this country. Colossal advance . . .

For further discussion of Margaret Thatcher's efforts to transform Victorian values "into a talisman for lost stabilities" see Raphael Samuel's "Mrs. Thatcher's Return to Victorian Values" in T. C. Smout's *Victorian Values: A Joint Symposium of the Royal Society of Edinburgh and the British Academy December 1990* (9–29). See also Simon Joyce's "The Victorians in the Rear View Mirror" (3–17) in Christine L. Krueger's *Functions of Victorian Culture at the Present Time* and Gary Day's mention of Thatcher and Victorian values in the introduction to *Varieties of Victorianism: The Uses of a Past* (1–2).

2. The expression "left behind" echoes George W. Bush's 2002 pledge to leave no child behind in the U.S. education system. It also echoes the apocalyptic *Left Behind* book series launched by writers Tim LaHaye and Jerry Jenkins.

Works Cited

Achebe, Chinua. "Colonialist Criticism." *Hopes and Impediments: Selected Essays.* New York: Anchor/Doubleday, 1989. 68–90.

———. "Named For Victoria, Queen of England." *Hopes and Impediments: Selected Essays.* New York: Anchor/Doubleday, 1989. 30–39.

Ackroyd, Peter. *Dickens.* New York: HarperCollins, 1991.

Adrian, Arthur A. "Dickens on American Slavery: A Carlylean Slant." *PMLA* 67.4 (June 1952): 315–29.

Andrews, William L. "William Wells Brown." *The Oxford Companion to African American Literature.* Ed. William L. Andrews, Frances Smith Forster, and Trudier Harris. New York: Oxford University Press, 1997. 106–7.

Angelou, Maya. *I Know Why the Caged Bird Sings.* 1969. New York: Bantam, 1971.

Anim-Addo, Joan. "Queen Victoria's Black 'Daughter.'" *Black Victorians/Black Victoriana.* Ed. Gretchen Holbrook Gerzina. New Brunswick, N.J.: Rutgers University Press, 2003. 11–19.

Armstrong, M. F., and Helen W. Ludlow. *Hampton and Its Students: With Fifty Cabin and Plantation Songs Arranged by Thomas P. Fenner.* New York: G. P. Putnam, 1875.

Arnold, Matthew. *Poetry and Criticism of Matthew Arnold.* Ed. A. Dwight Culler. Boston: Houghton Mifflin, 1961.

Aytoun, W. E. "The Scottish Universities." *Blackwood's Edinburgh Magazine* 83 (January 1858): 74–93.

Baker, William J. ed. *America Perceived: A View from Abroad in the 19th Century.* West Haven, Conn.: Pendulum, 1974.

Bay, Mia. *The White Image in the Black Mind: African-American Ideas about White People, 1830–1925.* New York and Oxford: Oxford University Press, 2000.

Bhabha, Homi. "Signs Taken for Wonders." *The Post Colonial Studies Reader.* Ed. Bill Ashcroft, Gareth Griffiths, and Helen Tiffin. London: Routledge, 1995. 29–35.

Blackburn, Robin. *The Overthrow of Colonial Slavery, 1776–1848.* London: Verso, 1988.

Blackett, R. J. M. *Beating Against the Barriers: The Lives of Six Nineteenth-Century Afro-Americans.* Ithaca, N.Y.: Cornell University Press, 1989.

———. *Building an Antislavery Wall: Black Americans in the Atlantic Abolitionist Movement, 1830–1862.* Ithaca, N.Y.: Cornell University Press, 1989.

Blassingame, John W., ed. *The Frederick Douglass Papers: Series One: Speeches, Debates, and Interviews: Volume 3: 1855–63.* New Haven, Conn.: Yale University Press, 1985.

Blassingame, John W., and John R. McKivigan, eds. *The Frederick Douglass Papers: Series One: Speeches, Debates, and Interviews: Volume 4: 1864–80.* New Haven, Conn.: Yale University Press, 1991.

Bolt, Christine. *Victorian Attitudes to Race.* London: Routledge and Kegan Paul, 1971.

Boyce, D. G. *The Irish Question and British Politics, 1868–1986.* New York: St. Martin's, 1988.

Boyd, Herb, ed. *The Autobiography of a People: Three Centuries of African American History Told by Those Who Lived It.* New York: Doubleday, 2000.

Brantlinger, Patrick. *The Spirit of Reform: British Literature and Politics, 1832–1867.* Cambridge, Mass.: Harvard University Press, 1977.

———. "Victorians and Africans." *"Race," Writing, and Difference.* Ed. Henry Louis Gates, Jr. Chicago: University of Chicago Press, 1985. 185–222.

Brebner, John Bartlet. *North Atlantic Triangle: The Interplay of Canada, The United States and Great Britain.* New Haven, Conn.: Yale University Press, 1945.

Brown, John. *Slave Life in Georgia: A Narrative of the Life, Sufferings, and Escape of John Brown, A Fugitive Slave, Now in England.* Ed. L. A. Chamerówzow. London: n.p., 1855.

Brown, Josephine. *Biography of an American Bondman* in *Two Biographies by African-American Women.* New York: Oxford University Press, 1991. 5–104.

Brown, William Wells. *The Travels of William Wells Brown, Including "Narrative of William Wells Brown, A Fugitive Slave" and "The American Fugitive in Europe. Sketches of Places and People Abroad."* Ed. Paul Jefferson. New York: Markus Wiener, 1991.

Browning, Elizabeth Barrett. "A Romance of the Ganges." *The Poetical Works of Elizabeth Barrett Browning.* Cambridge ed. Boston: Houghton Mifflin, 1974. 29–31.

———. "The Runaway Slave at Pilgrim's Point." *Victorian Women Poets: An Anthology.* Ed. Angela Leighton and Margaret Reynolds. Oxford: Blackwell, 1995. 80–88.

———. "A Vision of Poets." *The Poetical Works of Elizabeth Barrett Browning.* Cambridge ed. Boston: Houghton Mifflin, 1974. 127–40.

Butler, Judith. "Critically Queer." *Literary Theories: A Reader and Guide.* Ed. Julian Wolfreys. New York: New York University Press, 1999.

Byron, George, Lord. "Childe Harold's Pilgrimage." *The Complete Poetical Works of Lord Byron.* Ed. Paul Elmer More. Boston: Houghton Mifflin, 1905. 1–83.

Caesar, Terry. *Forgiving the Boundaries: Home as Abroad in American Travel Writing.* Athens: University of Georgia Press, 1995.

Campbell, Ian. "Carlyle and the Negro Question Again." *Criticism: A Quarterly for Literature and the Arts* 13.3 (Summer 1971): 279–90.

Caporale-Bizzini, Silvia, ed. *We, The "Other Victorians": Considering the Heritage of 19th-Century Thought.* Alicante, Spain: Universidad de Alicante, 2003.

Carby, Hazel. *Race Men.* Cambridge, Mass.: Harvard University Press, 1998.

Carlyle, Thomas. *Reminiscences.* Ed. C. E. North. London: n.p., 1932, 1972.

———. *Reminiscences.* Ed. K. J. Fielding and Ian Campbell. Oxford: Oxford University Press, 1997.

———. *Reminiscences of My Irish Journey in 1849.* New York: Harper and Bros. 1882.

———. *The Works of Thomas Carlyle in Thirty Volumes.* Rpt. Centenary Edition. Ed. H. D. Traill. New York: AMS, 1969. [Identified in the text as *CW*].

Carlyle, Thomas, and Jane Welsh Carlyle. *The Collected Letters of Thomas and Jane Welsh Carlyle.* Vols. 3, 28. Ed. Charles Richard Sanders et al. Durham, N.C.: Duke University Press, 1970–2000. [Identified in text as *CL*].

Carnegie, Andrew. "As Others See Us." *The Fortnightly Review* 31.182 (February 1, 1882): 157–65.

Clark, Thomas D. "Travel Accounts." *Dictionary of Afro American Slavery.* Ed. Randall M. Miller and John David Smith. Westport, Conn.: Praeger, 1997. 734–41.

Coben, Stanley. *Rebellion Against Victorianism: The Impetus for Cultural Change in 1920s America.* New York: Oxford University Press, 1991.

Combe, George. *Notes on the United States of North America during a Phrenological Visit in 1839-9-40.* 2 vols. New York: Arno, 1974.

Craton, Michael. *Sinews of Empire: A Short History of British Slavery.* Garden City, N.Y.: Anchor/Doubleday, 1974.

———. *Testing the Chains: Resistance to Slavery in the British West Indies.* Ithaca, N.Y.: Cornell University Press, 1982.

Crummell, Alexander. *Destiny and Race: Selected Writings, 1840–1898.* Ed. Wilson Jeremiah Moses. Amherst: University of Massachusetts Press, 1992.

———. "Our National Mistakes and the Remedy for Them." *Africa and America: Addresses and Discourses.* 1891. New York: Negro Universities Press, 1969. 165–98.

Curtis, Jr., L. Perry. *Apes and Angels: The Irishman in Victorian Caricature.* Rev. ed. Washington, D.C.: Smithsonian Institution Press, 1997.

Davis, Charles T., and Henry Louis Gates, Jr. *The Slave's Narrative.* Oxford: Oxford University Press, 1985.

Davis, David Brion. *Slavery and Human Progress.* New York: Oxford University Press, 1984.

Day, Gary. Introduction: Past and Present—the Case of Samuel Smiles' *Self Help. Varieties of Victorianism: The Uses of a Past.* Ed. Gary Day. London: Macmillan, 1998. 1–24.

Delany, Martin Robison. *The Condition, Elevation, Emigration, and Destiny of the Colored People of the United States.* 1852. New York: Arno Press and New York Times, 1969.

Desrochers, Jr., Robert. "'Surprizing Deliverance'?: Slavery and Freedom, Language and Identity in the *Narrative* of Briton Hammon, 'A Negro Man.'" *Genius in Bondage: Literature of the Early Black Atlantic.* Ed. Vincent Carretta and Philip Gould. Lexington: University Press of Kentucky, 2001. 153–74.

Dickens, Charles. *American Notes for General Circulation.* Ed. John S. Whitley and Arnold Goldman. New York: Penguin, 1972.

Dorr, David F. *A Colored Man Round the World.* Ed. Malini Johar Schueller. Ann Arbor: University of Michigan Press, 1999.

Douglas, Ann. *The Feminization of American Culture.* New York: Avon, 1977.

Douglass, Frederick. Address Delivered by Frederick Douglass at the Third Annual Fair of the Tennessee Colored Agricultural and Mechanical Association on Thursday, September 18, 1873, at Nashville, Tennessee. *The Frederick Douglass Papers.* Library of Congress. Reel 14 of 34.

———. *My Bondage and My Freedom.* 1855. Ed. William L. Andrews. Urbana and Chicago: University of Illinois Press, 1987.

———. *Narrative of the Life of Fredrick Douglass: An American Slave. Written by Himself.* Ed. David W. Blight. Boston: Bedford/St. Martin's, 1993.

———. The Papers of Frederick Douglass. Library of Congress. Reel 13. Travel. Folder 29.

Du Bois, William Edward Burghardt. *Against Racism: Unpublished Essays, Papers, Addresses, 1887–1961.* Ed. Herbert Aptheker. Amherst: University of Massachusetts Press, 1985.

———. *The Autobiography of W. E. B. Du Bois: A Soliloquy on Viewing My Life from the Last Decade of Its First Century.* n.p.: International Publishers, 1968.

———. "Behold the Land." *W. E. B. Du Bois: A Reader.* Ed. Andrew Paschal. New York: Macmillan, 1971. 361–67.

———. *Black Reconstruction in America, 1860–1880.* 1935. New York: Atheneum, 1992.

———. *Dark Princess: A Romance.* 1928. Jackson, Miss.: Banner Books, 1995.

———. *Darkwater: Voices from Within the Veil.* New York: AMS Press, 1969.

———. *Dusk of Dawn: An Essay Toward an Autobiography of a Race Concept.* New York: Harcourt, Brace, and Co., 1940.

———. *The Souls of Black Folk.* 1903. New York: Vintage/Random, 1990.

Dyson, Michael Eric. *The Michael Eric Dyson Reader.* New York: Basic Civitas Books, 2004.

Edwards, Brent Hayes. *The Practice of Diaspora: Literature, Translation, and the Rise of Black Internationalism.* Cambridge: Harvard University Press, 2003.

Eliot, George. "Thomas Carlyle." *Selected Essays, Poems and Other Writings.* Ed. A. S. Byatt and Nicholas Warren. London: Penguin, 1990. 343–48.

Epstein, Dena J. *Sinful Tunes and Spirituals: Black Folk Music to the Civil War.* Urbana: University of Illinois Press, 1977.

Ernest, John. "Economies of Identity: Harriet E. Wilson's *Our Nig.*" *PMLA* 109.3 (May 1994): 424–38.

Fedric, Francis. *Life and Sufferings of Francis Fedric; While in Slavery, An Escaped Slave After Fifty Years of Bondage.* Birmingham, Ala.: Thomas and Jones, 1859.

Fenton, Steve. *Ethnicity: Race, Class and Culture.* Lanham, Md.: Rowman and Littlefield, 1999.

Fisch, Audrey A. *American Slaves in Victorian England: Abolitionist Politics in Popular Literature and Culture.* Cambridge: Cambridge University Press, 2000.

FitzGerald, Edward, trans. *The Rubáiyát of Omar Khayyám.* New York: Collier, 1962.

Foner, Philip S. *The Life and Writings of Frederick Douglass: Volume I: Early Years, 1817–1849.* New York: International Publishers, 1950.

———. *The Life and Writings of Frederick Douglass: Volume IV: Reconstruction and After.* New York: International Publishers, 1955.

Fryer, Peter. *Staying Power: The History of Black People in Britain.* London: Pluto, 1984.

Fussell, Paul. *Abroad: British Literary Travellers Between the Wars.* Oxford: Oxford University Press, 1980.

Gates, Jr., Henry Louis. *Figures in Black: Words, Signs, and the "Racial" Self.* New York: Oxford University Press, 1987.

———. *The Trials of Phillis Wheatley: America's First Black Poet and Her Encounters with the Founding Fathers.* New York: Basic Civitas Books, 2003.

Gates, Jr., Henry Louis, and Cornel West. *The Future of the Race.* New York: Alfred A. Knopf, 1996.

George, Nelson. *Post-Soul Nation: The Explosive, Contradictory, Triumphant, and Tragic 1980s as Experienced by African Americans (Previously Known as Blacks and Before that Negroes).* New York: Viking, 2004.

Gervin, Mary A. "The Monodrama *Maud:* Tennyson's Little *Hamlet.*" *CLA Journal* 48.3 (March 2005): 274–89.

Gerzina, Gretchen Holbrook, ed. *Black Victorians/Black Victoriana.* New Brunswick, N.J.: Rutgers University Press, 2003.

Gikandi, Simon. "The Embarrassment of Victorianism: Colonial Subjects and the Lure of Englishness." *Victorian Afterlife: Postmodern Culture Rewrites the Nineteenth Century.* Ed. John Kucich and Dianne F. Sadoff. Minneapolis, Minn.: University of Minnesota Press, 2000. 157–85.

Gilroy, Paul. *The Black Atlantic: Modernity and Double Consciousness.* Cambridge, Mass.: Harvard University Press, 1993.

Glendinning, Victoria. *Anthony Trollope.* New York: Penguin, 1992.

Gohdes, Clarence. *American Literature in Nineteenth Century England.* Carbondale: Southern Illinois University Press, 1944.

Goldberg, Michael. *Carlyle and Dickens.* Athens: University of Georgia Press, 1972.

Green, Jeffrey. "Thomas Lewis Johnson (1836–1921): The Bournemouth Evangelist." *Under the Imperial Carpet: Essays in Black History, 1780–1950.* Ed. Rainer Lotz and Ian Pegg. Crawley, U.K.: Rabbit P. 1986. 55–68.

Gruesser, John. "Travel Writing." *The Oxford Companion to African American Literature.* Ed. William L. Andrews, Frances Smith Foster, and Trudier Harris. New York: Oxford University Press, 1997. 735–36.

Hall, Catherine. "The Economy of Intellectual Prestige: Thomas Carlyle, John Stuart Mill, and the Case of Governor Eyre." *Cultural Critique* 12 (1989): 167–96.

Hall, Stuart. "Frontlines and Backyards." *Black British Culture and Society: A Text Reader.* Ed. Kwesi Owusu. London: Routledge, 2000. 127–29.

Hammon, Briton. *Narrative of the Uncommon Sufferings, and Surprising Deliverance of Briton Hammon, a Negro Man. The Norton Anthology of American Literature.* Shorter Edition. Ed. Nina Baym. New York: Norton, 2003. 420–24.

Harrison, Frederic. "A Few Words about the Nineteenth Century." *The Fortnightly Review* 31 (April 1, 1882): 411–26.

Heffer, Simon. *Moral Desperado: A Life of Thomas Carlyle.* London: Weidenfeld and Nicolson, 1995.

Himmelfarb, Gertrude. *The De-Moralization of Society: From Victorian Virtues to Modern Values.* New York: Alfred A. Knopf, 1995.

Howard-Pitney, David. *The Afro-American Jeremiad: Appeals for Justice in America.* Philadelphia: Temple University Press, 1990.

Howe, Daniel Walker, ed. *Victorian America.* Philadelphia: University of Pennsylvania Press, 1976.

Huggins, Nathan Irvin. *Harlem Renaissance.* New York: Oxford University Press, 1971.

Hurston, Zora Neale. *The Sanctified Church.* Berkeley, Calif.: Turtle Island, 1981.

Hyam, Ronald. *Britain's Imperial Century, 1815–1914: A Study of Empire and Expansion.* 2nd ed. Lanham, Md.: Barnes and Noble, 1993.

Ignatiev, Noel. *How the Irish Became White.* New York: Routledge, 1995.

Jacobs, Harriet. *Incidents in the Life of a Slave Girl, Written by Herself.* 1861. Ed. Jean Fagan Yellin. Cambridge, Mass.: Harvard University Press, 1987.

James, C. L. R. *Beyond a Boundary.* 1963. London: Serpent's Tail, 1994.

Jones, Arthur C. "Upon This Rock: The Foundational Influence of the Spirituals." *The Triumph of the Soul: Cultural and Psychological Aspects of African American Music.* Westport, Conn.: Praeger, 2001.

Jones, Iva G. "Trollope, Carlyle, and Mill on the Negro: An Episode in the History of Ideas." *The Journal of Negro History* 52.3 (July 1967): 185–99.

Jordan, John O. "Dickens and Diaspora." *Dickens, Europe and the New Worlds.* Ed. Anny Sadrin. London: Macmillan, 1999. 239–50.

Joyce, Simon. "The Victorians in the Rearview Mirror." *Functions of Victorian Culture at the Present Time.* Ed. Christine L. Krueger. Athens: Ohio University Press, 2002. 3–17.

Kaplan, Fred. *Thomas Carlyle: a Biography.* Ithaca, N.Y.: Cornell University Press, 1983.

Kelley, Robin D. G. Foreword. *Dispatches from Durban: Firsthand Commentaries on the World Conference against Racism and Post–September 11 Movement Strategies.* By Eric Mann. Los Angeles: Frontlines Press, 2002.

Kemble, Frances Anne. *Journal of a Residence on a Georgian Plantation in 1838–1839.* Chicago: Afro-Am Press, 1969.

Kendrick, Robert. "Re-membering America: Phillis Wheatley's Intertextual Epic." *African American Review* 30.1 (Spring 1996): 71–91.

Kennedy, Adrienne. *In One Act.* Minneapolis: University of Minnesota Press, 1988.

———. *People Who Led to My Plays.* New York: Theatre Communications Group, 1987.

King, Lovalerie. "Adrienne Kennedy." *The Oxford Companion to African American Literature.* Ed. William L. Andrews, Frances Smith Foster, and Trudier Harris. New York: Oxford University Press, 1997. 418–19.

Kipling, Rudyard. *American Notes.* Boston: Brown and Co., 1899.

Krueger, Christine L., ed. *Functions of Victorian Culture at the Present Time.* Athens: Ohio University Press, 2002.

Kucich, John, and Dianne F. Sadoff, eds. *Victorian Afterlife: Postmodern Culture Rewrites the Nineteenth Century.* Minneapolis: University of Minnesota Press, 2000.

Landow, George P. *Elegant Jeremiahs: The Sage from Carlyle to Mailer.* Ithaca, N.Y.: Cornell, 1986.

Lewis, David Levering. *W. E. B. Du Bois: Biography of a Race, 1868–1919.* New York: Henry Holt, 1993.

———, ed. *W. E. B. Du Bois: A Reader.* New York: Henry Holt, 1995.

Loggins, Vernon. *The Negro Author: His Development in America to 1900.* Port Washington, N.Y.: Kennikat, 1931.

Lorimer, Douglas A. *Colour, Class and the Victorians: English Attitudes to the Negro in the Mid-Nineteenth Century.* Leicester, U.K.: Leicester University Press, 1978.

———. "Nature, Racism, and Late Victorian Science." *Canadian Journal of History* 25.3 (December 1990): 369–86.

Lotz, Rainer, and Ian Pegg, eds. Introduction. *Under the Imperial Carpet: Essays in Black History, 1780–1950.* Crawley, U.K.: Rabbit Press, 1986. 1–13.

Lovell, Jr., John. *Black Song: The Forge and the Flame: The Story of How the Afro-American Spiritual Was Hammered Out.* New York: Macmillan, 1972.

Lowell, James Russell. "The Present Crisis." *The Complete Poetical Works of James Russell Lowell.* Cambridge ed. Ed. Horace E. Scudder. Boston: Houghton Mifflin, 1925. 67–68.

Mackay, Charles. "The Negro and the Negrophilists." *Blackwood's Edinburgh Review* 99 (May 1866): 581–97.

Marable, Manning. *Race, Reform, and Rebellion: The Second Reconstruction in Black America, 1945–1990.* 2nd ed. Jackson: University Press of Mississippi, 1991.

Markus, Julia. *Dared and Done: The Marriage of Elizabeth Barrett and Robert Browning.* New York: Alfred A. Knopf, 1995.

Marryat, Frederick. *A Diary in America with Remarks on Its Institutions.* Ed. Sydney Jackman. New York: Alfred A. Knopf, 1962.

Marsh, J. B. T. *The Story of the Jubilee Singers with Their Songs.* Rev. ed. Boston: Houghton, Osgood, and Co., 1880.

Marshall, Herbert, and Mildred Stock. *Ira Aldridge: The Negro Tragedian.* 1958. Washington, D.C.: Howard University Press, 1993.

Martin, Jr., Waldo E. *The Mind of Frederick Douglass.* Chapel Hill: University of North Carolina Press, 1984.

Martineau, Harriet. *Retrospect of Western Travel.* 2 vols. London: Saunders and Otley, 1838.

Mason, Mary G. "Travel as Metaphor and Reality in Afro American Women's Autobiography, 1850–1972." *Black American Literature Forum* 24.2 (Summer 1990): 337–56.

Masson, David. Unsigned Review of *Latter-Day Pamphlets,* ed. Thomas Carlyle. *North British Review* 27 (November 1850): 1–22.

McFeely, William S. "Visible Man: Douglass for the 1990s." *Liberating Sojourn: Frederick Douglass and Transatlantic Reform.* Ed. Alan J. Rice and Martin Crawford. Athens: University of Georgia Press, 1999. 15–27.

McSweeney, Kerry, and Peter Sabor, eds. *Sartor Resartus* by Thomas Carlyle. New York: Oxford University Press, 1987.

Meer, Sarah. "Competing Representations: Douglass, the Ethiopian Serenaders, and Ethnic Exhibition in London." *Liberating Sojourn: Frederick Douglass and Transatlantic Reform.* Ed. Alan J. Rice and Martin Crawford. Athens: University of Georgia Press, 1999. 141–65.

Middleton, Dorothy. *Victorian Lady Travellers.* Chicago: Academy Chicago, 1965.

Mill, John Stuart. "The Negro Question." *Thomas Carlyle, The Nigger Question; John Stuart Mill, The Negro Question.* Ed. Eugene R. August. New York: Appleton Century-Croft, 1971. 38–50.

———. Unsigned Review of *The French Revolution: A History* by Thomas Carlyle. *London and Westminster Review* 27 (July 1837): 17–53.

Mitchell, Angelyn. "Introduction: Voices Within the Circle: A Historical Overview of African American Literary Criticism." *Within the Circle: An Anthology of African American Literary Critics from the Harlem Renaissance to the Present.* Ed. Angelyn Mitchell. Durham, N.C.: Duke University Press, 1994. 1–18.

Moody, William Vaughn. "The Brute." *Great Poems of the English Language: An Anthology.* Ed. Wallace Alvin Briggs and William Rose Benét. New York: Tudor, 1936. 1404–7.

Mooney, James E. Introduction. *Domestic Manners of the Americans* by Frances Trollope. Barre, Mass.: Imprint Society, 1969.

Morgan, Majorie. *National Identities and Travel in Victorian Britain.* Houndsmills, Basingstoke, Hampshire, U.K.: Palgrave, 2001.

Moses, Wilson Jeremiah. *Alexander Crummell: A Study of Civilization and Discontent.* New York: Oxford University Press, 1989.

———, ed. *Classical Black Nationalism: From the American Revolution to Marcus Garvey.* New York: New York University Press, 1996.

Moss, Sidney P. *Charles Dickens' Quarrel with America.* Troy, N.Y.: Whitson, 1984.

Nixon, Jude V. "Racialism and the Politics of Emancipation in Carlyle's 'Occasional Discourse on the Nigger Question.'" *Carlyle Studies Annual.* Special Issue, No. 16. 1996.

Norment, Jr., Nathaniel. "Addison Gayle, Jr.: "'The Consummate Black Critic' 1932–1991." *CLA Journal* 48.4 (June 2005): 353–86.

Ottley, Roi. *No Green Pastures.* New York: Charles Scribner's Sons, 1951.

Palmegiano, E. M. *The British Empire in the Victorian Press, 1832–1867: A Bibliography.* New York: Garland, 1987.

Palmer, Phyllis Marynick. "White Women/Black Women: The Dualism of Female Identity and Experience." *From Different Shores: Perspectives on Race and Ethnicity in America.* Ed. Ronald Takaki. New York: Oxford University Press, 1994. 167–74.

Paravisini-Gerbert, Lizabeth, and Ivette Romero-Cesareo, ed. *Women at Sea: Travel Writing and the Margins of Caribbean Discourse.* New York: Palgrave, 2001.

Paschal, Andrew, ed. *A W. E. B. Du Bois Reader.* New York: Macmillan/Collier, 1971.

Patterson, Orlando. *The Ordeal of Integration: Progress and Resentment in America's "Racial" Crisis.* Washington, D.C.: Civitas/Counterpoint, 1997.

Pease, Jane H., and William H. *They Who Would Be Free: Blacks' Search for Freedom, 1838–1861.* Urbana: University of Illinois Press, 1974.

Peck, John. "Racism in the Mid-Victorian Novel: Thackeray's *Phillip.*" *Varieties of Victorianism: The Uses of a Past.* Ed. Gary Day. London: Macmillan, 1998.

Pennington, J. W. C. *A Lecture Delivered Before the Glasgow Young Men's Christian Association; and Also Before the St. George's Biblical, Literary, and Scientific Institute, London.* Edinburgh: n.d.

Pettinger, Alasdair, ed. *Always Elsewhere: Travels of the Black Atlantic.* London: Cassell, 1998.

Pope-Hennessy, Una. *Three English Women in America.* London: Century, 1987.

Powell, Kevin. "The Word Movement." *Step into a World.* Ed. Kevin Powell. New York: John Wiley and Sons, 2000. 1–12.

Pratt, Mary Louise. *Imperial Eyes: Travel Writing and Transculturation.* London: Routledge, 1992.

Proctor, Jenny. "From Lay My Burden Down." *Autobiography of a People: Three Centuries of African American History Told by Those Who Lived It.* Ed. Herb Boyd. New York: Doubleday, 2000.

Quarles, Benjamin. *Black Abolitionists.* Rpt. 1969. New York: Da Capo, 1991.

Randall, Alice. *The Wind Done Gone.* Boston: Houghton Mifflin, 2001.

Raphael-Hernandez, Heike, ed. *Blackening Europe: The African American Presence.* New York: Routledge, 2004.

Rapson, Richard L. *Britons View America: Travel Commentary, 1860–1935*. Seattle: University of Washington Press, 1971.

Rentell, Philip. *Historic Cunard Liners*. Cornwall, U.K.: Atlantic Transport, 1986.

Rice, Alan J., and Martin Crawford, ed. *Liberating Sojourn: Frederick Douglass and Transatlantic Reform*. Athens: University of Georgia Press, 1999.

Richmond, M. A. *Bid the Vassal Soar: Interpretive Essays on the Life and Poetry of Phillis Wheatley and George Moses Horton*. Washington, D.C.: Howard University Press, 1974.

Ripley, C. Peter, ed. *The Black Abolitionist Papers: Volume I: The British Isles, 1830–1865*. Chapel Hill: University of North Carolina Press, 1985.

Robinson, Henry Crabb. *Henry Crabb Robinson on Books and Their Writers*. Ed. Edith J. Morley. Vol. 2. London: J. M. Dent, 1938.

Robinson, Randall. *Quitting America: The Departure of a Black Man from his Native Land*. New York: Dutton, 2004.

Said, Edward W. *Culture and Imperialism*. New York: Alfred A. Knopf, 1994.

Schiller, Friedrich. *Die Jungfrau von Orleans. Friedrich Schiller: Poet of Freedom*. Vol. 3. Washington, D.C.: Schiller Institute, 1990. 34–161.

Schriber, Mary Suzanne, ed. *Telling Travels: Selected Writings by Nineteenth-Century American Women Abroad*. DeKalb: Northern Illinois University Press, 1995.

———. *Writing Home: American Women Abroad, 1830–1920*. Charlottesville: University of Virginia Press, 1997.

Schueller, Malini Johar. Introduction. *A Colored Man Round the World* by David F. Dorr. 1858. Ann Arbor: University of Michigan Press, 1999. ix–xliii.

Sharp, William ["Fiona McCleod"]. "Dim Face of Beauty." *Poems and Dramas*. New York: Duffield & Company, 1910. 243.

Shields, John C. "Phillis Wheatley and Mather Byles: A Study in Literary Relationship." *CLA Journal* 23.4 (June 1980): 377–90.

Shyllon, Folarin. *Black People in Britain, 1555–1833*. London: Oxford University Press, 1977.

Slater, Joseph, ed. *Correspondence of Emerson and Carlyle*. New York: Columbia University Press, 1964.

———. "George Ripley and Thomas Carlyle." *PMLA* 67.4 (June 1952): 341–49.

Smith, Logan Pearsall. "Thomas Carlyle: The Rembrandt of English Prose." *Victorian Literature: Modern Essays in Criticism*. Ed Austin Wright. New York: Oxford University Press, 1961. 113–27.

Smout, T. C. *Victorian Values: A Joint Symposium of the Royal Society of Edinburgh and the British Academy, December 1990*. Oxford: Oxford University Press, 1992.

Sollors, Werner. Introduction. *The Adrienne Kennedy Reader*. By Adrienne Kennedy. Minneapolis: University of Minnesota Press, 2001.

Spiers, Fiona. "Black Americans in Britain and the Struggle for Black Freedom in the United States, 1820–1870." *Essays on the History of Blacks in Britain: From Roman Times to the Mid-Twentieth Century*. Ed. Ian Duffield and Jagdish Gundara. Aldershot, U.K.: Avebury, 1992. 81–98.

Spivey, Edward. "Carlyle and the Logic-Choppers: J. S. Mill and Diderot." *Carlyle and his Contemporaries: Essays in Honor of Charles Richard Sanders*. Ed. John Clubbe. Durham, N.C.: Duke University Press, 1976. 60–73.

Stepto, Robert B. *From Behind the Veil: A Study of Afro American Narrative.* 2nd ed. Urbana: University of Illinois Press, 1979, 1991.

Sterling, Dorothy, ed. *We Are Your Sisters: Black Women in the Nineteenth Century.* New York: Norton, 1984.

Stétié, Salah. "Géographie et Théologie du Voyage. *Écriture du Voyage et Mémoire Culturelle.* Vol. 9. Proceedings of the XVth Congress of the International Comparative Literature Association. Leiden 16–22 August 1997. Amsterdam: Rodopi, 2000. 7–21.

Stocking, Jr., George W. *Victorian Anthropology.* New York: Free Press/Macmillan, 1987.

Sundquist, Eric J. *To Wake the Nations: Race in the Making of American Literature.* Cambridge, Mass.: Harvard University Press, 1993.

Swinburne, Algernon. "Itytlus." Victorian Poetry and Poetics. 2nd ed. Ed. Walter E. Houghton and G. Robert Stange. Boston: Houghton Mifflin, 1968 [1959]. 671.

Symons, Arthur. "The Crying of Water." *Poems.* Vol. 2. New York: John Lane, 1902. 218.

Takaki, Ronald. ed. *From Different Shores: Perspectives on Race and Ethnicity in America.* New York: Oxford University Press, 1987.

Tate, Greg. Introduction: "Nigs R Us, or How Blackfolk Became Fetish Objects." *Everything But the Burden: What White People Are Taking from Black Culture.* Ed. Greg Tate. New York: Harlem Moon/Broadway Books, 2003. 1–14.

Tate, J. O. "Dress for Success." *National Review* 23 (August 1993): 60–61.

Taylor, Clare. *British and American Abolitionists, An Episode in Transatlantic Understanding.* Edinburgh: Edinburgh University Press, 1974.

Tennyson, Alfred, Lord. *Idylls of the King, and a Selection of Poems.* New York: Penguin, 2003. 5–286.

Thackeray, William Makepeace. *Thackeray's Letters to an American Family.* New York: Century, 1904.

———. *The Letters and Private Papers of William Makepeace Thackeray.* Ed. Gordon N. Ray. 4 vols. Cambridge, Mass.: Harvard University Press, 1946.

Thatcher, Margaret. TV Interview. By Brian Walden. London Weekend Television *Weekend World* (Thatcher Archive). London. 16 January 1983.

Thomas, Deborah A. *Thackeray and Slavery.* Athens: Ohio University Press, 1993.

Torpey, John. *The Invention of the Passport: Surveillance, Citizenship and the State.* Cambridge: Cambridge University Press, 2000.

Trollope, Anthony. *North America.* Ed. Donald Smalley and Bradford Allen Booth. New York: Da Capo Press, 1986.

Turley, David. "British Unitarian Abolitionists, Frederick Douglass, and Racial Equality." *Liberating Sojourn: Frederick Douglass and Transatlantic Reform.* Ed. Alan J. Rice and Martin Crawfore. Athens: University of Georgia Press, 1999. 56–70.

Walvin, James. *Black Ivory: A History of British Slavery.* Washington, D.C.: Howard University Press, 1994.

———. *England, Slaves, and Freedom, 1776–1833.* Jackson: University Press of Mississippi, 1986.

———. *Making the Black Atlantic: Britain and the African Diaspora.* London: Cassell, 2000.

Ward, Andrew. *Dark Midnight When I Rise: The Story of the Jubilee Singers Who Introduced the World to the Music of Black America.* New York: Strauss and Giroux, 2000.

Washington, Booker T. *Up from Slavery.* 1901. New York: Penguin, 1986.

Weisbuch, Robert. *Atlantic Double-Cross: American Literature and British Influence in the Age of Emerson.* Chicago: University of Chicago Press, 1986.

Wells, Ida B. *Crusade for Justice: The Autobiography of Ida B. Wells.* Ed. Alfreda M. Duster. Chicago: University of Chicago Press, 1970.

West, Cornel. *Race Matters.* Boston: Beacon, 1993.

Wheatley, Phillis. "To a Gentleman on His Voyage to *Great Britain.*" *The Poems of Phillis Wheatley.* Ed. Julian D. Mason, Jr. Chapel Hill: University of North Carolina Press, 1989. 91–92.

Whitley, John S. and Arnold Goldman. Introduction. *American Notes for General Circulation* by Charles Dickens. New York: Penguin: 1972. 11–36.

Whittier, John Greenleaf. "Howard at Atlanta." *The Complete Poetical Works of John Greenleaf Whittier.* Cambridge ed. Boston: Houghton Mifflin, 1894. 348–49.

———. *Literary Recreations and Miscellanies.* Boston: Ticknor and Fields, 1854.

Wright, Michelle M. "Others-From-Within From Without: Afro-German Subject Formation and the Challenge of a Counter-Discourse." *Callaloo* 26.2 (2003): 296–305.

Index

VANESSA D. DICKERSON is professor of English at DePauw University. She is the author of *Victorian Ghosts in the Noontide: Women Writers and the Supernatural,* the editor of *Keeping the Victorian House,* and, with Michael Bennett, coeditor of *Recovering the Black Female Body.*

The University of Illinois Press
is a founding member of the
Association of American University Presses.

University of Illinois Press
1325 South Oak Street
Champaign, IL 61820-6903
www.press.uillinois.edu